Art Encounters Deleuze and G

Renewing Philosophy

General Editor: **Gary Banham**

Titles include:

Kyriaki Goudeli
CHALLENGES TO GERMAN IDEALISM
Schelling, Fichte and Kant

Keekok Lee
PHILOSOPHY AND REVOLUTIONS IN GENETICS
Deep Science and Deep Technology

Jill Marsden
AFTER NIETZSCHE

Jean-Paul Martinon
ON FUTURITY
Malabou, Nancy & Derrida

Simon O'Sullivan
ART ENCOUNTERS DELEUZE AND GUATTARI
Thought Beyond Representation

Celine Surprenant
FREUD'S MASS PSYCHOLOGY

Alberto Toscano
PHILOSOPHY AND INDIVIDUATION BETWEEN KANT AND DELEUZE
The Thetre of Production

Vasiliki Tsakiri
KIERKEGAARD
Anxiety, Repetition and Contemporaneity

Philip Walsh
SKEPTICISM, MODERNITY AND CRITICAL THEORY

Martin Weatherston
HEIDEGGER'S INTERPRETATION OF KANT
Categories, Imagination and Temporality

Renewing Philosophy
Series Standing Order ISBN 0–333–91928–9
(*outside North America only*)

You can receive future titles in this series as they are published by placing a standing order. Please contact your bookseller or, in case of difficulty, write to us at the address below with your name and address, the title of the series and the ISBN quoted above.

Customer Services Department, Macmillan Distribution Ltd, Houndmills, Basingstoke, Hampshire RG21 6XS, England

Art Encounters Deleuze and Guattari

Thought Beyond Representation

Simon O'Sullivan

palgrave
macmillan

First published in 2006
This paperback edition first published 2007 by
PALGRAVE MACMILLAN

Palgrave Macmillan in the UK is an imprint of Macmillan Publishers Limited, registered in England, company number 785998, of Houndmills, Basingstoke, Hampshire RG21 6XS.

Palgrave Macmillan in the US is a division of St. Martin's Press LLC,
175 Fifth Avenue, New York, NY 10010.

Palgrave Macmillan is the global academic imprint of the above companies and has companies and representatives throughout the world.

Palgrave® and Macmillan® are registered trademarks in the United States, the United Kingdom, Europe and other countries.

ISBN-13: 978–1–4039–1809–3 hardback
ISBN-10: 1–4039–1809–0 hardback
ISBN-13: 978–0–230–57373–4 paperback
ISBN-10: 0–230–57373–8 paperback

This book is printed on paper suitable for recycling and made from fully managed and sustained forest sources. Logging, pulping and manufacturing processes are expected to conform to the environmental regulations of the country of origin.

A catalogue record for this book is available from the British Library.

Library of Congress Cataloging-in-Publication Data

O'Sullivan, Simon, 1967–
Art encounters Deleuze and Guattari : thought beyond representation / Simon O'Sullivan.
p. cm.—(Renewing philosophy)
Includes bibliographical references and index.
ISBN 1–4039–1809–0 (cloth); 0–230–57373–8 (pbk.)
1. Aesthetics. 2. Art – Philosophy. 3. Deleuze, Gilles. 4. Guattari, Fâlix. I. Title. II. Series.

BH39.O86 2005
111'.85'092244—dc22 2005049996

Printed and bound in Great Britain by
CPI Antony Rowe, Chippenham and Eastbourne

For Dan and Hazel O'Sullivan

Contents

Series Editor's Preface

The point of *Renewing Philosophy* is to present work that, whilst grounded in the traditions of European philosophy is capable of subjecting these traditions to a critique that will simultaneously open to a wider engagement with either the nature of modernity or some central aspect of the contemporary. Since modernism profoundly altered the nature of visual art in the early part of the twentieth century the connection between art and life has been a continuous site of engagement both within philosophical reflection and in the shaping of art works themselves. The encounter between philosophy and art works occurs principally through 'aesthetics', though the status of aesthetics itself has proved insistently problematic.

Nietzsche famously suggested that the world was only *bearable* as an aesthetic phenomenon indicating that the response to art is central to the way in which, at any time, a form of life can be regarded as one that is sustainable. The critique of social relations by means of aesthetic categories pre-dates Nietzsche as it stretches back to Schiller and the thinkers of the Romantic period. It also informs both the nature of a number of radical political movements and has been a stimulus to artistic creation from the Romantics to the present day. It is within this context that Simon O'Sullivan's engagement with the aesthetic project of Deleuze belongs. The traditions of avant-garde writing and theory have fallen into two main traps that O'Sullivan diagnoses and attempts here to escape. The first of these traps is the production of a mimetic relationship to that which is critically engaged with, a relationship that ensures that works either become as abstract as what they are attempting to displace or that they imbibe the 'cool' that is integral to modernity, ensuring their absorption as fashion. The second trap, conversely, would be that of melancholia, a trap that awaits those who remain committed to the seriousness of critique and are incapable of creating beyond a critical level. This second trap ensures reproduction of that criticised as it fails to point beyond it.

By contrast the Nietzschean pattern of thought would be based on an *affirmation* that would be the basis of a *gay science*. The contention of this work would be that the Deleuzian strain of French thought is the one that is capable of forwarding and prosecuting this endeavour. This work will be judged both by the degree to which it succeeds in inspiring further affirmations but also by the lucidity with which the art works that are here engaged with are made capable of creating a legacy of such affirmative resistance. Beyond the inheritance of the modern it would be necessary to shape a future that would be more than simply a retelling of the visions of the past. It will be the question for the readership of this work to determine whether such a future is given a first sketch here.

GARY BANHAM
Series Editor *Renewing Philosophy*

Acknowledgements

Many people have contributed to the writing of this book in many different ways. I would like to thank:

Tom O'Sullivan who read a draft of the whole book and made many insightful comments, and whose ongoing conversations and collaborative art practice, with Joanne Tatham, remains a continuing inspiration for my own thoughts about art and Deleuze. Ola Stahl, an ally in every sense of the word, and with whom many of the ideas of the book were argued over and expanded, who also read drafts of parts. The other members of C.CRED, Kajsa Thelin and Carl Lindh, for their ongoing inspiration and friendship. Brendan Prendeville who read parts of the draft with his usual eye for detail and generosity. Marcel Swiboda and John Lynch for their friendship and for numerous debates about Deleuze and art reaching back to our time together at Leeds. David Burrows for his conversations and collaboration. Robert Garnett for his always insightful comments on Deleuze and contemporary art. All of my colleagues in the department of Visual Cultures at Goldsmiths College, University of London. For our reading group at Goldsmiths, and other discussions: Phil Rudd, Simon Harvey, Erden Kosova and particularly Edgar Schmitz. Sara Ahmed, Pete Buse and Matt Hutt for their friendship and conversations reaching back to Cardiff. Felicity Coleman, Nick Thoburn and Andy Lowe for references. MA and BA students, at Leeds and Goldsmiths, who studied Deleuze with me, or whose own work offered inspiration (especially Valeria Graziano, Ditte Villstrup, Jim Backhouse, Catalina Lorenzo and James Hellings). The Bergson reading group at Leeds, and especially Michael Vaughan and Thomas Tyler. Keith Ansell Pearson and Philip Goodchild for the example of their own work and their support with mine. Adrian Rifkin for his ongoing support. Howard Caygill for his timely editorial advice. Gary Banham, and my editor at Palgrave, Daniel Bunyard, for making the publication process as smooth as it has been. The community at Padmaloka who generously hosted me whilst much of the book was being written, and especially Samudradaka, a true friend and Deleuzian in all but name. Nagapriya, for conversations, friendship, and the inspiration of his own writings. Last but by no means least I want to thank Shelley Budgeon for the adventures we shared, Thomas Mannion for the adventures we continue to share, Anna Weaver and Joe Collins for their ongoing friendship, Katie O'Sullivan for her love, and for the example of her own life and Jonathan O'Sullivan for being himself.

This book is dedicated to my parents Hazel and Dan O'Sullivan.

Much of the work for this book was carried out during two leaves of absence from Goldsmiths College. I would like to thank the latter for awarding me the Hoggart Scholarship for 2005 and acknowledge the support of the AHRC Research Leave scheme 2005.

Some of the material in Chapter 1 appeared in a much earlier form in my essay 'Cultural Studies as Rhizome; Rhizomes in Cultural Studies', *Cultural Studies and Interdisciplinarity*, Amsterdam: Rodopi, 2002. Parts of Chapter 2 have been taken from my article 'The Aesthetics of Affect: Thinking Art Beyond Representation', *Angelaki*, vol. 6, no. 3 (2001), 125–35. Parts of Chapter 3 have been taken from my article 'Notes Towards a Minor Art Practice', *Drain Magazine: A Journal of Contemporary Art and Culture*, 5 (2005), at http://www.drainmag.com. Earlier versions of Chapters 4 and 5 appeared as 'From Geophilosophy to Geoaesthetics: The Virtual and The Plane of Immanence vs. Mirror-Travel and The Spiral Jetty', *Pli: Warwick Journal of Philosophy*, 16 (2005), 27–55, and 'From Possible Worlds to Future Folds (Following Deleuze): Richter's Abstracts, Situationist Cities, and the Baroque in Art', *The Journal of the British Society of Phenomenology*, vol. 36, no. 3 (2005), 311–29. I would like to thank the editors of the above publications (Stefan Herbrechter, Pelagia Goulimari, Avantika Bawa, Celina Jeffery, Adrian Parr, Darren Ambrose and Ullrich Haase) for permission to republish. The last section of the conclusion was originally written as a catalogue essay, 'First Manifesto for the Guerrilla *Plastique Fantastique*', *David Burrows: New Life*, Warwick: Mead Gallery, 2004.

Abbreviations

Works by Gilles Deleuze

(*NT*) Deleuze, G. 'Nomad Thought', Trans. J. Wallace, *The New Nietzsche*, Ed. D. B. Allison (New York: Dell Publishing, 1977).

(*NI*) Deleuze, G. *Nietzsche and Philosophy*, Trans. H. Tomlinson (London: Athlone Press, 1983).

(*K*) Deleuze, G. *Kant's Critical Philosophy: The Doctrine of the Faculties*, Trans. H. Tomlinson and B. Habberjam (London: Athlone Press, 1984).

(*DI*) Deleuze, G. and C. Parnet. *Dialogues*, Trans. H. Tomlinson and B. Habberjam (London: Athlone Press, 1987).

(*B*) Deleuze, G. *Bergsonism*, Trans. H. Tomlinson and B. Habberjam (New York: Zone Books, 1988a).

(*FO*) Deleuze, G. *Foucault*, Trans. S. Hand (Minneapolis: University of Minnesota Press, 1988b).

(*PP*) Deleuze, G. *Spinoza: Practical Philosophy*, Trans. R. Hurley (San Francisco: City Light Books, 1988c).

(*C2*) Deleuze, G. *Cinema 2: The Time-Image*, Trans. H. Tomlinson and R. Galeta (London: Athlone Press, 1989).

(*LS*) Deleuze, G. *The Logic of Sense*, Trans. M. Lester with C. Stivale, Ed. C. V. Boundas (New York: Columbia University Press, 1990).

(*H*) Deleuze, G. *Empiricism and Subjectivity: An Essay on Hume's Theory of Human Nature*, Trans. C. V. Boundas (New York: Columbia University Press, 1991a).

(*M*) Deleuze, G. *Masochism: Coldness and Cruelty*, Trans. J. McNeil (New York: Zone Books, 1991b).

(*EX*) Deleuze, G. *Expressionism in Philosophy: Spinoza*, Trans. M. Joughin (New York: Zone Books, 1992a).

(*C1*) Deleuze, G. *Cinema 1: The Movement Image*, Trans. H. Tomlinson and B. Habberjam (London: Athlone Press, 1992b).

(*F*) Deleuze, G. *The Fold: Leibniz and the Baroque*, Trans. T. Conley (Minneapolis: University of Minnesota Press, 1993a).

(*LMM*) Deleuze, G. 'Language: Major and Minor', *The Deleuze Reader*, Trans. and Ed. C. V. Boundas (New York: University of Columbia Press, 1993b).

(*DR*) Deleuze, G. *Difference and Repetition*, Trans. P. Patton (New York: Columbia University Press, 1994).

(*N*) Deleuze, G. *Negotiations: 1972–1990*, Trans. M. Joughin (New York: Columbia University Press, 1995).

(*ECC*) Deleuze, G. *Essays Critical and Clinical*, Trans. D. W. Smith and M. A. Greco (London: Verso, 1998).

(*CH*) Deleuze, G. 'Cold and Heat', Trans. D. Roberts, *Photogenic Painting*, Ed. S. Wilson (London: Black Dog Publishing, 1999).

(*P*) Deleuze, G. *Proust and Signs*, Trans. R. Howard (London: Athlone Press, 2000).

(*I*) Deleuze, G. *Pure Immanence: Essays on A Life*, Trans. J. Rajchman (New York: Zone Books, 2001).

(*FB*) Deleuze, G. *Francis Bacon: The Logic of Sensation*, Trans. D. W. Smith (London: Continuum, 2003).

(*DES*) Deleuze, G. *Desert Islands and Other Texts: 1953–1974*, Trans. M. Taormina, Ed. D. Lapoujade (New York: Semiotext(e), 2004).

Works by Felix Guattari

(*CS*) Guattari, F. 'Cracks in the Street', Trans. A. Gibault and J. Johnson, *Flash Art*, 135 (1987).

(*SC*) Guattari, F. 'Space and Corporeality: Nomads, Cities, Drawings', Trans. H. and H. Zeitland, *Semiotext(e)/Architecture*, Ed. H. Zeitland (New York: Semiotext(e), 1992).

(*OM*) Guattari, F. 'On Machines', Trans. V. Constantinopoulos, *Complexity: Architecture/Art/Philosophy*, Ed. A. Benjamin (London: Academy Editions, 1995a).

(*C*) Guattari, F. *Chaosmosis: An Ethico-aesthetic Paradigm*, Trans. P. Bains and J. Pefanis (Sydney: Power Publications, 1995b).

(*S*) Guattari, F. 'Subjectivities: for Better and for Worse', Trans. S. Thomas, *The Guattari Reader*, Ed. G. Genosko (Oxford: Basil Blackwell, 1996a).

(*SS*) Guattari, F. *Soft Subversions*, Trans. D. L. Sweet and C. Wiener (New York: Semiotext(e), 1996b).

(*PM*) Guattari, F. 'Pragmatic/Machine: Discussion with Félix Guattari (19 March 1985)', in C. J. Stivale, *The Two-Fold Thought of Deleuze and Guattari: Intersections and Animations* (New York: Guilford Press, 1998).

(*TE*) Guattari, F. *The Three Ecologies*, Trans. I. Pindar and P. Sutton (London: Athlone Press, 2000).

Works by Gilles Deleuze and Felix Guattari

(*AO*) Deleuze, G. and F. Guattari. *Anti-Oedipus: Capitalism and Schizophrenia*, Trans. R. Hurley, M. Seem and H. R. Lane (London: Athlone Press, 1984).

(*K*) Deleuze, G. and F. Guattari. *Kafka: Towards a Minor Literature*, Trans. D. Polan (Minneapolis: University of Minnesota Press, 1986).

(*ATP*) Deleuze, G. and F. Guattari. *A Thousand Plateaus*, Trans. B. Massumi (London: Athlone Press, 1988).

(*WP*) Deleuze, G. and F. Guattari. *What is Philosophy?*, Trans. H. Tomlinson and G. Burchell (London: Verso, 1994).

Other Works

(*MM*) Bergson, H. *Matter and Memory*, Trans. N. M. Paul and W. S. Palmer (New York: Zone Books, 1991).

(*E*) Hardt, M. and A. Negri, *Empire* (Cambridge: Harvard University Press, 2000).

(*LYO*) Lyotard, J-F. 'Philosophy and Painting in the Age of Their Experimentation: Contribution to an Idea of Postmodernity', Trans. M. Minich Brewer and D. Brewer, *The Lyotard Reader*, Ed. A. Benjamin (Oxford: Basil Blackwell, 1989).

(*CW*) Smithson, R. *Robert Smithson: The Collected Writings*, Ed. J. Flam (Berkeley: University of California Press, 1996).

(*RIC*) Richter, G. 'Notes 1996–1990', *Gerhard Richter* (London: Tate Gallery, 1991b).

Introduction
Three Beginnings

In place of an introduction I want to offer three different beginnings.

About the encounter

> Something in the world forces us to think. This something is an object not of recognition but of a fundamental *encounter*. (*DR* 139)

An object of an encounter is fundamentally different from an object of recognition. With the latter our knowledges, beliefs and values are reconfirmed. We, and the world we inhabit, are reconfirmed as that which we already understood our world and ourselves to be. An object of recognition is then precisely a *re*presentation of something always already in place.[1] With such a non-encounter our habitual way of being and acting in the world is reaffirmed and reinforced, and as a consequence no thought takes place. Indeed, we might say that representation precisely stymies thought. With a genuine encounter however the contrary is the case. Our typical ways of being in the world are challenged, our systems of knowledge disrupted. We are forced to thought. The encounter then operates as a rupture in our habitual modes of being and thus in our habitual subjectivities. It produces a cut, a crack. However this is not the end of the story, for the rupturing encounter also contains a moment of affirmation, the affirmation of a new world, in fact a way of seeing and thinking this world differently. This is the creative moment of the encounter that obliges us to think otherwise. Life, when it truly is lived, is a history of these encounters, which will always necessarily occur beyond representation.

Rupture and affirmation are then two moments of the same encounter, two moments that only seem opposed if considered in the abstract, outside of actual experience. Art, in breaking one world and creating another, brings these two moments into conjunction. Art then is the name of the object of an encounter, but also the name of the encounter itself, and indeed of that which is produced by the encounter. Art is this complex event that brings about the possibility of something new.

This book explores a variety of just such event-encounters with a diversity of objects. Objects that I have chosen, or that in some senses, have chosen me. My encounter with these objects has helped form who I am. To this extent the book is a kind of personal archive, a history of my encounters within the expanded field of modern and contemporary art. Indeed, I would argue that exploring these event-encounters can only be written about on such a basis, from personal experience. Another way of saying this is that I am presenting an inventory of works that have forced me to thought, in the sense that they have offered a moment of inspiration or enthusiasm, or have provoked a question – set a challenge – to what was already in place. In much of what follows these objects and practices are only implicit (more often than not they appear in the footnotes), and lead instead to general statements concerning art. It is only in the last three chapters that I look in depth at three specific practices that have been important to me, and that I would say operate 'beyond' representation. These latter practices are either non-figurative, located outside the gallery, or simply outside the field of 'art' as it is typically understood. They are all involved in questioning accepted assumptions about the world. We might even say that each produces a different kind of world, whether it be through a painting, an earthwork or indeed a form of collective collaboration.

However, there is also a second encounter that this volume tracks. An encounter with the thought of Gilles Deleuze and Felix Guattari.[2] It is in this sense that Chapter 1 operates as yet another introduction, concerned as it is with my own context and investments in the Deleuzoguattarian project. Deleuze and Guattari's writing can itself be positioned as an experiment in thinking differently, 'beyond' representation. Their collaborative projects, and their single authored works, offer us a 'new image of thought', one in which process and becoming, invention and creativity, are privileged over stasis, identity and recognition.[3] My own encounter with this new image of thought has itself had a rupturing and creative effect on me. It has challenged previous ideas I had about art, about philosophy, and indeed about my self, and in so doing has produced a new way of looking at the world and of positioning my own practices within that world. It is in this sense that I feel it is crucial always to foreground how we encounter Deleuze and how we think about his thought. This is especially the case given the increasing growth in 'Deleuze studies'. Indeed, it seems to me to be of critical importance to keep alive a certain style of Deleuze's thought without over-academicising his writings or endlessly repeating his own words. We need to repeat the energy and style of his writings without merely representing his thought. For me this difficult project, to which I contribute here, entails giving attention to the pragmatic and constructive nature of Deleuze's thought whilst at the same time creatively bringing it into contact with other worlds and always with our own projects and our own lives. If such an encounter ruptures, then it also entails the opening up of new worlds, new territories.

A third encounter therefore follows from the first and second, namely one between Deleuze's thought (and specifically the concepts he created) and the expanded field of modern and contemporary art. Indeed, it is a key assumption of mine that many of such practices require a turning towards conceptual resources that themselves question traditional philosophical assumptions and procedures (and in this respect I attend also to some of those whom we might call Deleuze's allies, those figures who also think art differently (again, more often than not these parallel encounters appear in the footnotes)). We might note an apparent contradiction inherent in this third encounter. On the one hand it implies an attempt to set out what might be called a Deleuzian methodology, especially insofar as this might relate to the visual arts. And yet it also foregrounds those very assemblages that always and everywhere disrupt pre-established methods and systems and in so doing put new conditions into play (Deleuze's thought itself being one of those new assemblages).[4] Indeed, the desire to outline a Deleuzian methodology is to my mind somewhat wrong headed. One might be able to extract such a method or system but this would be to render Deleuze's thought inoperative, to freeze it in, and as, a particular image of thought, to capture its movement, precisely to *re*present it. It would, in the final analysis, be to make an object of recognition out of what has the potential to disrupt this self-confirming mechanism. In order to avoid this systematisation of Deleuze the book proceeds in a rather piecemeal fashion, jumping from one aspect of Deleuze's thought to another, picking up the same threads in different contexts and repeating key notions with different emphases. Indeed, rather than giving a systematic overview of Deleuze, the volume offers a series of thought experiments – different attempts at bringing Deleuze into contact with different milieus. In fact, the volume, and especially the last two chapters, might be said to attend to certain *resonances* between the field of philosophy (specifically Deleuzian) and the field of art and art history (specifically modern and contemporary).[5] The idiosyncratic nature of these encounters and conjunctions is a result of my own particular orientation, my own particular 'situatedness' within both of these fields. Each chapter is then also the record of a particular development – a journey – in my own ongoing project of attempting to think art beyond representation.

Relations of adjacency/intention

> The ideal for a book would be to lay everything out on a plane of exteriority of this kind, on a single page, the same sheet: lived events, historical determinations, concepts, individuals, groups, social formations ... The war machine-book against the State-apparatus-book. (*ATP* 9)

Forward looking art history and theory has often focussed on, and utilised, models from psychoanalysis or post-structuralist notions of textuality and allegory – on the one hand Jacques Lacan, on the other Jacques Derrida and Paul de Man. Indeed, this 'linguistic turn', originally of literary theory, has itself radically redefined the objects and practices of art history, as evidenced for example by the publication in the 1980s of *The New Art History* and the ongoing debates of *October* journal.[6] However, it might be argued that this radicality has in some cases become a new kind of orthodoxy and that its conceptual resources are less relevant to many modern and contemporary practices that operate away from this textual paradigm. As such, one of the intentions of this volume is to explore, via Deleuze, another way of thinking art, beyond the 'horizon of the signifier', beyond textuality, but *not* through a return to traditional aesthetic theory or indeed to previous artist-centred models. We might say that this involves a further turn from the linguistic, a turn towards matter and to the expressive potentialities of the latter.

This book might then be positioned at the intersection of two fields: the ever-growing secondary texts on Deleuze's writings and the field of modern and contemporary art theory. As regards the first context the book might be said to operate as a corrective to those that focus exclusively either on the philosophical or the scientific aspects or implications of Deleuze's thought, and in so doing often relegate (or indeed disavow) the contributions Guattari made to their joint projects, especially in his focus on the pragmatic and aesthetic business of producing ones own subjectivity.[7] In terms of the second context, it is hoped that the book might operate as an introduction to Deleuze and Guattari for those working within the field of art history and theory. The book is also an intervention into this latter field, hence its sometimes polemical tone. It makes the argument that there are possibilities for art and thought beyond representation, and indeed beyond the latter's critique and crisis (those deconstructive approaches which almost despite themselves can stymie thought). In relation to this, a further intention of the volume is to attend to art not considered by Deleuze himself, in fact to utilise Deleuze's concepts in general (and not just his own writings on art) to think through more recent practices (practices that perhaps Deleuze himself, with his particular tastes in art, would have been less inclined to explore). It is only through such an act of betrayal, I would argue, that Deleuze's real relevance to the expanded field of visual art can be mapped out.

What follows is then in part a commentary and introduction but only in so far as this allows other adventures to be put in motion.[8] As far as this goes the volume is certainly not typical art history, but it is not purely philosophical either. In fact it operates as a kind of bastard take on philosophy, a smearing or blurring of certain conceptual resources into other specifically non-conceptual areas (precisely in order to renew thought). In relation to this the volume is itself strategic. It is less concerned with 'getting Deleuze right' than in producing compatibilities and alliances. As Deleuze and Guattari remark, a book 'is not an image of the world' but rather 'forms a rhizome with the world' (*ATP* 11). It is hoped that this book, at least in part, might do justice to this notion connected as it is to other milieus and orientated as it is against a certain state formation: representation.

Synopsis

> If you don't admire something, if you don't love it, you have no reason to write a word about it. (*DI* 144)

The book then is a journey through the work of Deleuze, which involves five 'takes' on the conjunction 'Deleuze *and* art'. Each take is of a different nature, one might even say of a different speed. Certainly the first two chapters, which were written much earlier than the last three, are more polemical, more position statements than anything else. They also, I think, capture some of the excitement I felt when coming into contact with Deleuze for the first time. They are written from 'within' – and against – a certain style of art history, one that, as the first chapter makes clear, I had become increasingly hemmed in by. All art history might be said to operate through representation (it reads its objects), but it was particularly a more deconstructive attitude – that representation was always already in crisis – that produced the *cul de sac* I found myself in. We might say then that the first two chapters perform the same argument – against/beyond representation (and its critique) – but from two different directions. Chapter 3 shifts the terrain somewhat and also the style of the book. In this chapter I continue to think about Deleuze and art, but in a less obvious, one might even say more transversal, manner. The final two shorter chapters change the style again. They are more philosophical and might be considered more case study based in that they attempt to produce an encounter between some of Deleuze's conceptual resources and specific examples of art practice. A word also about the footnotes. They record my readings around art and Deleuze and as such constitute an archive project in themselves. They are also often quite lengthy. I would ask the reader to indulge this and only follow these digressions when they constitute a point of interest.

Chapter 1 begins with an account of my own beginning in relation to Deleuze's thought. I make no apologies for this except to say, again, that as a reader of Deleuze my personal investment inevitably orientates my attitude to, and 'application' of, Deleuze, and, as such, requires at least some foregrounding. In this chapter I introduce the encounter between art and Deleuze via a working through of the concept of the rhizome and a broad thinking through of how this might relate to the practices of art and of art history understood together as a form of expanded art practice. We might say that the principle of this chapter is connectivity, which in itself involves the theorisation of art practice as a form of *bricolage*. I am particularly interested here in developing a machinic notion of art as that which operates on a variety of signifying but also asignifying registers. The chapter in general operates as an intervention (within the field of art history) and also as a manifesto (for future art practices and histories perhaps) rather than as a description of those practices already in place. In relation to the rest of the volume, this is where I deal with Deleuze and Guattari's joint project of *Capitalism and Schizophrenia*.

In Chapter 2 I switch my focus to Deleuze's concept of affect. This chapter also looks briefly at two of Deleuze's philosophical precursors, Henri Bergson and Baruch Spinoza, and at some of those individuals that we might call Deleuze's contemporary allies, specifically Georges Bataille, Michel Serres and Jean-François Lyotard (the latter is in fact a constant presence throughout the book). In this chapter affect is thought in two ways: as the effect of art on the body and as that which constitutes the art object. In both cases affect is orientated against an overemphasis on signifying regimes, but also against habit and opinion. In the first part of this chapter the approach is to build up a polemical case for introducing a notion of affect into the discourse of art history. I am keen here to correct the overemphasis on ideological critique and semiotic approaches to art by attending to the affective dimension of the art experience. We might see this as a return to a notion of the aesthetic albeit a specifically immanent one. The second section of this chapter narrows the focus further to the actual art object. In particular, it involves a reading of Deleuze's book on Francis Bacon, a working through of the chapter on art in *What is Philosophy?*, and some ideas on how to take these two philosophical analyses further. This is particularly the case with the notion of 'probe-heads', a strange quasi concept that I return to in the final section of the book. This chapter ends with a very brief coda, as a short corrective, on the allegorical aspects of art.

Chapter 3 concerns itself with ideas of the political within art practice. Here I attempt to theorise the political effectiveness of art beyond what might be called typical Marxian frameworks. The chapter begins with a working through of Deleuze and Guattari's important notion of the minor (from their book on Kafka) and some thoughts on how this might be usefully 'applied' to contemporary art. I am interested here in an art practice that calls its audience into being, and in so doing produces a different kind of (political) subjectivity. The chapter goes on to briefly look at Michael Hardt and Antonio Negri's *Empire*, and specifically at ideas of dissent and affirmation. The second section of this chapter changes tack somewhat and involves an excursus away from art. Here I look at Deleuze and Guattari's important notion of the war machine, and at a historical example of guerrilla warfare, the Red Army Faction. I am interested here in what lessons might be learnt for an artistic war machine from this specifically politically engaged formation. In general, this means attending once more to the 'production of subjectivity', and it is to this that the third and last section of the chapter turns (Guattari's ethicoaesthetic project and Deleuze's own thoughts on a 'world without others').

With Chapter 4 the terrain becomes more philosophical. Here I am interested in working through Deleuze's concept of the virtual (borrowed from Bergson) and of the 'plane of immanence'. At the same time I attempt to bring these into contact with a specific art practice, in this case the work of the artist Robert Smithson. For me Smithson's work operates as an exemplar for much of what I say about art in this book, perhaps especially because it involves such a focus on the matter of art (whether that be rocks, words or film), and also because of its creative power of fabulation. Smithson's work might also be positioned on that edge between the virtual and the actual, a place that for me very much defines art's field of operation. This chapter then is about a moment, the late 1960s, when both an expanded art practice (Smithson's) and a new image of thought (Deleuze's) were being produced. In this chapter I might be accused of deliberately misreading Deleuze in so far as I utilise his ideas on philosophy to think about art. In a sense then the chapter is an experiment in taking Deleuze's philosophical concepts into other realms, other milieus, and in allowing these other fields to 'feed back' on Deleuze.

The fifth and final chapter attends to perhaps Deleuze's most complex work, *The Fold*. Once more I attempt to produce an encounter between this most difficult of concepts and an art practice, in this case the paintings of Gerhard Richter. I am interested here in the notion of painting, and especially the act of painting, as a kind of folding. I am also interested in Deleuze's idea of the Baroque as a fractal account of the world and of subjectivity (the two floors of the Baroque house). It is specifically through Richter's 'Abstracts' that I attempt to think this Baroque texturology. This experiment involves attention being given to the future-orientated nature of Richter's Abstracts and to what we might call their world-building character. We might also see this as an attempt to rescue Richter's paintings from that melancholy apparatus of capture that positions them as works of mourning. In choosing to write on Richter I realise that I enter into an already well-constituted discursive field situated around the paintings, and, as such, my remarks are often made in opposition to other commentaries (again, especially in the footnotes). The chapter goes on to read the last sections of *The Fold* alongside certain ideas of the Situationist city, for it seems to me that Deleuze's notion of a 'new' and expanded Baroque parallels, and can be productively conjoined with, the unitary urbanism of Ivan Chtcheglov, Guy Debord and others. This particular encounter also returns us to the terrain of Chapter 1 and to notions of interconnectivity. The chapter ends with a very brief consideration of art and new technologies in relation to Deleuze's closing comments in the book on *Foucault*. This last area demands a book in itself and I attend to it only to mark the possibility of this future project.

The book concludes with three endings. The first involves a brief consideration of fabulation, or what we might call the myth-making character of particularly contemporary art (and an even briefer look at two case studies). The second involves some reflections on the book itself, and on what it means to write a book on Deleuze. The third is an attempt at a different style of writing, something more inventive: a manifesto of an imagined future collective that restates the arguments of the book in programmatic, aphoristic and fictionalised form.

1
Rhizomes, Machines, Multiplicities and Maps
Notes Toward an Expanded Art Practice (Beyond Representation)

Rhizomes

Context-Investment

For many readers *A Thousand Plateaus* is a notoriously difficult volume, full of strange jargon, unfamiliar terminology and bizarre cross fertilisations. For others it is a surprisingly easy and exciting read, in spite of, and in some cases perhaps because of, the above. Indeed, it is almost as if one has already to be in a certain space in order to understand, or rather utilise, this complex and unusual collaborative work, which is to say that the most striking effect of reading *A Thousand Plateaus* is that it encapsulates a certain attitude, or one might say style, of intellectual work and indeed of life in general. It is a style that is at odds with much academic writing, especially that utilised by art theory, inasmuch as its *modus operandi* is affirmation and creation rather than negation and critique. Equally important, and as Brian Massumi points out in the translator's foreword, is to remember that *A Thousand Plateaus* is very much a pragmatic work.[1] To read it as a purely scholarly text, to read it simply for *meaning*, is to position it always already within that field that it writes against – representation.

How then to approach this strange book that the authors argue is not a book? Again, Massumi suggests that you treat it as you would a record. Some tracks will leave you cold, others you will want to keep returning to (*ATP* xiii–xiv). For you these latter tracks 'work', they activate something. The possibility of a different kind of thought perhaps? Certainly for myself 'Rhizomes', the first plateau of *A Thousand Plateaus*, had just such an effect – although not at first. I first read *A Thousand Plateaus* back in the 1980s whilst immersed in a reading programme of Critical and poststructuralist theory. At that time it made no sense to me whatsoever. I was reading Jacques Derrida, Jacques Lacan and those writers that wrote on them – 'signifier enthusiasts' as Deleuze and Guattari might call the latter – and thinking about how this broadly deconstructive model might be 'applied' to art and to art history. Compared with these writers Deleuze and Guattari seemed hopelessly chaotic and anarchic. Indeed, this was the general attitude within literary and art theory at the time, that Deleuze and Guattari had abandoned, in fact had possibly never been involved in, a left-wing oppositional practice. Put bluntly, Deleuze and Guattari did not seem to offer anything to ideological critique (and at that time deconstruction, along with Lacanian psychoanalysis, was allied with Frankfurt School Critical Theory in what might be called an expanded critique of ideology).[2]

There is much that could be said here about Deleuze and Guattari's specific context of writing (post-1968 France), and the changing notion of what, for them, constituted political strategy; about Deleuze's own philosophical non-representational project (the monographs he wrote on that 'bastard line' of philosophers that are his precursors) and not least about the speed, and order, in which his books, and his collaborations, appeared in English translation. Guattari's own context is equally relevant – his practice within psychoanalysis (the break with Lacan), and his own involvement with radical politics and questions to do with the production of subjectivity. And then there was my own context, working as I was within the hegemony of deconstruction and ideological critique of the Academy with my own investments in what I subsequently recognised as projects of negative critique (and indeed the production of a certain kind of neurotic subjectivity).

Instead I want to jump forward to the writing of my doctoral thesis, a project which lasted six years, and one in which I wrote myself into, and then out of, a *cul de sac*. My project was a reading, and deconstruction, of various discourses on art, from traditional aesthetic theory through to the Social History of Art. To cut a long project short, I produced a map of some of the terrain of representation. Each chapter of the thesis considered a particular model for thinking the art object and although some of the chapters were affirmative and creative, in general I conducted a negative critique, through close readings, on the texts I thought important to, in fact that philosophically 'underpinned', typical art history and theory. My argument back then was that these theories of representation tended always to be in crisis. They would posit a system – of representation – that would become undone in the very exposition of that system. This was all well and good, except it got me nowhere. By the end of this project I was exhausted with this deconstruction of representation that to begin with I had found so beguiling and so urgent.

Enter Deleuze and Guattari, and my second, in fact my third or fourth attempted reading of *A Thousand Plateaus*. On reflection I must have been looking for something, some other way of understanding my intellectual project beyond that of critique, and Deleuze and Guattari seemed to offer this to me. As I have already suggested, what I found in their writing was a different conception of what intellectual work might involve; no longer the endless critique of previous bodies of knowledge (or not just this) but the creative invention of concepts and the intensive mapping of affects and events. I recognised then, as I do now, a different possibility, another avenue, for thinking art and culture away from the horizon of the signifier. I also resonated with their different style of writing. It had itself an affective or intensive character, which is to say *A Thousand Plateaus* was one of the first books I had looked at that successfully performed its content. *A Thousand Plateaus* was for me a living landscape peopled by different characters, animals, plants and even stranger life forms. And then it was also something more ethereal, even elemental – a book with different rhythms and refrains, with different regions of intensity and different rates of flow. All this has been said before, not least by the authors themselves, but I think it is worth remarking that there is a kind of molecularity to the style of *A Thousand Plateaus* that escapes molar capture (the latter understood here as our dominant and habitual systems of reading and interpretation). In fact, and to pre-empt slightly my argument below, we might say that it is this contact with an outside, with the *forces* of the outside, that gives the book its particular character.

It is also important for me to say that Deleuze and Guattari's concept of the world as mapped out in *A Thousand Plateaus* appeared to fit more closely with how I was understanding and moving through my own world. I was turning away, for a variety of reasons and through a variety of strategies, from what I now understand as an overly signifying register. I had in fact already made moves, outside the Academy as it were, to circumnavigate the alienation that my doctoral project had forced me into. Deleuze and Guattari came at me then as an affirmation of an intuition I had already had and of conditions I had already put in place. I was, if you like, ready to read *A Thousand Plateaus*.

An idiosyncratic and confessional introduction perhaps, but I think it is important to lay out how one comes to Deleuze, and thus how one reads him. Other commentators for example highlight a logic of dissolution in Deleuze's work, but for me his books – and especially those written with Guattari – have always had this creative and fundamentally constructive character.[3] Deleuze's books then have operated as a sort of manual, but also as a kind of work of art in themselves inasmuch as they have proved a challenge, a problem, but also worked as a point of inspiration. This is particularly the case, as I have suggested, in that I resonated, and still resonate, with *A Thousand Plateaus* on an affective level.[4]

I also wanted to begin this first chapter with my own context and investments to demonstrate that I do not think it enough just to read *A Thousand Plateaus* without understanding the difference between it and say *Of Grammatology* by Derrida. There are of course many similarities.[5] Both are involved, albeit from different directions, in the critique, one might say crisis, of representation. Both explore difference. However, whereas Derrida's project is precisely one of reading another's texts (as is some of Deleuze's writings before his collaboration with Guattari), Deleuze and Guattari's collaboration, particularly in *A Thousand Plateaus*, is something else altogether: an attempt to reconfigure the way we think about the world in an affirmative and creative manner. In this sense *A Thousand Plateaus* might be understood as a box of psychic tools, or strategies, to help us construct our lives differently. Indeed, Michel Foucault once referred to *Capitalism and Schizophrenia* as an '*Introduction to the Non-Fascist Life*' (*AO* xiii). Fascism here refers not just to those who wear the Black shirts – but to the micro fascisms in everyone's head; the propensity for hierarchy, fixity and stasis (or simply representation) with which we are all involved, but which, for Deleuze and Guattari, can stifle creative, and we might even say ethical, living.

This project is nowhere more apparent than in the first plateau of *A Thousand Plateaus*, 'Rhizome', where what is essentially a biological term used to describe an acentred root system (couch grass, for example) is put to theoretical work. A rhizome is a system, or anti-system, without centre or indeed any central organising motif. It is a flat system in which the individual nodal points can be, and are, connected to one another in a non-hierarchical manner. A rhizome, then, fosters transversal connections and communications between heterogeneous locations and events. Indeed a rhizome, ultimately, is composed not of points but of the lines between these points. The rhizome is a paradigmatic example of the invention of a concept. In its expanded sense it might also be understood as the presentation of a new 'image of thought' inasmuch as it allows us to think thought differently, in this case to think differently and in opposition to root-like, or tree-like, structures, which, as Deleuze and Guattari demonstrate in this first plateau, are ubiquitous within Western thought and culture.

This new image of thought has parallels within many new 'representational' technologies and indeed with those habits of thought inextricably linked to such technologies. This is not to say that philosophy is determined by technological development, or that technology follows philosophy, but rather that both feed into, and open up possibilities for, one another (they are both part of the same historical moment, both formative of our particular consciousness).[6] Deleuze and Guattari's increasing relevance, and indeed popularity, cannot be divorced from the switch from analogue to digital that perhaps more than anything else characterises our contemporary world.[7] The best example of rhizomatics within our so-called information age is then the emergence of the World Wide Web as an omnipresent force, at least in the West. The much heralded, but now seemingly defunct, 'Information Super Highway' is then precisely a root structure (all information coming from one direction). The emergence of the Web is not without its problems, not least in its utilisation for profit and control (precisely blockages). However, despite these moments of capture, the Web remains a space of creativity, invention and expression. It allows for a certain amount of individual freedom, or simply self-organisation (open source software developments would be a case in point). It is in this sense that the Web is paradigmatically a rhizome. It is a 'bottom up' system rather than a 'top down' one, a grass roots system of 'organisation'.[8]

On a rather banal level then it might be argued that the most obvious 'application' of Deleuze and Guattari's rhizomatics to art is in emergent Web-based and other digital practices, and there are certainly examples of creative practices that utilise the Web and digital technology in general.[9] However, we might also look to 'older' technologies: the free radio networks in existence since the 1960s, or the continuing experiments in mail art. Indeed, it is important to remember that Web-based activities are merely continuing, at an accelerated pace, the construction of decentred rhizomatic networks that was already going on, utilising existing communications systems and more informal modes of contact and connection.

On a broader level we might position the system of arts in general as rhizomatic, each of the arts, and indeed each individual art work, connecting, or having the potential to connect, to every other. In fact, the arts themselves might be said to be in rhizomatic contact and communication with other man-made, or indeed 'natural' systems.

Indeed, from this perspective, everything is, or has the potential, to be rhizomatically connected to everything else.[10] Restricting our notion of rhizomatics to the situation of contemporary art practices, to the field of what has become known as 'relational aesthetics', we might understand a rhizomatics as operating between different practices, but also between those involved in such practices, and this would include those who were hitherto considered consumers of art.[11] We need also to allow the notion of the rhizome to somewhat collapse our art–art history distinctions, or at least to see each as being in rhizomatic connection with the other. This is very much the subject of this first chapter – a mapping out of the parameters, via the rhizome, of an expanded art practice, between art and its participants, and between art and art history.[12]

Beyond this the implications of rhizomatics for art can only be mapped out by appreciating its more philosophical aspect, as an image of thought at odds with representation and as a challenge to traditional philosophical assumptions and procedures such as hierarchy and interpretation. This is the second intention of this chapter – to position the rhizome as a new way to think art in general, a turn from transcendence to a kind of 'thinking immanence'. All of this inevitably involves a critique of structure (structures requiring centres, points of control). The rhizome is then, at least in this sense, a specifically poststructuralist concept.

Before going into the characteristics of the rhizome, and into its relevance for thinking art *and* art history, it is worth briefly demarcating the differences between this flat concept and the typical representational models that we find in Western metaphysics and paradigmatically in Western accounts of art and aesthetics. Here is not the place to go into this fully, Derrida does this succinctly in the *Truth in Painting*, nevertheless a general point is worth noting: discourses around art tend to be premised on a binary – meaning versus object or, if you prefer, content versus form. Derrida demonstrates that all discourses on art (and this includes the so-called New Art History as well as the Social History of Art) are premised on this binary, as indeed are all accounts of meaning in general.[13] You ask the question 'what is the meaning of art?' or 'what does that painting mean?' and automatically, perhaps unintentionally, you have reactivated the conceptual opposition between object/form and meaning/content, an opposition which itself sets up the promise that art will 'mean' anything at all.[14] Art becomes predetermined by the question you have asked. This is representation, an operation that produces a kind of hollowed out entity, in this case 'art' objects.[15] The terms may change depending on the theoretical orientation but the conceptual opposition, being nothing if not resilient, remains in place. Philosophically speaking the mechanism is the same whatever the answer to the above question; the 'conditions of production' occupies the same 'other place' as the 'aesthetic' (both provide the final signified, the final cause, to the circumstance of the object being talked about). Derrida points out – as does Paul de Man in his own parallel project of deconstruction – that these promises are always being broken.[16] We never actually get to that place beyond the circumstances of the object being talked about. Art, for both Derrida and de Man, leads towards, and then stymies, presence.[17] We might say that for these two melancholy scientists art is like a fallen angel, or, less poetically, simply a form of writing.

The rhizome allows us to avoid this conceptual model or procedure of representation and also its critique. This is an easy thing to say, but it is a difficult thing to think. After all we live, particularly in academia, even more particularly within art history, in a representational world. We are used to thinking in binaries: content/form, but also depth/surface, essence/appearance, soul/body, author/book, signified/signifier, speech/writing, unconscious/conscious, reality/ideology and so on. Poststructuralism, at least from a certain perspective, is a critique of these binaries. However, this critique often merely entails the reversing of the binary, or the putting under erasure (the deferral) of the privileged term. Thus, for each of the binaries above we have respectively a poststructuralist critique such as Jean Baudrillard and the simulacra (critique of depth/surface and reality/image), Roland Barthes and the move from work to text (critique of the author book binary), Lacan's critique of Freud, Derrida's critique and reversal of the speech writing dyad, or even Louis Althusser's problematisation of the base superstructure model (reality/ideology). All of these bodies of poststructuralist theory – to lump them together – provide a critique of origins, a critique of the origin's privileged position and ultimately a critique of representation.

However, these projects, important though they might be, are, in one sense, just readings of other theories. To be somewhat reductive, we might say that each of the writers above *reads* and problematises a previous discourse or system of thought. In itself this is not necessarily a bad thing. Both deconstruction and ideological critique are valid and important critical resources, particularly in critiquing transcendent claims to authority and in 'revealing' the exclusions and marginalisations inherent in such claims. However, what can happen, as Jean-François Lyotard once remarked, is that the critique gets ensnared by the object of its criticism: 'the thing criticised holds back and even consumes the one who criticises' (1989b, 155).[18] In this case the critique of representation takes place within, and is determined by, the field of representation itself, albeit a representation that is in crisis.[19] We might say that the critique itself polices the possibilities of thought. In passing, it is worth noting a further observation Lyotard once made about those who refuse to concern themselves with these systems of representation (for example in talking about art). They will be labelled as 'naïve', 'not up to speed' with the 'traps of representation', the workings of ideology (*LYO* 193).

It is important to remind ourselves again that this representational model, this representational way of thinking, is not confined to academia. Indeed, it is the way we all tend to think ourselves and our relation to the world. We are, if you like, representational creatures with representational habits of thought. We inhabit an internal and an external world. We separate ourselves as subjects from the object world. Indeed, this alienated state is the very precondition of self-consciousness. Art, at least as it is figured within representation, is complicit in this dynamic. Art mirrors back an apparently reassuring image of our own subjectivity (an outer form and an inner content). As such, a transformation in how we think about art will necessarily alter the topology of how we think ourselves and *vice versa*.[20] It is in this sense that the crisis of representation is also a crisis in typical subjectivity. It is also in this sense that Deleuze and Guattari's rhizome is not just a critique of representation, but also an active attempt to think our own subjectivities differently. Importantly, this is not to argue for some kind of 'return' to a pre-Oedipal 'Oneness'. We are who we are and there is no use pretending that we are not essentially divorced from the world. Representation is the condition of our subjectivity and as such has to be 'gone through' as it were. It is here that thought and the possibilities of thought are crucial. We can *think* the world and ourselves differently. This is not to champion an idealism over materialism, to side ourselves with the young Hegelians against Marx, for thinking differently, in Deleuze and Guattari's terms, is very much a materialist practice (after all what else could it be?). And of course thought must always be accompanied by other kinds of practice. Transforming oneself and creatively producing ones own subjectivity involves a complex of techniques and strategies.

And so, back to the rhizome, and as way in I want to go through the main principles as Deleuze and Guattari portray them of this concept-tool. What I also want to do below is map out the rhizomes' rhizomatic connections with some other Deleuzian concepts from *A Thousand Plateaus* (particularly notions of the machine and of multiplicity) in order to see how these might aid our project of thinking an expanded art practice understood as a form of thought and as a technology of subjectivity.

Connectivity-Intensity

> 1 and 2. Principles of connection and heterogeneity: any point of a rhizome can be connected to anything and must be ... A rhizome ceaselessly establishes connections between semiotic chains, organizations of power, and circumstances relevant to the arts, sciences, and social struggles. (*ATP* 7)

The rhizome names a principle of connectivity. It implies a contact, and movement, between different milieus and registers, between areas that are usually thought of as distinct and discrete. Such a smearing is creative; it can produce surprising compatibilities and novel synthesis. In fact, the making of connections in this sense might be understood as a key modality of creativity in general. In life this leads to a less one-dimensional and straitjacketed existence. Connections and alliances can be made between different people, different objects and different practices, which in itself allows for more flexibility, more fluidity. It is in this sense that a rhizomatics might then be characterised as the practice of the amateur involving as it does a certain *bricolage*, or 'Do-It-Yourself' logic.

Although 'art' can name an object, we might also use it as a name for these pragmatic processes of connectivity and interpenetration. Instead of pointing to a beyond, to a 'somewhere else', as is often the case with art positioned in aesthetic discourse, art might be a name for this moving sideways, for the fostering of specifically transversal connections. Here the experience of art is not one of a transportation (art is no longer a 'vehicle' in this sense) but one of more and more connectivity. Again, we might place here the recent turn to 'relational aesthetics' in art and in writings about art. This is a turn towards those practices that precisely connect different semiotic regimes with different organisations of power as well as connecting practitioners and producers of art with spectators and beholders. Indeed, this turn to participatory practices involves precisely a paradigm of relationality and connectivity.[21] It is important to remark that not all connections will be equally as relevant, or strategically as useful. In fact, we might want to demarcate an 'engaged' and creative rhizomatics from those more typical and habitual relations of everyday life. Hence a rhizomatic art practice might be best understood as the production and utilisation of alternative or 'counter' networks 'outside' those of the dominant. Again, we might note here the importance of the Internet for many artistic collaborations in this sense – the production of micro communities and local alliances even on a global scale.[22] These alternative and counter cartographies might also involve a more haptic, 'on the ground', local mapping of connections as opposed to those legislated for by the state (the latter operating through a more 'distant' and optical spatialisation). Following Deleuze and Guattari we might call this a more supple form of mapping.[23] Such rhizomatic practices will also involve the 'mapping' of different speeds and durations, the mobilisation of different temporalities to those typically proffered by our commodity-led society. I will be returning to this last point in Chapter 2.

We can, however, also recognise these principles of connectivity in all art. The frame is not a boundary in this sense, but that which opens the art work to the world 'outside' (including the spectator). Indeed the frame, however it is thought, operates as very much a 'connector' in this sense, and this frame might include other elements, such as writing on art, that were hitherto considered extraneous to the work itself. Indeed, writing on art might itself be a rhizomatic project; after all why not connect different signifying regimes together, smear the new sciences over into the humanities for example?[24] Or connect the writing of science fiction with the writing of art history?[25] By blurring discrete categories, producing new encounters and fostering monstrous couplings, new kinds of writing and new kinds of thought become possible. Importantly, this need not necessarily result in a kind of postmodern 'free for all'. Certainly 'history' as the transcendent signified of art might be dislodged, but mapping the rhizomatic connections an art practice might or might not make between different milieus does not necessarily involve a lack of rigour. Indeed, thinking art rhizomatically in this sense involves a more careful and thorough thinking through of art's realm of effectivity. Art's connections with the ever expanding fields of production and circulation of information for example, or more generally art's 'connection' to, but also disruption of, the dominant mode of production. An art work – or indeed an art history – would only ever be one point, one moment, in this general economy (and neither would have a necessary privilege over the other).

This principle of connectivity operates on a molecular as well as a molar level. Deleuze and Guattari's well-known example here is the wasp and the orchid, each involved less in a game of mimesis than in a network of becoming. The wasp becomes orchid, just as the orchid becomes wasp; they each form a rhizome with the other, an exchanging, or capturing of each other's codes (*ATP* 10). We might say that all true encounters involve this molecular blurring. The rhizome then announces a *general* principle of connectivity, not just with other subjects and different signifying regimes, but also with other organic (and inorganic) compounds and forces. As Deleuze and Guattari remark: 'semiotic chains of every nature are connected to very diverse modes of coding (biological, political, economic etc.), that bring into play not only different regimes of signs but also states of things of differing status' (*ATP* 7).[26] Once more, the most important connection is always with an outside. It is in this respect that Deleuze and Guattari suggest we should look to the 'wisdom of plants', whereby 'even when they have roots, there is always an outside where they form a rhizome with something else' (*ATP* 11). I will be looking at this molecularity in relation to art in more detail in the next chapter. Suffice to say here that art operates on an intensive register; it involves affective capture. In this place art might still be understood as a sign of sorts, but as not merely a signifying one.

Guattari in his own writings pays particular attention to this notion of art operating on a variety of regimes – signifying but also asignifying and intensive, which is to say that art, for Guattari, produces affects on and in the body that are irreducible to signification or representation. Here is Guattari talking (from an interview) about these multiple registers:

> The same semiotic material can be functioning in different registers. A material can be both caught in paradigmatic chains of production, chains of signification [under the cardologic], but at the same time can function in an a-signifying register [the ordologic]. So what determines the difference? In one case, a signifier functions in what one might call a logic of discursive aggregates, that is, a logic of representation. In the other case, it functions in something that isn't entirely a logic, what I've called an existential machinic, a logic of bodies without organs, a machinic of bodies without organs. (*PM* 219–20)

As we shall see in Chapter 4, the 'Body without Organs' is Deleuze and Guattari's name for this intensive register, this experimental milieu that operates beyond representation. The Body without Organs is a kind of strategy, or practice, that allows an opening onto the realm of affect. Following Guattari, we might say it is the same signifier, the same material as it were, that operates with different logics depending on our attitude and approach to it. Thinking art rhizomatically might then involve foregrounding those art works that have a specifically affective function, or simply foregrounding the affective character of all art (its power to effect us on a molecular level, to make us become other).[27] Art history might then still be involved in a kind of semiotic project of and for art, but it might also think the sign differently, as having an intensive register too. Indeed, the line between art and writing on art becomes blurred as both foreground, produce and register different kinds and degrees of affect. Usefully, Lyotard gives this intensive register of the sign a name, the *tensor*, and outlines what is at stake in this turn from signification:[28]

> First therefore, a different reaction, a different reception. We do not suppose, to begin with, that the signs ... transport messages which are communicable in principle. We don't start off by saying to ourselves: there is someone or something that *speaks* to us. I must understand them. To understand, to be intelligent, is not our overriding passion. We hope rather to be set in motion. Consequently our passion would sooner be the dance, as Nietzsche wanted, and as Cage and Cunningham want. (1993, 51)

Here the sign becomes an intensity, a trigger point for movement. Reading, if this is still a relevant term, is reading in order to be moved, to be 'set in motion'. Indeed, the tensor can be understood as precisely the affective side of the sign. Understanding art practice rhizomatically then entails attending to what we might call its performative aspect, what it does and what it makes us do, as well as to its 'knowledge producing' aspects.

A materialist meaning

For Massumi, following Deleuze and Guattari, and in particular following their Spinozist leanings, the sign can also be understood in very much this material sense – away from a horizon of signification and a logic of logocentricism. In *A User's Guide to Capitalism and Schizophrenia* Massumi defines meaning as a 'network of enveloped material processes' (1993, 10). To paraphrase Massumi, meaning is figured as the envelopment of a potential, a contraction of the past, and the future, in an event/object that has the capacity to affect or be affected. Here it is the work of 'interpretation' to unravel these 'virtual' processes encapsulated in the object.[29]

This notion of meaning is not based on identity thinking, on a correspondence between the object and the subject (the object treated as subject, as that which has an 'inner' essence), but rather is a relation of a non-relation between two (or more) forces acting on one another in a reciprocal and transformative relationship. For Massumi, 'meaning' is this process, an encounter between forces, or lines of force (which themselves are complexes of other lines), an event, dynamic rather than static, and in a constant process of becoming. Here meaning is a material process, the expression of one force on another. To quote Massumi: 'the expressed is not fundamentally a signified caught in an interplay of signifiers. It is a function involving a real transformation' (1993, 18). It is worth quoting Massumi further here, for the definition he gives of this 'meaning encounter' is particularly appropriate to art practice as we have been exploring it so far:

> The thinking-perceiving body moves out to its outer most edge, where it meets another body and draws it into an interaction in the course of which it locks onto that body's affects (capacities for acting and being acted upon) and translates them into a form that is functional for it (qualities it can recall). A set of affects, a portion of the object's essential dynamism, is drawn in, transferred into the substance of the thinking-perceiving body. From there it enters new circuits of causality. (1993, 36)

Massumi gives us the example of the carpenter, and his or her skills, competences and tools, 'meeting' a piece of wood, itself already the contraction of a past and of future potentialities. We might think of the artist's 'meeting' with his or her materials, a more complex encounter perhaps, but of the same fundamental nature. This is a confrontation between a specific artist-subjectivity and specific materials, each of which themselves are already the envelopment of a potential.[30] We might also move away from Massumi a little and think about the 'finished' art work's encounter with a beholder who again is the envelopment of a potential, a set of capacities to affect and be affected. In fact 'art' might be the name for both of these encounters, a meeting, or collision, between two fields of force, transitory but ultimately transformative. Both of these encounters are precisely moments of production. The encounter, between participant and art work, is as productive, albeit in a different sense, as that between artist and material. 'Meaning' might then be thought as this productive 'event', this 'moment' of meeting, ungraspable in its moment of occurrence, but real in its effects. Following Massumi, we might also use the term 'meaning' as the name for a suspension of this becoming, the 'pinning down' of a dynamic process, a kind of map, or diagram, of a procedure. If art history has a role to play in this rhizomatics of art practice it might be to explore meaning in this latter diagrammatic sense.

Machines

Machines against meaning

Another way of thinking this change in approach to art is as a move towards a more machinic understanding, one in which we are less involved in questions of definition and more with notions of function. We no longer ask the interminable question: 'what does art, what does this art work, *mean*?' But rather, 'what does art, what does this art work, *do*?' Or, again, following Lyotard, 'what does this art work set in motion?' Thinking art as a machine in this way, literally and not just as metaphor, side steps many of the problems and *cul de sacs* of aesthetic and art theory, particularly as Derrida reads it. Instead of offering us access to 'presence' (and then denying it to us), we can think of the art-machine as producing a number of effects, one of them perhaps being understood as a kind of aesthetic effect. In fact, it is here that we begin to modify the notion of the aesthetic, to pull it away from the metaphysics of presence, away from a transcendent horizon, towards a field of immanence. Indeed, aesthetics might be understood as simply the name for an affective deterritorialisation, a becoming. The aesthetic effect – or simply *affect* – as precisely a break in habit. Again, I will be returning to this point in the next chapter.

Staying with the notion of effects, we might say that signification is only one set of effects which the object, or machine we call art, produces. It is also important to remember that it is not just our art-machine that produces these effects, but our art-machine in conjunction with a subject-machine. For the signification effect, or indeed the aesthetic effect, does not come from the object, but from the object being confronted by (coupled with) a beholder, and a very particular kind of beholder, for it is not everyone who 'gets' the meaning, 'feels' the effect. Art is produced by the coupling of two very specific kinds of machine. We might note here that the subject-machine operates as very much a 'limit point' to the ever expanding circuits of effects generated by the art work and in this sense constitutes, at least in part, that very work.[31]

Strictly speaking other kinds of machine might also offer us an aesthetic effect in the above sense. For some subject-machines it might be the 'drug-machine', for others it will be a 'music-machine' or 'meditation-machine', or simply the coupling with another kind of subject-machine. Likewise, we might see certain kinds of art as not producing an aesthetic effect at all, or producing a *weak* aesthetic effect along with a *strong* signifying effect (certain practices of conceptual art for example). All sorts of combinations are possible. We might also think about objects that have become redundant, which are broken machines. Machines that are no longer working in terms of producing an aesthetic effect, but are perhaps working to produce other (unintended?) effects depending on what else (and who else) they are connected to – broken machines producing random effects, broken machines fixed but producing side effects. Indeed, we might say that an effective art practice, paradoxically, often relies on not knowing exactly in advance what effect the practice might have (and that effect may be so small as to be almost imperceptible, a tiny affective deviation that nevertheless begins a landslide and the production of a new world).

Again, to a certain extent this machinic paradigm allows us to escape the definitional problem with art that haunts modernism. We will call art that which produces an aesthetic effect, although this will be contingent and strategic. The same object 'plugged' into another kind of subject-machine may produce another kind of effect altogether (or not produce any effect at all). Likewise, a different (non-art) object plugged into a certain kind of subject-machine may produce what we would recognise as an aesthetic effect. As such, and to the extent that it produces such an effect, it would become, for that time, 'art'. Art here is less a label for an object than a name for a specific kind of coupling. This is not necessarily to override other factors – the specific location and context of the object, or indeed the specific socio-economic and cultural background of the participant, but it is to place both of these within a larger machinic economy of the art work.

Is an aesthetic effect the only effect we are interested in? Are there other asignifying and signifying effects we might desire our art-machine to produce? For example political and/or critical effects? What kinds of machine would be capable of producing these effects? What kinds of strange couplings, or machinic assemblages, would we need to construct or initiate? I look into this a little further in Chapter 3. Suffice to say here – and despite what I have said above – that artistic strategy might also involve, as a first moment, identifying the effect desired and then locating, or constructing the appropriate machine (Chapter 3, for example, is concerned with the construction of a 'dissenting-machine').[32] Conversely, and in the spirit of *bricolage*, we might look to the machines we already have and see if they can be made to produce other effects. Machines no longer working that could be reactivated, or machines working and producing certain effects that could be tinkered with, unplugged and re-plugged, redirected. Using a machine in a contrary way to that for which it was intended, as is the case with the Duchampian Readymade (and here Duchamp's insight is less to do with the institutional definition of art *à la* Peter Bürger and more to do with the machinic functions of different objects, subjects, spaces and places). Here, a notion of found images and found objects, of encounters and confrontations, is less the sole remit of specific practices and more the general condition of all art.

Desiring machines

We are moving towards a notion of the art experience, of art practice, whether it be making it, seeing it, or writing about it, as complex and expanded. No longer the static production, distribution and consumption of an object, but art practice as a process, as a 'desiring-machine', always 'in' production.[33] In *Anti-Oedipus* Deleuze and Guattari characterise these desiring-machines as flow producing and flow interrupting.[34] A machine produces a flow, another machine coupled to this interrupts the flow, draws it off, and in doing so produces a temporary halt, an aggregate, an 'object' or frozen event.[35] Art, for example, which envelops a potential to affect, to be 'plugged' into another machine, to be reactivated and redirected. Deleuze and Guattari, in *Anti-Oedipus*, are writing about the construction or formation of the subject-machine. Their project in this first volume of *Capitalism and Schizophrenia* is to give a different account, to offer an alternative framework, for thinking subjectivity away from that Oedipal theatrical configuration that tends to determine our lived life. They write of subjects, or protosubjects, as desiring-machines. Later, in the second volume of *Capitalism and Schizophrenia*, this theory of production is extended out to the 'natural' world. Indeed, no fundamental distinction is drawn between man as machine and nature as machine. The photosynthesising leaf for example is involved in the interrupting of flows, the production of production. In fact, even inorganic matter is included within this general economy of production.[36] There is no problem in understanding art in this way, for art too is involved in production. Art as a desiring-machine, or as the platform for a desiring-machine, is involved in the: '*production of productions*, of actions and passions; *productions of recording processes*, of distributions and of co-ordinates that serve as points of reference; *production of consumptions*, of sensual pleasures, of anxieties, and of pain' (*AO* 4).

In *Anti-Oedipus* Deleuze and Guattari specify two types, or levels, of desiring-production which are in fact two modalities of the same desire and which as such intersect – social-production (institutional and *supra*-individual) and the desiring-production of individuals. Sometimes (individual) desiring-production can work to destabilise social-production as a whole ('desiring-production is used to short circuit social-production, and to interfere with the reproductive function of technical machines by introducing an element of dysfunction' (*AO* 31)). This interference, or disjunction, is a breakdown of the machine's institutional function. It is equivalent to a kind of schizophrenia, which, for Deleuze and Guattari, involves the scrambling of existing codes – or the setting up of autonomous codes that operate independently of any social coding.[37] This is a definition of art practice as we have been describing it. Art practice functions as a kind of blockage in the smooth running of larger institutional, and indeed global, coding machines. It is in this sense that 'the artist is the master of objects; he puts before us shattered, burned, broken-down objects, converting them to the regime of desiring machines ... so as to cause desiring-machines to undermine technical machines' (*AO* 32). In this place:

> the value of art is no longer measured except in terms of decoded and deterritorialized flows ... It is here that art accedes to its authentic modernity, which simply consists in liberating what was present in art from its beginnings, but was hidden underneath aims and objects, even if aesthetic, and underneath recodings or axiomatics: the pure process that never ceases to reach fulfilment as it proceeds – art as 'experimentation'. (*AO* 370–71)[38]

This experimentation involves the release of desire (a desire for more and more connectivity) from beneath the repressive apparatus of representation. It is also the blueprint for a new and different kind of politics, a new militancy. This is the production of an affirming, laughing militant whose individual mappings and machines escape societal limitations and habitual restrictions, and which, it is to be hope, can be conjoined with other such machinic mappings in the construction of larger collectivities or simply the war machine.[39] This might well involve, as Deleuze suggests it did with Nietzsche, 'an *absolute* decoding', and not just the 'relative decoding which would consist in deciphering antiquated, current or future codes' (*NT* 144). It might also involve the introduction of something that is not encodable, the jamming of all codes (*NT* 144). We might note in passing the increasing importance of this disruption, given the nature of what Deleuze has called our 'control societies' that operate increasingly through coding mechanisms.[40] As Deleuze remarks in relation to Nietzsche (and Kafka), it is style that produces this jamming. Style (and we might say art in general) operates here as a 'political instrument' (*NT* 144).

All of this is to foreground the 'sharpness', interventionary, or simply bothersome nature of art practice. Indeed, art practice might involve the positioning of an object in such a way that it disrupts the situation that surrounds it. It is in this sense that art can have such a disproportionately large effect on its 'context'. To say the same differently, an art object might be relatively simple but produce a large number of complex effects placed as it is within a complex situation (and here attention would need to be given to the specific situation, or milieu, into which the object is inserted). Art can be like the pebble dropped in still water; large effects rippling out from an apparently minor event (effects which are as much to do with the water as the pebble). For committed artists questions of strategy become important here. Does this object work for this milieu? Does this milieu demand a different object? Where to drop the pebble? Or again, how to smuggle in the dangerous object? How to provide camouflage, to dissimulate the dynamite? We might call this a reverse strategy to the principle of connectivity given earlier, a strategy of anti-connectivity, of deviation, disjunction and disruption.

From machines to machinic assemblage

Machines as we have been portraying them are never in isolation, but are always and everywhere in relation to larger machinic circuits of production. Again, Guattari is particularly attentive to this in his own writings, in which the world is rethought as a collection of machines, or more accurately a collection of machinic assemblages (*OM*). This is not to think the machine in the merely industrial and technical sense, rather, and like the rhizome, the machinic assemblage is to be thought of as a kind of concept tool that enables a thinking through of expanded connectivity. For Guattari (following Pierre Levy) this is particularly important in terms of 'trying to break down the ontological iron curtain between being and things' (*OM* 8). This curtain is our alienated consciousness which everything from Kantian aesthetics through to Marxist revolutionary praxis is intent on overcoming. For Guattari it is in fact not so much a question of overcoming alienation but rather of reordering ourselves and our relationship to the world, a question of reconfiguration.

Once more, we might call this an aesthetic project inasmuch as it involves a break in our habitual sense of self and in our habitual responses to the world (and is, in this sense, specifically disinterested). Instead of offering an apparent reconciliation, art might be involved in enabling these 'new' kinds of relations with the world. In such a machinic remapping subject and object become less fixed, both being moments in a network of continuous contact and communication between different kinds of machinic assemblages. A good example of this project of rhizomatic remapping is Guattari's work at *La Borde* clinic, at least as it is written about in *Chaosmosis*. Here Guattari is interested in what he calls 'resingularisation', the ability individuals have to creatively remap their world (we might call this a rhizomatics of subjectivity). Here is Guattari writing about this process:

> certain psychotic patients, coming from poor agricultural backgrounds, will be invited to take up plastic arts, drama, video, music, etc., whereas until then, these universes had been unknown to them. On the other hand, bureaucrats and intellectuals will find themselves attracted to material work, in the kitchen, garden, pottery, horse riding club. The important thing here is not only the confrontation with a new material of expression, but the constitution of complexes of subjectivation: multiple exchanges between individual-group-machine. These complexes actually offer people diverse possibilities for recomposing their existential corporeality, to get out of their repetitive impasses and, in a certain way, to resingularise themselves. Grafts of transference operate in this way, not issuing from ready-made dimensions of subjectivity crystallised into structural complexes, but from a creation which itself indicates a kind of aesthetic paradigm. One creates new modalities of subjectivity in the same way an artist creates new forms from a palette. (*C* 6–7)

The possibility of making transversal connections between people, and between people and things, is, for Guattari, not so much a cure for neurosis/psychosis, even less a reintegration of the neurotic/psychotic back into society (the re-oedipalisation enacted by psychoanalysis), rather it is a means by which individuals can reorganise, or resingularise themselves in a creative, affirmative, and self-organising manner. For Guattari, *La Borde* is a machinic assemblage, a space in which different complexes can aggregate together.[41] Importantly, and like the rhizome, this assemblage, as well as having an internal consistency, is always opening up to an outside (the wider social field, the even wider natural world). Indeed, the machinic assemblage can best be understood as a function, a fluid function of connectivity involving an internal cohesion (autopoiesis, or the production of a territory) but also an external openness (allopoiesis, or a deterritorialisation). It is in this sense, as Guattari remarks elsewhere, that the rituals of archaic societies (complexes of signifying and asignifying functions, of auto and allopoiesis) are as much machines as the city mega-machine (*OM* 11). And so the rhizome is in this sense machinic, or the machine is rhizomatic; both foster connections, both deterritorialise, and in both it is the connection with an outside that is crucial.

Multiplicities

Against theology

> 3. Principle of multiplicity: it is only when the multiple is effectively created as a substantive, 'multiplicity', that it ceases to have any relation to the One as subject or object, natural or spiritual reality, image and world ... A multiplicity has neither subject nor object, only determinations, magnitudes, and dimensions ... . (*ATP* 8)

As we move through the plateau the notion of the rhizome becomes more complex and of a decidedly more philosophical nature. The rhizome is a multiplicity, that operates without reference to the One as subject or object. We are moving away from representation here and indeed away from any theological accounts or images of the world. A multiplicity must be understood without reference to an organising or classifying referent. The puppet master's strings are tied not to the 'will of an artist or puppeteer but to a multiplicity of nerve fibres, which form another puppet in other dimensions connected to the first' (*ATP* 8). There is no end to this rhizomatic network, this weave, no origin or final cause. It is in this sense that the rhizome operates without points of transcendence. It never allows itself to be over coded; it never has a supplementary dimension over and above the number of lines from which a unity might be projected.

This notion of multiplicity then announces a different attitude to the world; an understanding of the latter as a plane of immanent connectivity and complexity. Indeed, this multiplicity is not going on 'elsewhere', in some 'other place', but is here, in our world, albeit 'seen' differently. Our world 'seen' without the spectacles of representation. In this sense Deleuze and Guattari are offering us a kind of fiction, after all we are representational beings, but it is a productive fiction. It allows us to imagine our world differently, and as such it offers escape routes,

Deleuze and Guattari might call these lines of flight, from our representational and often over stratified sense of self. As Deleuze says in an interview:

> What we're interested in, you see, are modes of individuation beyond those of things, persons or subjects: the individuation, say, of a time of day, of a region, a climate, a river or a wind, of an event. And maybe it's a mistake to believe in the existence of things, persons, or subjects. (*N* 26)

We might see one of the roles of art as being an entry point on/into this smooth space, a line of flight from representational habits of being and thought on/into the multiplicity of the world.[42] Aesthetics would name the 'science' of 'seeing beyond' our habitual tendency to individuate on a recognisable and reassuring molar level. Art might name the mechanism of reindividuating at a different level, precisely the constitution of new composites, new assemblages.

This notion of multiplicity is key to Deleuze's, and to Deleuze and Guattari's, writings. But it is not without its problems, problems of a distinctly philosophical nature. How to think this multiplicity? Or, in the terms of this chapter, how to think the rhizome (or rhizomes) without reference to a single unifying principle, without reference to a subject or object? How to think this multiplicity of which we are part without reducing it to the simple? How to think an 'original' complexity that does not arise from, or return to, the One? How in fact to think beyond representation? This will be a recurring question throughout the following chapters of this book. Suffice to say at this stage, and in this plateau, it must involve a subtraction: always subtract the leader, the general. Always subtract the centre, always n-1 (and the question of how to ensure such a multiplicity still operates intentionally or has direction might be seen as one of the key political questions of our time).

As a brief aside, it is worth noting the name of Michel Serres, who, as an ally in our rhizomatic project, attempts a similar task of thinking the multiple in his poetic book *Genesis*. Serres is particularly wary of the hegemony of the concept, which he characterises as a mechanism of classification, a technology that distributes and produces unities. For Serres, instead, a kind of quasi concept is needed to think the work of the multiple:

> Time-as-weather, fire-as-heat are not concepts in the usual sense. Clock-time is such a concept, entropic time is, perhaps, another such,

> and temperature as well. A cloud is an aggregate, a nebulous set, a multiplicity whose exact definition escapes us, and whose local movements are beyond observation. A flame is an aggregate ... that is even more nebulous. Here then are a couple of concepts in which the multiple reveals itself as such. Heat and flame, cloud and wind, climate and turbulences, we could refer to them as concepts of multiplicities. (Serres 1995, 103)

Like Deleuze and Guattari, Serres attempts to individuate the world on a different register, to 'free' the multiplicity from the shelter of the unifying concept. Indeed, for Serres the world is made up not from 'well formed' objects but by aggregates, which require a different kind of thought altogether. We might turn to Lyotard here, yet another ally in thinking multiplicity, for whom thoughts are themselves cloud-like multiplicities:

> Thoughts are not the fruits of the earth. They are not registered by areas, except out of human commodity. Thoughts are clouds. The periphery of thoughts is as immeasurable as the fractal lines of Benoit Mandelbrot. Thoughts are pushed and pulled at variable speeds. They are deep, although core and skin are of the same grain. Thoughts never stop changing their location one with the other. When you feel like you have penetrated far into their intimacy in analysing their so-called structure or genealogy or even post structure, it is actually too late or too soon. (Lyotard 1988, 5)

For both Serres and Lyotard, thought, when it really is thought (and not just a habitual response or reaction), is decidedly non-representational. Such a rethinking of thought involves a rethinking of the *cogito*. The 'mind' is no longer the origin of thought as such, but operates as a kind of threshold, or temporary turbulence, within a thought cloud-field. Here thought, thinking, is itself a multiplicity. Creative thinking then involves an openness to, a reconnection with, this nebulous realm of potentialities beyond (in fact, always parallel to) the subject.

In *What is Philosophy?* Deleuze and Guattari are interested specifically in demarcating different forms of thought; for example science understood as that which involves function (we might say, involves a machinic mapping of the world); or art, involving blocs of affects (I will be exploring this further in the next chapter). When concepts are considered (in the philosophical project *per se*) they are understood creatively; active concept creation as a means of problem solving, precisely to 'get something done'. I go into this in more detail in Chapter 4, but it is worth briefly pointing here to a pertinent concept that Deleuze 'constructed' (borrowed and made his own) before his collaboration with Guattari, the concept of difference. Here the world is no longer thought as being comprised of distinct entities, not even of aggregates of smaller and smaller parts. Instead a notion of difference becomes the condition of possibility for phenomena. But this difference is not that between already demarcated signifiers (it is not a semiotic) rather it is a difference in intensity:

> Every phenomenon refers to an inequality by which it is conditioned. Every diversity and every change refers to a difference which is its sufficient reason. Everything which happens and everything which appears is correlated with orders of differences: differences of level, temperature, pressure, tension, potential, *difference of intensity*. (*DR* 222)

Again, such a reconceptualisation allows us to move from a signifying register to an asignifying one. The world, as multiplicity, is constituted by moments of, and differences in, intensity. The world is not, or not only, a book to be read. To a certain extent this is not a new idea, indeed it may involve a return to a pre-theological, a pagan, mapping of the world (and certainly a more artistic mapping). Deleuze has himself positioned his work in a genealogy of 'bastard' pagan philosophers from Heraclitus to Nietzsche, a line of nomadic thought everywhere accompanying state philosophy as its mutant double. We might also turn away here from the West to the East and to the immanent religions. In fact, with Deleuze we are not even in the realm of Pantheist religion (for example the multiplicity of Hinduism which nevertheless comes from, and returns to, the One), rather the world is positioned as conditioned reality. In this world (our world seen differently) there are only conditions that produce other conditions. Here process (movement) replaces stasis (fixity) as the world's, and the subject's, *modus operandi*. We are quite close to the Buddhist or the Taoist here: no essences, indeed no theology (no representation), but a 'fundamental' insubstantiality, impermanence and interpenetration of all phenomena. The world as a vortex of energy. The world, and ourselves within that world, as a 'region in flames' (Lyotard 1993, 56).

Maps

Strategy-Cartography

'Multiplicities are defined by the outside, by the abstract line, the line of flight or deterritorialization according to which they change in nature and connect with other multiplicities' (*ATP* 9). We can understand an art practice, whether it is that of an individual, a collaboration or group, or even a specific 'work', as a kind of multiplicity in this sense. An art practice is a fluid, dynamic system always in connection with a number of different regimes and registers and always in contact with an outside however this latter is theorised. What an art practice 'is' then is defined by its outermost edge, its boundary line or simply its line of flight, understood as the furthest point from within its territory. Indeed the artist, when he or she is an artist, is this line of flight, or more accurately operates on this line and at this edge. An art practice is then a specifically open system in this sense, one that changes its nature as the number of its dimensions increase (as it crosses into other milieus). In this place art is less the name for an object or a discipline as such but again a name for a function of deterritorialisation.

> 4. Principle of asignifying rupture: against the oversignifying breaks separating structures or cutting across a single structure. A rhizome may be broken, shattered at a given spot, but it will start up again on one of its old lines, or on new lines ... Every rhizome contains lines of segmentarity according to which it is stratified, territorialized, signified, attributed, etc., as well as lines of deterritorialization down which it constantly flees. (*ATP* 9)

So the rhizome is not the opposite of the root, rather the rhizome is within the root, just as the root is within the rhizome. In fact, in a sense the root and the rhizome are less distinct spaces but rather two different strategies or attitudes. We might even say they operate as two different kinds of speed. As a case study of this two-faced assemblage we might look to any of the institutions that surround us, for example a university. The latter can be seen as a root- or tree-like structure, organised and hierarchised around a central point (ultimately the vice - chancellor). A top down organisation with communication – and pedagogy – generally proceeding in one orderly direction. But within this hierarchical formation there will be burgeoning rhizomes – creative practices and lines of flight (transversal reading groups, alliances between staff, students, staff and students, and so on). Another example might be an academic discipline such as philosophy or art history, organised, centralised around certain institutions, editorial boards, and the like and also around central concepts (for example representation). There will be rhizomes here too. We might want to extend this principle outwards, away from specific institutions to the more general networks and pathways that determine our lived lives. A burgeoning rhizomatics will operate within and between these more fixed networks (friendship might be a name for these more spontaneous and non-legislated connections and relationships). The practice of rhizomatics is then precisely strategic, indeed, as Deleuze and Guattari remark: 'a new rhizome may form in the heart of a tree, the hollow of a root, the crook of a branch. Or else it is a microscopic element of the root-tree that gets rhizome production going' (*ATP* 15). We might add that of course, the opposite can also happen; multiplicities can become frozen, the rhizome can become blocked. Time to switch to another opening, to find another line of flight.

Art practice here is then both rhizomatic and tree-like, indeed, one does not come about without the other. One requires some kind of territory before deterritorialising. Art practice is not, and cannot be, a wild destratification. As Deleuze and Guattari remark in another plateau, 'staying stratified – organized, signified, subjected' is not the worse that can happen: 'the worse that can happen is if you throw the strata into demented or suicidal collapse, which brings them back down on us heavier than ever' (*ATP* 161). Indeed:

> You have to keep enough of the organism for it to reform each dawn; and you have to keep small supplies of signifiance and subjectification, if only to turn them against their own systems when the circumstances demand it, when things, persons, even situations, force you to; and you have to keep small rations of subjectivity in sufficient quantities to enable you to respond to the dominant reality. Mimic the strata. You don't reach the BwO [Body without Organs], and its plane of consistency, by wildly destratifying. (*ATP* 160)

The watchword in this rhizome project is caution. It is not a question of completely abandoning structure or following an absolute deterritorialisation, indeed, in such cases your work might move too close to chaos. In fact, this is the difference, ultimately, between art and illness. To produce the former you need a territory, a consolidated base; you need the root to produce the rhizome:

> This is how it should be done: Lodge yourself on a stratum, experiment with the opportunities it offers, find an advantageous point on

> it, find potential movements of deterritorialization, possible lines of flight, experience them, produce flow conjunctions here and there, try out continuums of intensity segment by segment, have a small plot of new land at all times. It is through a meticulous relation with the strata that one succeeds in freeing lines of flight. (*ATP* 161)

This is a programme for an expanded notion of art practice *and* for living our lives as an art practice.[43] Such a practice does not arrive from some other place but is produced with available materials, from an archive, a territory, which itself offers up the possibilities of deterritorialisation. As far as actual art history goes such a strategy will involve close attention to already existing structures, a meticulous relation with the strata. For it is through this work that the line of flight, understood as a creative line, is located and followed. An art history rhizome in this sense is not an abandonment of, but a reengagement with, the matter of representation, albeit representation thought in a different way.

We might say then that art practice names the careful process by which within a striated space (organised, regimented and representational) a smooth space is opened up. Inevitably these lines of flight from 'territorialised regimes of thought' can be destructive or are reterritorialised. However, new lines of flight, new possibilities of movement, will then emerge in a constant process of opening and closure. This is not a programme of escapism, even less the outline of a utopian metaphysics. Rather it is a call for attention to be focused on the actual, if only to unlock the potential becomings, the virtualities encapsulated within every moment. It is here that the 'in-between' nature of art practice again becomes important. Art is always situated between the actual and the virtual, in fact we might say operates itself as a kind of 'actualising-machine' (I will be looking at a case study of this in Chapter 4).

Another way of saying this is that an expanded art practice becomes diagrammatic, and begins to operate as an abstract and future-orientated machine: 'The diagrammatic or abstract machine does not function to represent, even something real, but rather constructs a real that is yet to come, a new type of reality' (*ATP* 142). Again, this 'new type of reality' is not utopian, at least not in a transcendent sense, and neither is it endlessly deferred. Rather it is immanent to this reality, made of the same stuff, the same materials as it were. The abstract machine is in fact that which connects any given assemblage to an outside, the latter understood ultimately as the realm of future potentialities:

> Abstract machines operate within concrete assemblages: They are defined by ... the cutting edges of decoding and deterritorialization.

> They draw these cutting edges. Therefore they make the territorial assemblage open onto something else, assemblages of another type, the molecular, the cosmic; they constitute becomings. Thus they are always singular and immanent. (*ATP* 510)

Back to the rhizome for the last time:

> 5 and 6. Principle of cartography and decalcomania: a rhizome is not amenable to any structural or generative model. It is a stranger to any idea of genetic axis or deep structure ... The rhizome is altogether different, *a map and not a tracing* ... What distinguishes the map from the tracing is that it is entirely orientated towards an experimentation in contact with the real ... The map is open and connectable in all of its dimensions; it is detachable, reversible, susceptible to constant modification. It can be torn, reversed, adapted to any kind of mounting, reworked by an individual, group, or social formation. It can be drawn on a wall, conceived of as a work of art, constructed as political action or meditation. (*ATP* 12)

A rhizome, as a map, is to do with experimentation. It does not trace something that came before (again no *re*presentation) rather it actively creates the terrain it maps – setting out the coordination points for worlds-in-progress, for subjectivities-to-come. This is opposed to a tracing that 'injects redundancies and propagates them' (*ATP* 12). What the tracing reproduces of the map or rhizome are only the 'impasses, blockages, incipient tap roots, or points of structuration' (*ATP* 13). A map on the other hand is creative, constructive and always in process. With maps, as Deleuze remarks elsewhere:

> The trajectory merges not only with the subjectivity of those who travel through a milieu, but also with the subjectivity of the milieu itself, insofar as it is reflected in those who travel through it. The map expresses the identity of the journey and what one journeys through. It merges with its object, when the object itself is movement. (*ECC* 61)

Again, this is not a binary opposition between mapping and tracing, for one can always become the other ('You may make a rupture, draw a line of flight, yet there is still a danger that you will re-encounter organizations that restratify everything' (*ATP* 9)). It is in fact a question of method: *'the tracing should always be put back on the map'* (*ATP* 13).[44] Replacing representation here is a notion of pragmatics; the rhizome map is made to get things done, to move us onwards. Art practice as a form of cartography then, the creative mapping of our connections and potentialities, a mapping that pays attention to regions of intensity (the distribution of affects) and to trajectories of future becomings, as well as to those already delineated continents of representation and signification.

In the essay 'What Children Say' Deleuze in fact characterises these kinds of maps as precisely those made by children, but also by art. Maps 'made up of trajectories and becomings ... both extensive and intensive' (*ECC* 65–6).[45] Such maps are always impersonal and anti-commemorative. This is a cartography art as opposed to an archaeology art (the latter obsessed with origins, with long-term memory). Deleuze makes the point that these maps are also internal to the work of art itself or are determined by the work of art: 'A map of virtualities, drawn up by art, is superimposed onto the real map, whose distances it transforms' (*ECC* 67). Such internal paths are, as Deleuze remarks, particularly implied in modern sculpture (the internal lines determine the external ones), but also in any work of art. Indeed any work of art is a kind of sculpture in one sense: an assemblage of elements in the world that in itself allows for different affects and possible trajectories to arise:

> Every work is made up of a plurality of trajectories that coexist and are readable only on a map, and that change direction depending on the trajectories that are retained. These internalised trajectories are inseparable from becomings. *Trajectories and becoming:* art makes each of them present in the other, it renders their mutual presence perceptible. (*ECC* 67)

The rhizome announces this mapping project, this endless connectivity and becoming that has always already been going on in the interstices of the world, and in the imaginations of those who inhabit it. This is also a call for a rhizomatics of art, of art practice, with art history as no longer, or not just, a critical project but an affirmative and creative one as well; a creative project that parallels the work of its objects. Would the terms art and history still be applicable, still be useful? In fact, I suspect that a kind of rhizomatics has always been going on in between the various objects and practices of canonical art history; a secret and nomadic art history of sensation and becoming, and that likewise, art practice when it truly is an art practice, is always already rhizomatic. For wherever there are roots there are burgeoning rhizomes, wherever there is strata there is, locked within, possibilities of movement, of destratification. Perhaps this might then be a job for a kind of art history, to reactivate the frozen event that is art, to map out the 'past' of the object but also the future potentialities; to map out the rhizomatic connections through time and space, and at the same time, everywhere and always to think about ourselves as being in rhizomatic connection with our objects of study and to allow these creative connections, these mappings, to transform such objects and ourselves. It is in this sense, once more, that the practice of rhizomatics can be understood as a specifically aesthetic project. A certain notion of politics might strategically disappear here (the 'subject' of politics himself disappears). Indeed, this project might also be characterised as ethical inasmuch as it involves exploring our potential for becoming and our potential for self-overcoming. This is not necessarily to completely disavow the political project, the work of representation and of representational critique, rather it is to reconfigure these projects as molar, which, important though they might be, when focused on exclusively, efface the molecular of which they are effectively constituted.

2
The Ethicoaesthetics of Affect and the Bloc of Sensations
Reaffirming the Specificity of Art (Against Representation)

In this chapter I put forward a polemical argument for a kind of 'return' to aesthetics, the latter understood here as the deterritorialsing function of art, its power to take us outside our 'selves' – a return, via Deleuze and Guattari and a number of different allies and precursors, which reaffirms the specificity of art. It is then a return to the terrain of the previous chapter in terms of its utilisation of an expanded and immanent notion of aesthetics and a foregrounding of art's asignifying potential, but it is also a turn away, one might even say a revision, in terms of its focus on the art object understood as a particular kind of 'made' thing. One might also think of this latter turn as a strategic move from opening to closure, or even from speed to slowness (in this sense it tracks the move Deleuze and Guattari themselves made from the wildness of *Capitalism and Schizophrenia* to a more sober account of the impasses and possibilities of thought in *What is Philosophy?*).[1] As with the previous chapter I do not refer to specific practices, rather, my argument is directed at the field of contemporary art in general as well as at certain theoretical preoccupations of art history.

The first half of the chapter then makes a case for attention to be paid to the *affective* side of the art experience. Affect here is understood, via Deleuze–Spinoza, as the effect a given object or practice has on its beholder, and on its beholder's 'becomings'. Important here is also what we might call that 'affective-gap', or 'hesitancy' as Henri Bergson understood it, between stimulus and response, which in itself allows creativity to arise. A third moment is provided by both Georges Bataille and

Jean-François Lyotard each of whom in their own way see art as a form of affective, or ritual practice that accesses a realm beyond the known. In each case affect is to do with the body and with thought, and with what a body–thought is capable of.[2] As with the previous chapter I make this argument against the backdrop of deconstruction (or 'signifier enthusiasm') and against what we might call the melancholy science of a more Adornian attitude towards art.

The chapter then turns to Deleuze and Guattari's own chapter on art in *What is Philosophy?* and looks at how a notion of affect (along with a notion of percept) might be deployed in thinking about the actual work of art, itself understood as a specific form of thought. In particular I am interested in how this 'Deleuzian' attitude differs from the more usual (in terms of art history) representational models or languages (and especially the 'Social History of Art'). Affect here is used slightly differently in that it names not only intensities in or on the body but also self-sufficient elements in the world (that which 'makes up' art). I also make a detour at this point to Deleuze's book on Francis Bacon, and specifically to concepts of the *figural*, the *diagram*, and *probe-heads*, each of which deform figuration and disrupt representation. This leads on to the last section, a brief consideration, as a corrective, of what we might call contemporary art's allegorical qualities.

The ethicoaesthetics of affect

Apartness against deconstruction

> Art is thus confused with a cultural object and may give rise to any of the discourses to which anthropological data in general lend themselves. One could do a history, sociology, or political economy of it, to mention just those few. One can easily show that its destination, anthropologically speaking, undergoes considerable modification depending on whether the artwork 'belongs' to a culture that is tribal, imperial, republican, monarchical, theocratic, mercantile, autarkic, capitalist, and so on, and that it is a determining feature of the contemporary work that it is obviously destined for the museum (collection, conservation, exhibition) and for the museum audience. This approach is implied in any 'theory' of art, for the theory is made only of objects, in order to determine them. But the work is not merely a cultural object, although it is that too and always has been, and if it holds out or is able to hold out a promise of an infinity of forms and commentaries, and through this infinity, a promise of community of feeling, it is because it harbours within it an excess, a rapture,

a potential of associations that overflows all the determinations of its 'reception' and 'production'. (Lyotard 1999, 93)

And so, we might ask, how could it happen? That in thinking about art, in *reading* the art object, we missed that which art does best, in fact we missed that which defines art: the aesthetic. Because art is not an object amongst others, at least, not an object of knowledge (or, not only an object of knowledge), rather, art 'does something else'. Indeed, art is precisely antithetical to knowledge, if by knowledge we understood the accretion of information about 'reality' as we typically experience it. It is in this sense that art works against what Lyotard once called 'the fantasies of realism' (1984, 74).[3] This amounts to saying that art might well be *a part* of the world (after all it is a 'made' thing in the world), but at the same time it is *apart* from the world, and this 'apartness', however it is theorised, is what constitutes art's importance and its specificity as art. I want to explore this apartness, this 'excess', or 'rapture', which, as Lyotard remarks above, constitutes art's effectivity over and beyond its existence as a cultural object. I want to claim that this excess need not be theorised as transcendent, but that we can think the aesthetic power of art in very much an immanent sense, as offering an excess not somehow beyond the world but an excess of the world, the world here understood as the sum total of potentialities of which our typical experience is merely an extraction.

Before moving on however, a quick backward glance. What happened? What caused this aesthetic blindness? In the discipline of art history there were (at least) two factors in play: (1) Marxism (or the 'Social History of Art') and the propensity to historically explain, or interpret, art through recourse to its moment of production and (2) deconstruction (or the 'New Art History') and the propensity to stymie manoeuvres such as the first, whilst still inhabiting their general conceptual framework. With the first factor, art is figured as representation *par excellence*. With the second, the very notion of representation is problematised. We might say that with the first factor there is an appeal to origins as final explanation, whilst with the second the very notion of an origin is put under erasure. Aesthetics fell foul first to the first factor. A disinterested beauty? A transcendent aesthetic? Both were seen as ideological.[4] Aesthetics then fell foul to the second factor – that 'apparatus of capture' which we might characterise as broadly deconstructive. As we saw in Chapter 1, deconstruction figuring aesthetics as a discourse of or on representation, albeit one in crisis. In this latter case the aesthetic moment is denied (or deferred) and art becomes a broken promise.[5] Both the factors were, and still are, powerful critiques (critiques that are specifically techniques of reading). However, the second especially is critique *par excellence*; indeed, the second is implicitly a critique of the first (hence Marx and Derrida will always be troublesome bed mates, at least in this sense).

It is not as if this deconstructive reading-machine is itself a bad thing. As was pointed out in the previous chapter it might be strategically important to employ deconstruction precisely to counteract the effects – to disable – a certain kind of aesthetic discourse (again, deconstruction operates here as a kind of 'expanded ideological critique'). Often such critiques, that inhabit the object of criticism (in this case discourses of representation), are the only way to strategically engage with an enemy, at least at first, but after the deconstruction the art object remains. Life goes on. Art, whether we will it or not, continues producing affects. So, what is the 'nature' of these affects, and can they be deconstructed? Well, they are certainly extra-discursive and may well be extra-textual.[6] Affects are passages of intensity, a reaction in or on the body at the level of matter.[7] We might even say that affects are immanent to matter. They are certainly immanent to experience. In fact, following Deleuze–Spinoza, we might define affect as the effect another body (for example an art object) has upon my own body, and upon my body's duration (*ECC* 139).

Spinoza: joyful encounters

An affect is then not simply a given intensity, although in a sense it begins with this. For Deleuze–Spinoza the latter is in fact termed *affection*, or the actual 'state of the *affected* body' (which in itself 'implies the presence of the *affecting* body' (*PP* 49)). These affections 'express our state at a given moment in time ... they are a slice of our duration' (*ECC* 139). However such affections also determine a passage to a 'more' or to a 'less'. They are, if you like, always experienced *in* time, *as* duration. Thus, affect, understood here as precisely the body's passage from one state of affection to another (*PP* 49). Affect then, for Deleuze–Spinoza, names the risings and fallings – the becomings – of my own body, especially when it encounters another body. It follows that different encounters will have different characters, and indeed that certain encounters will be more productive, others less so. Hence Spinoza's comment (quoted by Deleuze): 'By affect I understand affections of the body by which the body's power of acting is increased or diminished, aided or restrained' (*PP* 49).

For Deleuze–Spinoza the science of affect is called ethics; the organisation of one's world so as to produce joyful encounters, or affects which are of the 'joy-increasing type', those which increase our capacity to act in the world. Art practice as it was mapped out in the previous chapter, might be a name for a kind of ethics in this sense, in fact for a kind of ethicoaesthetics; the organisation of productive encounters 'through' art. These productive encounters themselves allow for the generation of 'common notions', understood simply as the concepts we form about the world when we experience the joy of two bodies that agree coming together. As Deleuze remarks: 'The common notions are an Art, the art of the *Ethics* itself: organising good encounters, composing actual relations, forming powers, experimenting' (*PP* 119). In such a creative mapping of experience:

> The important thing is to understand life, each living individuality, not as a form, or of a development of form, but as a complex relation between differential velocities, between deceleration and acceleration of particles. A composition of speeds and slownesses on a plane of immanence. (*PP* 123)

This physics of life applies to the artist, to the spectator – indeed to all the participants 'with' art – but also to the object itself, which, as we shall see below, might itself be understood as a complex composite of different speeds and rhythms.

In a sense then affects as they are typically experienced *are* disparaged even by Spinoza. They invariably involve random compounds, mixtures of bodies, which are 'inadequate ideas'. 'Common notions', or adequate ideas, are inevitably privileged over these. However, as Deleuze points out in his short essay on 'Spinoza and the Three "Ethics"', such mixtures operate as the 'springboard', giving us the 'necessary vitality' to form 'common notions', or concepts about the world (*ECC* 144). Indeed, it is the selection of augmentative affects that is the very precondition of such concept creation (*ECC* 144). These affects then are the 'dark precursors' of our conceptual system, precursors that subsist alongside the production of knowledge. We might argue here that the terrain of the dark precursor is the terrain of art, the production of new mixtures and new affective assemblages, although art can also be involved in the production of 'common notions' that lead on from this. In passing it is important to note that this 'conceptual system' is itself nothing but the precursor for a third kind of knowledge, a knowledge of what Deleuze–Spinoza calls 'Essences or Singularities' (*ECC* 148). This knowledge involves a further, almost meditative, self-reflection on the common notions themselves. In fact, a movement from the relative speed of the latter (the reflection on relations of movement and rest, or simply on encounters) to an absolute speed that occupies space all at once, 'a speed of absolute survey' (*ECC* 150). As Deleuze remarks: 'Absolute speed is the manner in which an essence surveys its affects and affections in eternity' (*ECC* 149). We might say that this third kind of knowledge, or special kind of thought, that arises from the second, and that collapses distances and operates through leaps and hiatuses, has also a privileged relation with the first, albeit the first seen with clarity and precision (it is, if you like, ourselves seeing ourselves clearly). The joy produced by this third kind of knowledge is a kind of auto-affect (a beatitude). It is a place in which everything in the world agrees with oneself (and thus produces joy). This is a state of involved disinterestedness and compassion – looking out on a world of pure intensities. It is also the experience of eternity within duration (we might even say the deployment of the eternal *against* duration).[8]

Affects then are not to do with signification or 'meaning' as such. Indeed, they occur on a different, asignifying register. In fact this is what differentiates art from language, although language can and does have an affective register (for example, we have an affective relationship with writing – as Deleuze often reminds us, not least in his book on Kafka, writing always involves becomings). From a deconstructive perspective it might be argued that 'affects' are only 'meaningful' 'within' language. Here the realm of affect is positioned as an unreachable (and unsayable) origin (the 'before' of language if you like). And yet affects are also, and primarily, felt experience. There is no denying – or deferring – them. They are what make up life and art.[9] For there is a sense in which art is itself made up of affects. Affects frozen in time and space that maintain a certain cohesiveness, however temporary. Affects are then, to use a Deleuzian term, and to move the register away from deconstruction and away from representation, the molecular 'beneath' the molar, the molecular understood here as life and art's intensive quality, the stuff that goes on 'beneath', in fact that always parallels, signification.[10]

But what can one say about affects? Indeed, what needs to be said about them? Certainly, in a space (art history) where deconstructive approaches, let alone semiotic ones, to art have become hegemonic, their existence, and their central 'role' in art needs asserting. For again this is what art is: a bundle of affects, or, as Deleuze and Guattari would say, a *bloc of sensations*. It is also what art does, that is, produces affects. Indeed, you cannot 'read' affects in this sense, you can only experience them. Which brings us to the whole crux of the matter: experience. Here is Paul de Man, a more or less typical spokesperson for that melancholy science that is deconstruction:

> It is a temporal experience of human mutability, historical in the deepest sense of the term in that it implies the necessary experience of any present as a *passing* experience that makes the past irrevocable and unforgettable, because it is inseparable from any present or future. (1983b, 148–9)[11]

As with Derrida, so with de Man: present experience – the moment – is inaccessible to consciousness. All we ever have is its trace (we experience passing moments). As such, and if affect 'is' precisely present experience, it might be argued, following de Man *et al.*, that all we ever have is a kind of echo, the *re*presentation, of affect. Here a notion of affect is given a logocentric spin; affect becomes synonymous with presence. But is the affect really of this type? Is the affect transcendent in this sense (beyond experience)? Or rather, is it not the case that affects make up experience, and that all this writing about affect is really just that: writing. Writing that produces an effect of representation. Bastardising Derrida a little, we might say that by asking the question 'what is an affect?' we are already presupposing that there is an answer (an answer that must be given in language). We have placed the affect in a conceptual opposition that always and everywhere promises, and then frustrates, presence.

So much for writing and for art as a kind of writing. In fact, an affect is something else entirely, precisely an event, or 'happening'. Indeed, this is what defines affect. Affects *are* directly experienced, or rather they are given in experience (they are what makes up our world and our selves).[12] In fact, for Deleuze–Spinoza ethical living does involve a kind of abstraction from this experience. As beings in the world we are caught up in our immediate, often random, encounters, thus we tend not to see what causes different affects (the specific character of specific encounters). Knowledge then is important, but this knowledge is not the accretion of signifying sedimentations, but, as we have seen, the formation of adequate ideas which themselves arise from affects. This is to experientially 'understand' the conditions and causes of specific encounters, and then to utilise such knowledge in organising one's life. If one does still ask what an affect 'means' then, the answer is not to be given in terms of signification (there is no rhetoric of affect) but rather in terms of causes and conditions. The focus is less on writing and on the present moment as always already passed (a lament), but on experience, and on the present moment as the product of a particular type of encounter (an analysis).

It is not that de Man (or Derrida for that matter) is wrong. As subjects we can certainly be positioned – and indeed position ourselves – in de Man's temporal predicament (a name for which is representation). This has often been the way in the West, in modernism and in postmodernism. Indeed, we might say, following Michael Fried and his detractors, that this oscillation between aesthetics and the latter's deconstruction has animated the discourse of art history right up to today.[13] But this deconstructive 'mechanism', this way of thinking art (and indeed ourselves) inevitably closes down the possibility of approaching the encounter or event that is art. Indeed, within this mechanism art is either situated as transcendent, or, with deconstruction, is always already predetermined by the discourse that surrounds it. The event as always already 'captured' by representation. Again, art here becomes a broken promise, a fallen angel.

Might there be a way of rescuing art and the event from this predicament, this double bind, without necessarily returning to a traditional and transcendent aesthetic? This is a slippery area, indeed, it is almost a question of faith.[14] Either you side with deconstruction: the event as always already constituted, determined by the *scene* of the event (the impossibility of improvisation as Derrida once remarked), or you get a little more optimistic: the event as something genuinely unexpected.[15] Importantly, this need not involve a transcendent aesthetic. In fact, there may be a way of reconfiguring the event as immanent to this world, as not arriving from any kind of transcendent plane (and as not transporting us there) but as emerging from the realm of the virtual.[16] In this latter place art – or art work – is no longer an object as such, or not only an object, but also a space or a zone from which creativity emerges.[17] An 'event site' as Alain Badiou might call it: 'a point of exile where *it is possible* that something, finally, might happen' (Badiou 1999, 84.5). At any rate a place where one might encounter affects.

Bergson: the gap

Such an encounter, or 'accessing' of the event, might involve what Henri Bergson calls attention; the suspension of normal motor activity which in itself allows other 'planes' of reality to become perceivable (this is an opening up to the world beyond utilitarian interests) (*MM* 101–2). The event then emerges from the world but from a world usually imperceptible. For Bergson this event is also an event 'from' memory, not habitual memory but what we might call pure, ontological memory. Indeed, one of the aspects that most interests Deleuze about Bergson's thesis is how this memory penetrates lived life and in so doing brings about the possibility of creativity, or simply the breaking of habit. The realm of affect understood in Spinoza's sense as the plane of becoming is here a realm of potentiality located in a kind of gap between action and reaction.[18]

For Bergson it is the brain, understood as complex matter, which opens up this gap. The brain functions as an exchange system, receiving sensations and producing reactions, and yet because of its complexity (there are a multiplicity of possible pathways through which the brain–body configuration can react) an interval is opened up between excitation and reaction.[19] It is into this interval that memory, understood as the pure past, enters and as such the possibility of circumnavigating typical responses – of creatively responding to the world. We might say that this is the definition of freedom, a disinterestedness which allows access to something bigger, more expansive, than one's self. It is in this gap then that genuine events emerge. In fact, Bergson goes further, and, as Deleuze points out in *Bergsonism*, extends this principle to society's organisation, and to the possibility of creative emotion within the latter (precisely a liberation from habit). Another name for this creative emotion might be revolutionary potential, inasmuch as it is this 'pure memory' that liberates us from our present plane of experience:

> The little interval 'between the pressure of society and the resistance of intelligence' defines a variability appropriate to human societies. Now, by means of this interval, something extraordinary is produced or embodied: creative emotion. This no longer has anything to do with the pressures of society, nor with the disputes of the individual. It no longer has anything to do with an individual who contests or even invents, nor with a society that constrains, that persuades, or even tells stories. It has only made use of their circular play in order to break the circle, just as Memory uses the circular play of excitation and reaction to embody recollections in images. And what is this creative emotion, if not precisely a cosmic Memory that Actualises all the levels at the same time, that liberates man from the plan (*plan*) or the level that is proper to him, in order to make him a creator, adequate to the whole movement of creation. (*B* 111)

For Bergson, ultimately, it is the mystic who embodies this creative emotion, but art has a role to play too. In fact, art, understood here as fabulation, is a kind of platform. It allows for a 'slowing down' (in itself an interesting operation in our increasingly accelerating technocratic world), which prepares the ground for the arising of creative emotion.[20] Ultimately art, in this story-telling mode, is transcended by genuine creation. As Deleuze remarks in a footnote to the above: 'It will be noted that art, according to Bergson, has two sources. There is a *story-telling* art, sometimes collective, sometimes individual. And there is an *emotive* or *creative* art. Perhaps all art presents these two aspects, but in variable proportions' (*B* 134–5, n36). Indeed, we might say that visual art encapsulates both these forms (it is situated between the novel and music in this sense). We might say that the *story-telling* aspect is art's signifying aspect, whereas the *creative* aspect is art's asignifying potential. The former might also be understood as art's allegorical nature. Here then it becomes a question of attitude, of what one is open to experience, or of what one 'takes' from the art experience, and it would seem likely, to agree with Deleuze–Bergson, that this state of affairs is always mixed; we are always dealing with complex assemblages. I will return to this point at the end of the chapter.

Ritual

Following Bergson then we might say that we are caught, as beings in the world, on a certain spatio-temporal register: we 'see' only what we have already seen. We see only that which we are *interested* in. At stake with art might be an altering – a switching – of this register. New (prosthetic) technologies can do this: switching temporal registers (time lapse photography producing firework flowers and flows of traffic; slow motion film revealing intricate movements which otherwise are a blur), and switching spatial ones too (microscopes and telescopes revealing the molecular and the super-molar). Indeed, at this point 'new' media coincides with art, taking on an aesthetic, or what we might call deterritorialising function. These new universes are not somehow beyond the world but very firmly in and of the world, albeit a world normally invisible.

However, we need not turn to new technologies.[21] Painting, for example, might also be seen as the making perceptible of the imperceptible, as the making visible of affect. Deleuze's book on Bacon, as we shall see, makes precisely this argument. In fact, we can go further than this. The realm of affect is all around us and there are as many different strategies for accessing it, as there are subjects. Deleuze and Guattari pay particular attention to this in *A Thousand Plateaus*. Here it is a question of making yourself a 'Body without Organs', the latter understood, in this context, as a strategy for accessing that which is normally 'outside' yourself (that is, outside your signifying self), your 'experimental milieu' which everywhere accompanies your sense of identity.[22] Sadomasochistic practices, meditation, drugs, and so on, all in different ways open up these molecular worlds.[23] It goes without saying that this is very much a pragmatic project: you do not just read about the Body without Organs, you make yourself one. I will be looking at a case study of this in relation to Robert Smithson's earthworks in Chapter 4.

We might also productively turn here to Georges Bataille, who writes about this pragmatic and affective nature of art in his book on the Lascaux cave paintings. For Bataille the practice of cave painting is specifically ritualistic, involving the creation of a sacred space. Indeed, art, for Bataille, is a mechanism for accessing a kind of immanent beyond to everyday experience. Here, art operates as a form of play that takes the participant out of mundane consciousness, hence Bataille's understanding of the Lascaux cave paintings as specifically performative. This involves a switching of temporal modes, a move from 'work time' (to do with utility; with being human) to 'sacred time' (a transgression of this norm; a move 'into' the natural – cosmic – realm). As Bataille remarks:

> in every ritual operation, the seeking after a specific end is never but one amongst a number of its operators' motives: these motives derive from the whole of reality, its religious and sensible (aesthetic) sides alike. In every case they imply what has always been art's purpose: to create a sensible reality whereby the ordinary world is modified in response to the desire for the extraordinary, for the marvellous, a desire implicit in the human being's essence. (1980, 34)

This operation might involve a representational function, after all we can recognise the animals at Lascaux, but representation is not these paintings' sole purpose and we miss something essential about them if we attend merely to their signifying function (if we simply read them). We might note the connections with Bergson here: art utilises the mundane to produce something *extra* mundane.

This is to understand art as ritual or rather to understand all art as having a ritualistic component. In some senses it is also a return to pre-modern notions of magical causality. Magic is to be understood here as a specific technique of connecting with the world.[24] Interestingly, it is often the doyens of modernity who are most attuned to this 'aesthetic' connection. Thus, we have Aby Warburg and his account of (and attraction to) the serpent rituals of the Pueblo Indians and concomitant ambivalence towards technological progress.[25] We also have Walter

Benjamin's ambiguous lament that the sorcerer has been replaced by the surgeon (the oft quoted loss of aura which might be understood here as the loss of the specifically affective power of the work of art).[26] The parallels between Warburg and Bataille in particular are striking, for both it is the capturing of affect through the dance and the wearing of masks that they are attracted to as an alternative to their typical modern milieu and habitual subjectivities. Indeed, for both, ritual is a form of becoming, and specifically a form of becoming animal, at least as a threshold to other (non-human) becomings. We must be wary here, as Theodor Adorno would remind us, of getting too caught up in the 'jargon of authenticity'. There is no sense in which we can, nor should we want to, move to some fantasy pre-modern world of the noble savage (we are after all modern subjectivities in a modern world). On the other hand, we should always be alert to other kinds of possibilities for mobilising alternative practices to those typically offered to us (the dominant paradigm in our techno-scientific world being one of spectatorship and consumption). Such resistant practices and alternative temporalities, as Raymond Williams once reminded us, are to be found as much in residual cultures as in those more emergent ones (at least when the residual has not been completely co-opted by the dominant).[27] As well as looking to the future then, art might strategically also have one eye on the past.

We might also look to Jean-François Lyotard again here. Indeed, Lyotard seems to be the poststructuralist theorist who is most attuned to this experimental and rupturing quality of art. In *Peregrinations* Lyotard in fact calls for a practice of patience and of listening, a kind of meditative state which again builds a platform as it were, allowing for an experience of affect understood here as an event in experience. As Lyotard, remarks:

> to become open to the 'It happens that' rather than the 'What happens', requires at the very least a high degree of refinement in the perception of small differences ... In order to take on this attitude you have to impoverish your mind, clean it out as much as possible, so that you make it incapable of anticipating the meaning, the 'What' of the 'It happens ...' The secret of such ascesis lies in the power to be able to endure occurrences as 'directly' as possible without the mediation of a 'pre-text.' Thus to encounter the event is like bordering on nothingness. (1988, 18)[28]

This perception of small differences without pretext is the perception of affect. We might say then that art, understood as an affect-event, and as

Bataille also teaches us, is not really about self- consciousness – the representation of experience to oneself, the self as constituted through representation. In fact, we might say that affect is a more brutal *a*personal thing. It is that which connects us to the world. It is the matter in us responding and resonating with the matter around us. Affect is, in this sense, *trans*human. Indeed, with affect what we have is a kind of transhuman aesthetic. De Man might figure art as a shield from mortality, a reassuring mirror to a fearful subject (and then, of course, demonstrate that the shield is *always already* broken), but in fact art is something much more dangerous: a portal, an 'access point' to another world of molecular becoming (our world experienced differently). As Deleuze and Guattari say, this, ultimately, is what makes art abstract: the 'summoning' and making visible of otherwise imperceptible forces (*WP* 181–2).[29]

This world of affects, this universe of forces, is our own world seen without the spectacles of habitual subjectivity. But how to remove these spectacles, which are not really spectacles at all but the very condition of our subjectivity? How, indeed, to side step our selves? In fact, we do it all the time. We are involved in molecular processes that go on 'beyond' our subjectivity. Indeed, we 'are' these processes. We 'are', as well as subjects (bound by strata), bundles of events, bundles of affects.[30] At stake here then is the initiation of practices and strategies that reveal this 'other side' to ourselves, which dismantle the molar aggregates of our subjectivity – modern rituals that imaginatively and pragmatically switch the register.[31] In such a place one is less a speaking subject, or not only a speaking subject, but 'becomes a set of liberated singularities, words, names, fingernails, things, animals, little events' (*N* 7). Art, understood in this ritualistic sense, might be said to reconnect us with the world, opening us up to the non-human universe that we are part of but typically estranged from. We might say then that art, as well as having a representational function (after all art objects – like everything else – can be read), also operates as a fissure in representation.[32] And we, as participants with art, as representational creatures ourselves, are involved in a dance with art, a dance in which, through careful manoeuvres, the molecular is opened up, the aesthetic is activated and art does what is its chief *modus operandi*. It transforms, if only for a moment, our sense of our 'selves' and our experience of our world.

This is to claim quite an importance for art. Certainly, it is to move far away from those postmodernists who assert that it is time for art to be included within the 'broader picture of representational practices in contemporary society' (Burgin 1986, 161). Indeed, it is to reclaim a kind of autonomy for art. But this autonomy is not the same as, for example, Adorno's, although it might appear similar. It is, in fact, a reconfiguration of aesthetics away from Adorno (and to some extent the whole Kantian heritage). I go into this in more detail in Chapter 4. Suffice to say here that with our turn from Adorno to Deleuze we have moved towards a more affirmative notion of the aesthetic impulse. Here, instead of the existent and the possible as ontological categories and coordination points for art, we might utilise Deleuze's categories of the actual and the virtual. Art is that genuinely creative act that actualises the virtual, the virtual here being understood as the realm of affect. This gives art an ethical imperative, for it involves a 'moving beyond' the already familiar (our 'actual' selves), a kind of 'self-overcoming'.

Again, this is to take art away from a Frankfurt School register. For Adorno, art's importance lay, at least in one sense, in its 'uselessness', its irreducibility to conceptual thought. Art did not partake in, and thus provided a critique of, instrumental reason and its accompaniment, the world commodity system. With Deleuze, Guattari and with their allies, we have a different mapping of the world – and of philosophy and art's role within it. Philosophy is no longer to be understood as a utopian pursuit (at least in a defeatist, melancholy sense) but is rather to do with pragmatics: active concept creation in order to solve problems.[33] Likewise with art. Art is not 'useless' but performs very specific roles.[34] These roles or functions differ depending on the kind of art being looked at and the milieu that a specific work of art exists within. Indeed, conceptual art might have more in common with what Deleuze and Guattari call philosophy (I will return to this briefly below). Installation art on the other hand might be a paradigmatic case of art as access point to 'other worlds'. In fact, Julia Kristeva arrives at precisely this latter conclusion. Here she is writing about the contemporary installations at the Venice Biennale:

> In an installation it is the *body* in its entirety which is asked to participate through its sensations, through *vision* obviously, but also *hearing, touch*, on occasions *smell*. As if these artists, in the place of an 'object' sought to place us in a space at the limits of the sacred, and asked us not to contemplate images but to communicate with beings. I had the impression that [the artists] were communicating this: that the ultimate aim of art is perhaps what was formerly celebrated under the term of *incarnation*. I mean by that a wish to make us feel, through the abstractions, the forms, the colours, the volumes, the sensations, a *real experience*. (Quoted in Bann 1998, 69)

For Kristeva art, in this case installation, is a bloc of sensations, made up of abstractions, forms, colours and volumes whose point is to make us feel a real and multi-sensory experience. Indeed, Kristeva writes about these installations not in terms of representation but in terms of their function, a function of incarnation. For Kristeva, this aesthetic function is the 'ultimate aim of art'. This is, in a sense, to move to a post-medium notion of art practice, in that it is not so important what the specifics of a medium might be (no Greenbergian truth to materials, again, no more asking the question 'what is art?', or 'what is painting?' (thus, no more deconstructions)), rather it becomes important what a particular art object can do.[35] In relation to aesthetics and affects, this function might be summed up as the making visible of the invisible, the making perceptible of the imperceptible, or, as Deleuze and Guattari might say, the 'harnessing of forces'.[36] Another way of saying this is that art is a deterritorialisation, a creative deterritorialisation into the realm of affects. Art then might be understood as the name for a function, a magical and aesthetic function of transformation, less involved in a making sense of the world and more involved in exploring the possibilities of being in – and becoming with – the world. Art is less involved in knowledge and more involved in experience – in pushing forward the boundaries of what can be experienced. And finally, it is less involved with shielding us from death, than in actualising the possibilities of life.

This notion of an 'aesthetic function' might well lead us to a productive utilisation of the term 'visual culture', understood as the field of expanded practice of Chapter 1, but it will be a return marked by its passage through a notion of affect. Indeed, in such a passage the aesthetic becomes dislodged from its attachment to certain objects and especially the canonical objects of art history. This immanent aesthetic as function can now be thought in relation to a variety of objects and practices in connection with a diversity of different subjects. So, perhaps a kind of general visual culture after all, but not through notions of a general semiotics, rather through notions of a general aesthetic.

The bloc of sensations

Monuments

So far in this chapter I have been predominantly employing a notion of affect in terms of our interaction with art. Art here has generally been thought as the name of an interaction or an encounter, the effect of one body on another. However, art also names an object, or we might say names a principle of internal cohesiveness. Indeed, as was alluded to above, art itself might be understood as a kind of affective assemblage. What is the relation of this bodily definition of affect with affect as it is incarnated in art works, and perhaps more importantly, how do we demarcate art from non-art (or even 'good' art from 'bad')? In a sense, with our definition of affect and aesthetics, we have already moved away from this kind of delimiting exercise. The lines of demarcation are still there but they are more complex and contingent. That which operates as a creative deterritorialisation (in Spinoza's terms, a joyful encounter) for one individual might not work for another (the question of the spectator's specific production of subjectivity – his or her investment with a particular object – becomes important here). This definition of art arising from the spectator, however, seems unsatisfactory (Barthes' death of the author notwithstanding). Is there not something that also 'defines' art from the perspective of its manufacture? Indeed what is that thing that constitutes art 'beyond' its existence as brute matter? Deleuze and Guattari, in *What is Philosophy?*, give us a kind of answer: style. It is style that organises matter. Style that takes lived perceptions and affects into the realm of art: 'In each case style is needed – the writer's syntax, the musician's modes and rhythms, the painter's lines and colours – to raise lived perceptions to the percept and lived affections to the affect' (*WP* 170). It is style that produces art, style that produces, and preserves, a particular combination of sensations and as such is opposed to opinion, which produces only mediocre work – understood as typical bundles of affect. Style, as Deleuze and Guattari remark, quoting Giacometti, are precisely 'those visions fixed in time and space' (*WP* 171).

Art then is to be understood as a composed thing that preserves otherwise passing sensations. 'What is preserved – the thing or the work of art – is a *bloc of sensations, a compound of percepts and affects*' (*WP* 164). Percepts are perceptions that no longer rely on their origin, that are 'independent of a state of those who experienced them' (*WP* 164). Affects, as they are discussed in *What is Philosophy?*, are likewise independent of where they came from. They are 'no longer feelings or affections; they go beyond the strength of those who undergo them' (*WP* 164). Together these two make up art works, or blocs of sensation whose 'validity lies in themselves and exceeds any lived' (*WP* 164). As Deleuze and Guattari remark, this is also what makes art a kind of 'being' which 'could be said "to exist" in the absence of man because man, as he is caught in stone, on the canvas, or by words, is himself a compound of percepts and affects' (*WP* 164).

'The artist creates blocs of percepts and affects, but the only law of creation is that the compound must stand up on its own' (*WP* 164).

Art then has an independent and self-sustaining existence in the world and as such 'works' independently of its producer. Here art is to be understood as a kind of monument, even if it is composed of only a few lines. However, this is not a monument commemorating the past; an art work has less to do with origins in this sense (in the subjective state of the artist, in the mode of production of the time and so on). Indeed, the monument is not summoning or 'conjuring up' a once present absence; it is not 'in' memory in this sense that the materials for art are to be found, but rather in that 'complex material' of 'words and sounds' or of 'tones and colour' (*WP* 164). We have moved away here from a deconstructive paradigm, from the 'absent presence' of the artist, from art as a kind of trace or signature. Indeed, we have moved out of representation altogether. A new vocabulary is needed, a vocabulary not from semiotics, not to do with representation, and Deleuze and Guattari give us one. Here they are writing about the three 'great monumental types', or 'varieties', of 'compounds of sensation' (*WP* 168). They think these through in relation to sculpture, but are clear that they relate to all forms of art:[37]

> Vibrating sensation – coupling sensation – opening or splitting, hollowing out sensation. These types are displayed almost in their pure state in sculpture, its sensations of stone, marble, or metal, which vibrate according to the order of strong and weak beats, projections and hollows, its powerful clinches that intertwine them, its development of large spaces between groups or within a single group where we no longer know whether it is the light or the air that sculpts or is sculpted. (*WP* 168)

There is no rhetoric or 'reading' of the art object here.[38] We might note in passing that Deleuze and Guattari's 'language' of movement and matter, as well as their general characterisation of art as a bloc of sensations, is precisely not the language of art history, at least as far as the former attends to art's signifying character. Indeed, we might say that this language of movement and matter is the object of art history's secret desire and fear, in the sense that it provides a 'language' of art which is no longer to do with signifiers and signifieds (poached, as T. J. Clark once remarked, from film theory (Clarke 1992)).[39]

For Deleuze and Guattari then, art is a composition of percepts and affects brought together in a certain rhythm. Artists are those who add these new varieties or compounds of affects to the world, they are the makers of new rhythms.[40] Another way of putting this is that art is the production of other possible worlds (after all what else is this world but a bloc of sensations, an assemblage of affects?). These are worlds that incorporate the virtual – the realm of affect – as a key component: 'The monument does not actualise the virtual event but incorporates or embodies it: it gives it a body, a life, a universe ... These universes are neither virtual nor actual; they are possibles, "the possible as aesthetic category" ' (*WP* 177). In fact, in the next chapter I attempt to think art precisely as an actualisation of the virtual (art as form of geophilosophy); here, however, art is the embodiment of other possible worlds, other universes. This is almost a return to Adorno and to the notion of the 'utopian blink' (art as a promise, as *the* promise, of another world). But these worlds, for Deleuze and Guattari, are not to be somehow presented negatively. Art is *not* the negative representation of these possible worlds. Indeed, they are not utopian worlds in this sense but worlds that are very much here and now, albeit they are worlds that must summon their own audience into being.

Becomings

The art work is then not a representation but rather the expression of a specific world-view. Here the artist is reinstated in a position of importance, not as the font of meaning of his or her art, but as an individual who has glimpsed the 'great health', the realm of affect: 'what little health they possess is often too fragile, not because of their illness or neuroses but because they have seen something in life that is too much for anyone' (*WP* 172). It is in this sense that the artist 'is a seer, a becomer' (*WP* 171). The creative individual is here given an explicitly Nietzschean formation.[41] He or she has seen the force of life – the world of inorganic forces – underlying the world as it is typically experienced *and* through artistic method is able to give this experience to us as a bloc of percepts and affects. On a more mundane level we might say that the artist is simply he or she who has seen 'beyond' those already given signifying formations and affective assemblages – and who is able to offer up new ones.

'Percepts' can be understood as the '*non-human landscapes of nature*'; as that which deterritorialises the human (*WP* 169). 'Affects' can also be understood as the '*non-human becomings of man*' (*WP* 169). Throughout *A Thousand Plateaus* becoming replaces the more typical mimesis as an articulation of relationships in the world. As we saw in Chapter 1, the wasp and the orchid do not imitate one another, rather they 'become' one another. They are involved in a form of affective capture. Man, too, participates in these becomings, becoming women as the threshold becoming to other stranger becomings: 'becoming animal', 'becoming plant', ultimately, as with Henri Michaux, 'becoming molecular'.[42] In one sense notions of 'becoming' can be understood as a critique of notions of 'Being'. Whereas 'Being' is static and fixes identities for all time, becomings are fluid and dynamic. Representation is all to do with Being. The *re*presentation of truths, of origins, of essences: *B*eing *re*presented in *b*eings. *Art re*presented in *art works*. For Deleuze and Guattari this was never really the case. There is no Being, or at least no Being which is separate from the processes of becoming. Our world consists of moments of becoming, the mingling of bodies, the meeting of forces, a constant interpenetration and interconnection of all phenomena. There is no beginning or end to this process. As Deleuze and Guattari remark: 'We are not in the world, we become with the world; we become by contemplating it. Everything is vision, becoming. We become universes. Becoming animal, plant, molecular, becoming zero' (*WP* 169).

> It should be said of all art that, in relation to the percepts or visions they give us, artists are presenters of affects, the inventors and creators of affects. They not only create them in their work, they give them to us and make us become with them, they draw us into their compound. Van Gogh's sunflowers are becomings, like Dürer's thistles or Bonnard's mimosas. (*WP* 173)

Van Gogh becomes sunflower in painting the sunflowers, we become sunflower in beholding, in encountering Van Gogh's painting. 'We become' meaning we go through the sensations: 'Whether through words, colours, sounds, or stone art is the language of sensations' (*WP* 176). Again, it is through an artist's style that this becoming is achieved. Becoming in this sense is a capture of sensations, a 'passing between things': 'Life alone creates such zones where living beings whirl around, and only art can reach and penetrate them in its enterprise of co-creation' (*WP* 173). Art then is the 'living on' of these zones of indetermination (although this does not necessarily mean that a work of art will physically last) and as such it requires a ground. This is the specific contribution of the art work, understood as that plane of composition in which the material has passed into sensation. If meaning has any use or sense here it is to describe this meeting between the material and sensation, which is to say meaning is no longer logocentric, or indeed rhetorical: 'Aesthetic figures, and the style that creates them, have *nothing to do with rhetoric*. They are sensations: percepts and affects, landscapes and faces, visions and becomings' [my italics] (*WP* 177). We might say then that art is that which freezes, then releases, becomings.

Against figuration

In *What is Philosophy?* it is often literature, and the 'literary moment' in art, that Deleuze and Guattari reference. In a sense this might appear to be shortcoming, for theories of art that rely on the figurative tend to be theories of signification. That is to say it might be argued that the art which Deleuze and Guattari look to needs to be seen and 'recognised'; must in fact, before it is anything else, be about representation. There is then a contradiction here or at least a problem that needs unravelling. For when Deleuze and Guattari discuss Van Gogh's *Sunflowers* it would seem that presupposed is a moment of 'recognition' or precisely of 'reading' (in order to become sunflowers do we need first to identify them?) Is there a becoming that does not involve figuration? What about the non-figurative, the abstract?

In fact, in *What is Philosophy?*, Deleuze and Guattari are less forthcoming, and somewhat disparaging, about abstract (and conceptual) art – which they see as the linking of art with philosophy: 'Abstract art and conceptual art are two recent attempts to bring art and philosophy together, but they do not substitute the concept for the sensation; rather they create sensations and not concepts' (*WP* 198). Abstract art is, for Deleuze and Guattari, a dematerialisation of sensation (in fact the sensation of a concept). Conceptual art on the other hand 'seeks an opposite dematerialisation through generalisation, by installing a sufficiently neutralised plane of composition' (*WP* 198). This latter art, they argue, is in danger of becoming 'informative': 'the sensation depends upon the simple "opinion" of a spectator who determines whether or not to "materialise" the sensation, that is to say, decides whether or not it is art' (*WP* 198). Indeed, this counteracting 'opinion' is one of the objectives of *What is Philosophy?* Before turning to abstract art we might make a brief corrective to Deleuze and Guattari's notion of conceptual art here. For, to a certain extent this reliance on the 'opinion' of the beholder to 'materialise' the art – or rather to make a decision as to whether it is art or not – was one of the declared purposes of conceptual art. As such, Deleuze and Guattari's theory of art (and specifically of painting) might be understood as a 'return' to that which conceptual art deliberately distanced itself from (the 'aesthetic' or expressive object). What we can also say however is that Deleuze and Guattari might have got conceptual art wrong. Indeed, I would argue that conceptual art, as it was most rigorously practiced, had more to do with what Deleuze and Guattari call philosophy than with what they say about art (although Deleuze and Guattari's tripartite division of thought into science, philosophy and art might well render the label 'conceptual art' redundant). I go into the workings of the concept as it is worked out in *What is Philosophy?* in Chapter 4, although it is worth noting here that the formation of concepts has a lot to do with the posing of problems, and the creation of 'solutions' attendant on this: 'All concepts are connected to problems without which they would have no meaning and which can themselves only be isolated or understood as their solution emerges' (*WP* 16). Conceptual art, I would argue, is also connected to the posing of problems in this sense, specifically to do with problems as regards the definition of 'art'.

Back to abstract art then which Deleuze and Guattari argue

> seeks only to refine sensation, to dematerialise it by setting out an architectonic plane of composition in which it would become a purely spiritual being, a radiant thinking and thought matter, no longer sensation of thought or tree, but a sensation of the concept of sea or tree. (*WP* 198)

Is this indeed a kind of blind spot? Does a theory of the non-figurative have to return via the concept to figuration ('sensation of the concept of sea or tree')? Or, in other words, does the abstract have to move away from art to the concept? In fact, we can use Deleuze and Guattari to get out of this aporia. We must learn to think art, including abstract painting, as a constellation of 'forces':

> And this, first of all, is what makes painting abstract: summoning forces, populating the area of plain, uniform colour with the forces it bears, making the invisible forces visible in themselves, drawing up figures with a geometrical appearance but that are no more than forces – the forces of gravity, heaviness, rotation, the vortex, explosion, expansion, germination, and time. (*WP* 181–2)

Non-figurative art might then be seen to be 'about' forces, about making 'perceptible the imperceptible forces that populate the world, affect us, and make us become' (*WP* 182). Again, this is a characterisation of art at odds with much art history, a 'language' of forces that points beyond representation. In this place art is about experiencing sensations, allowing the force(s) of art to act upon the force(s) of our subjectivity: 'Like all painting, abstract painting is sensation, nothing but sensation'

(*WP* 183). It is in this sense that the history of painting might be renamed a logic of sensation, a logic that opens us up to the realm of inorganic 'life'.

However, this is not a complete answer, for the abstract painting of forces is not, for Deleuze anyway, the high point of a kind of inorganic painting. Such painting needs the figure, or the *figural*, in order that it is made relevant, and indeed that it impact directly on ourselves (and on our nervous system). The figural is not figuration. Indeed Deleuze, in his book on Francis Bacon, specifically writes against figuration, understood as narration and illustration, as one of the key tropes of representation. But it is not pure abstraction either. Rather, the figural is a deterritorialisation of the figure (a kind of middle way), but, as such, needs the figure as its point of departure. How then does the figural work to disrupt representation? At this point a detour through the book on Bacon becomes necessary.

The figural

The figural for Deleuze–Bacon is that which deforms, or does violence to, the figurative. We might understand the latter here as the typical way we are represented and represent ourselves within the world, or simply those forms that reassure us of our identity.[43] The figural does this, first, through a mechanism of isolation; the figure is presented as a 'matter-of-fact', detached from narration or indeed any illustrative function. As Deleuze remarks:

> Isolating the figure will be the primary requirement. The figurative (representation) implies the relationship of an image to an object that it is supposed to illustrate; but it also implies the relationship of an image to other images in a composite whole which assigns a specific object to each of them. Narration is the correlate of illustration. A story slips into, or tends to slip into, the space between the two figures in order to animate the illustrated whole. (*FB* 2–3)

We might say then that by placing the figure within the frame of 'art', narration, and indeed representation, is disabled. But this isolation is only one moment in a process, for this figure also operates as a point of departure for deterritorialisations, for a moving beyond the figure. In this sense, the figural is between the figurative and the non-figurative. Put differently the figural involves a becoming of the figure. A becoming animal ('in place of formal correspondences what Bacon's painting constitutes is a *zone of indiscernability or undecideability* between man and animal' (*FB* 21)), and ultimately a becoming imperceptible ('whatever its importance becoming-animal is only one stage in a more profound becoming-imperceptible in which the figure disappears' (*FB* 27)). We can see this in relation to Bacon's portrayal of heads where, in the terms of *A Thousand Plateaus*, Bacon attempts to disrupt the processes of faciality, understood here as that abstract machine of modernity that produces signifiance (the white wall) and subjectification (the black hole). As Deleuze and Guattari remark in *A Thousand Plateaus*:

> if human beings have a destiny, it is rather to escape the face, to dismantle the face and facializations, to become imperceptible, to become clandestine, not by returning to animality, nor even by returning to the head, but by spiritual and special becomings-animal, by strange true becomings that get past the wall and get out of the black holes. (*ATP* 171)

Bacon's heads are then 'probe-heads', lines of escape from the face and from faciality. Crucially, they are not a return to some kind of primitive pre-faciality. They are in fact an escape that takes place from within the terrain of the face, a kind of stammering from within. We might add that probe-heads need not necessarily be pictures of heads but rather any device that disrupts faciality, for the latter applies not just to heads but to most of the mechanisms that produce signifiance and subjectivity, from faces and landscapes within painting to facialisation and landscapification within the world:

> You will be pinned to the white wall and stuffed in the black hole. This machine is called the faciality machine because it is the social production of the face, because it performs the facialization of the entire body and all its surroundings and objects, and the landscapification of all worlds and milieus. (*ATP* 181)

Facialisation then must be understood as precisely a, if not *the*, system of human organisation. Indeed, facialisation is representation *par excellence*. In passing we might note that the affective assemblage of the mass media is an increasingly powerful component – we might even say an acceleration – of this faciality-machine as it operates today.

A probe-head is then that which explores the terrain beyond the face, the terrain from which the face is nothing more than an extraction or crystallisation. Probe-heads are in this sense a move into chaos. Probe-heads are those devices: 'that dismantle the strata in their wake, break through walls of signifiance, pour out of the holes of subjectivity, fell trees in favour of veritable rhizomes, and steer the flows down lines of positive deterritorialization or creative flight' (*ATP* 190). But they are also, as the name suggests, productive of other, stranger and more fluid modes of organisation: 'Beyond the face lies an altogether different inhumanity: no longer that of the primitive head, but of "probe-heads"; here, cutting edges of deterritorialization become operative and lines of deterritorialization positive and absolute, forming strange new becomings, new polyvocalities' (*ATP* 190–1).

Probe-heads might then be a name for more experimental, non-traditional art practices. Such practices might not seem to be defacialisations, but, with the systems of facialisation becoming increasingly complex (one thinks here of new communications technologies) then the lines of flight from these will themselves become increasingly complex and unfamiliar, as will the territories produced on the other side of the 'white wall'. A case study of this new production of subjectivity might be collective and collaborative practices, those that deliberately turn away from the production of individualist and atomised subjectivities. I will be returning to this in the next chapter with what might be seen as a case study of a probe-head. Importantly, probe-heads do not arrive from some other place. They are in fact made from the same stuff as faces, indeed, we might say that the same machines that produce probe-heads also produce faces, the latter being subjectivities and assemblages that are 'useful' (for example in terms of our capitalist mode of production), the former often appearing as redundancies or dead ends.

In relation to Bacon's paintings this defacialisation, or deployment of the figural, involves a very particular system, consisting of a ground or colour field (we might call this the world), a contour or membrane, and the figure itself. The contour in particular plays a crucial role for it is that which isolates the figure, producing a territory, but also that which allows a contact and communication with the outside or ground. The contour operates as the 'deterritorializer' in this sense (*FB* 32). Bacon's paintings picture the relationship between these three elements and the movements between them. Indeed, this constitutes the particular *rhythm* of each particular painting. In terms of what we have already said about percepts and affects, we might say that the percept is the ground, the landscape, whereas the affect is the figure. Their interrelation would then constitute the subject matter of art. All art has a rhythm in this sense, relations between a territory and an outside to this territory. Of particular interest then will be to locate the deterritorialiser, the line of flight that connects an image, object or practice with its outside.

Deleuze and Guattari make a similar point in *What is Philosophy?* in relation to the framing and deframing functions of art. Art involves framing, the marking out of a territory, or the building of a house, but this house is always open to an outside, to the universe (the inorganic world of forces) (*WP* 182).[44] Art is a form of territorialisation that in turn allows for, and produces the conditions for, deterritorialisation. It is in this sense that all art begins with the animal and with the marking out of a territory (*WP* 183). Indeed, it is not so much the animal, or the artist, that produces the territory but rather the territory that produces the animal, or indeed the artist. It is also in this sense that art might be thought as a kind of refrain. A local refrain that opens out onto the cosmic refrain (as Deleuze and Guattari remark one must always leave a gap in the circle (*ATP* 311)). Music must then be seen as exemplary of all art involving as it does the specific production of local refrains within larger ones. Likewise, architecture might be positioned as the first of all arts involving as it does the production of a territory, of a *habitus*, that defines us as human (*WP* 186). We might say the visual arts moves between these two poles (and indeed, within the expanded field of contemporary art, utilises both of them).

For Deleuze–Bacon it is the diagram that enables this deterritorialisation of the figure, this production of the Body without Organs (the latter understood here as that which lies 'under' the organism/organisation (*FB* 50)). In painting, and specifically Bacon's painting, the diagram involves the making of random marks that allow the figural to emerge from the figure: 'The diagram is ... the operative set of asignifying and nonrepresentative lines and zones, line-strokes and colour-patches' (*FB* 101).[45] We might apply this rule of the diagram to other kinds of art, all of which must involve this play with chance, this contact and utilisation with that which goes beyond conscious control (in Bataille's terms this is the move beyond mundane reality). Here random occurrences are ontologically constitutive of art (and not an accident that befalls it). It is in this sense that art can never be wholly predetermined or worked out in advance but must involve this productive encounter with chaos.

The diagram is then 'a chaos, a catastrophe, but it is also a germ of order or rhythm. It is a violent chaos in relation to the figurative givens, but it is a germ of rhythm in relation to the new order of the painting' (*FB* 102).[46] The diagram is a manipulation of chance in order to suggest the 'emergence of another world' (*FB* 100). As Deleuze remarks: '... the law of the diagram, according to Bacon, is this: one starts with a figurative form, a diagram intervenes and scrambles it, and a form of a completely different nature emerges from the diagram, which is called the

Figure' (*FB* 156). All art might be said to produce or suggest worlds in this sense, worlds hitherto unseen but always produced from within the seen.

Within painting the figural works in an analogical fashion, producing resemblances through non-resembling means (*FB* 115). Ultimately this analogical system works through colour and through the modulation of colour. The figural is that territory, that form of resemblance, produced by colour. The diagram is then also a colour map, or a map of sensation. Sensation is understood here as the action of forces upon the body (*FB* 45). It is precisely so that these forces might 'communicate' (that they work directly on our nervous system) that they need to be 'contained' within a territory however fluid this might be. Again, we might also call this territory, this complex of sensation, a rhythm.[47]

However, this is all not without its dangers. Indeed, for Deleuze–Bacon there are two 'wrong' positions as it were, which the middle way of the figural must avoid. Figuration (narration and illustration: *representation*) but also the absolute deterritorialisation of the figure, the move to total abstraction (we might call these the twin dangers of moving too slow, of remaining within representation, and of moving too fast, a line of abolition). Figuration operates through cliché, understood as those signifying formations that surround us everyday: 'We are besieged by photographs that are illustrations, by newspapers that are narrations, by cinema-images, by television-images' (*FB* 87). These are the clichés – physical, though there are also psychic ones ('ready-made perceptions, memories, phantasms' (*FB* 87)) that fill the canvas even before the artist has dipped his brush. Another way of understanding these clichés is as habits, habits of sight and habits of thought. Art opposes these habits, these clichés, with its own logic.[48]

The other way, abstraction, can be divided further into two modalities. The first is pure or geometric abstraction, which elevates the optical and ultimately returns to figuration inasmuch as it contains a code (visual and spiritual) or, to say the same differently, passes through the brain (as is the case, Deleuze–Bacon argues, with Kandinsky) (*FB* 104–5). This is a signifying art, waiting to be read. Indeed, in this regard, the same criticism can be made against both figurative painting and geometric abstract painting: 'they pass through the brain, they do not act directly on the nervous system, they do not attain the sensation, they do not liberate the Figure – all because they remain at *one and the same level*' (*FB* 36). The second form of abstraction, action painting, paradigmatically the case with Jackson Pollock, provides an all-over diagram (a purely haptic space) but in so doing, according to Deleuze–Bacon loses its capacity to act on our nervous system (*WP* 109). The figural avoids these, although it is, according to Deleuze–Bacon, no less radical in its 'path'. We might say then that the figural within Bacon parallels Deleuze's own philosophical project – especially in *A Thousand Plateaus* – of thinking beyond the human, understood here as a habitual mode of being (a representational mode). Both projects do not involve a simple turning away from the figure or from the human, but a kind of stretching or twisting of it, a rupturing and stammering, a releasing of forces from within and the contact of forces that are without (both in fact being the same operation). Both Bacon and Deleuze are specifically mannerist in this sense (*FB* 161). Both are interested in revealing the figural 'behind' the figure, the invisible 'behind' the visible.

Abstraction and the gothic line: Pollock versus Bacon

In the book on Bacon, Deleuze remarks that there are two ways in which 'Barbarian Art' goes 'beyond organic representation': 'either through the mass of the body in movement, or through the speed and changing direction of the flat line' (*FB* 129). This flat line is also known as the 'northern line', that 'which goes to infinity either by continually changing direction, perpetually twisting, splitting, and breaking off from itself; or else by turning back on itself in a violent peripheral or whirling movement' (*FB* 129). This would seem to be a description of Pollock's paintings and indeed Deleuze does reference these. However, for Bacon, as for Deleuze, Michaux remains the master of abstraction and of the abstract, nomadic line, because unlike Pollock he 'remained master of the diagram' (*FB* 110). The all-over paintings of abstract expressionism are instead composed of a diagram that merges with the totality of the painting ('somewhat like a map this is as large as the country' (*FB* 104)). Such paintings produce 'a haptic, manual space', that delimits nothing (no inside/outside), they are made up only of patches of colour and the gothic line:

> with Pollock, this line-trait and this colour-patch will be pushed to their functional limit: no longer the transformation of the form but a decomposition of matter, which abandons us to lineaments and granulations. The painting thus becomes a catastrophe-painting and a diagram-painting at one and the same time. (*FB* 105)

Certainly Pollock would seem to be *the* nomadic painter of modern times. The inheritor of Worringer's northern, gothic line, the painter who has done most to deterritorialise painting. As Deleuze remarks, an important question then is why Bacon did not follow this path, the path of the Gothic. The answer, for Bacon at any rate, is that although sensation is achieved with Pollock it 'remains in an irremediably confused state' (*FB* 109): 'the diagram covers the entire painting and because of this proliferation creates a veritable "mess" ' (*FB* 109). For Bacon the watchword is caution; always save the contour. The painting must remain limited in this sense; the diagram must remain localised, operative and controlled (*FB* 110). Pollock then might be said to have flown too close to the sun, for although it is here, in the confrontation with chaos, in the closest proximity to catastrophe, that the germ of a new world appears, Pollock's paintings go too far for Bacon.[49]

It might be argued however that Bacon did not pay enough attention to Pollock's paintings, for of course they are controlled, and as other commentators have pointed out, were not just the record of a single encounter, a single 'frenetic dance' (although they may contain elements, moments, of this) (*FB* 106).[50] In fact, they were the product of a series of reflections and modifications – involving pauses and repaintings. Nevertheless we must ask whether the diagram remains operative in the sense that Deleuze–Bacon uses the term? Does it allow the figural, understood as another world, to emerge? Two relatively recent commentators on Pollock give us an affirmative answer to this question. First, Kristeva, who argues that in a painting such as *Blue Poles* we precisely see Pollock producing figures, although Kristeva is clear that the earlier all-over paintings of Pollock, are for her, precisely non-figurative, and one must assume non-figural too.[51] But then what is the figural if not a territory of some kind? Pollock's paintings may not be figural in the sense of the human form, or indeed any other 'recognisable' form, but they do contain different aggregates and demarcated territories, albeit fluid ones. They are not chaos, and certainly not a mess. In fact, it might be productive to extend the figural out into that which constitutes art's ability to *interpellate* us in general. All art, to be art, must have an element of figurality in this sense, an intimation of order emerging from chaos, something that looks back as it were (not necessarily a face, but certainly a 'head'). This 'order' might involve the repetition of marks, precisely a rhythm, and certainly Pollock's paintings can be thought of as containing repetitions and refrains in this sense.

A second perhaps more interesting argument that would also seem to contradict Deleuze–Bacon, and to open out the figural into a more complex field is T.J. Clarke's writings on Pollock, and specifically the painting *Number One*. In *Farewell to an Idea* Clarke attends to this painting's peculiar character as a kind of limit point between representation and all over abstraction.[52] The figural elements are in fact the gestural marks, the handprints and whip lashes or loops of paint, particularly as they appear at the top of the painting (evidencing a kind of flailing movement or moment). It is Clarke's conviction that the painting thus maintains a kind of human scale, and yet is *almost* non-human. Is this Pollock's painting as figural, a figurality that lies with the gestural mark itself? Figurality might then be understood as a characteristic of art as a made thing, a characteristic of the style of the artist, and not necessarily limited to the portrayal – however deformed and disrupted – of the human form. We might also think of the expanded practices emerging in the 1960s and 1970s as figural in this sense – performance art, for example, in which the human body itself becomes figural, or installation art and 'Happenings' in which the figural is maintained with just the minimum of technique. And then there are also more recent art practices that although lacking a figure certainly involve a complexity and intentionality – albeit one that is difficult to reconcile with our habitual facialising tendencies.[53]

Coda: on allegory and art's future orientation

Although this chapter has been written against a certain notion of art as representation, it is nevertheless important to note that art, and in particular contemporary art, does operate through the manipulation of signifying material, and indeed that it is the specific character of this manipulation that at least in part sets art apart from other aspects of culture. This is not to return to Craig Owens *et al.* and to identify a general postmodern allegorical impulse within art, but it is to note that contemporary art is involved in multiple regimes of signs.[54]

We might note also that contemporary art often refers to previous art or involves a repetition of previous artistic forms, and indeed forms from more popular and sub cultures.[55] For Deleuze, specifically in the Bacon book, this utilisation of previous form would be a utilisation of cliché even (in fact especially) when it attempts to appropriate and parody cliché (it is in this sense that irony gets caught in the regime it attacks, trapped in the 'milieu of the cliché' (*FB* 87)). Art, here painting, is for Deleuze, specifically *not* to do with the manipulation of already existing signs or codes but precisely in accessing that wildness which is always already underneath these systems. Likewise, in *What is Philosophy?* art disrupts cliché understood as opinion – our typical ways of seeing and speaking – and this realm of opinion will include previous art.

Nevertheless it might be the case that art requires some kind of repetition of previous forms to operate. Here the question of the archive becomes crucial, and of artists working over their archives (whatever and wherever these might be). Bacon's interest in collecting photography would be a case in point (and indeed Deleuze does attend to this). Indeed, art is made from matter in the world and the staging posts for the figural, for deterritorialisation, is always ourselves understood as a bundle of clichés, or simply a territory, within the world. Perhaps then art is always facing in two directions – towards cliché and towards the figural. Or, to put it in terms of *A Thousand Plateaus*, and the previous chapter:

> one side of a machinic assemblage faces the strata, which doubtless makes it a kind of organism, or signifying totality, or determination attributable to a subject; it also has a side facing a *body without organs*, which is constantly dismantling the organism, causing asignifying particles or pure intensities to pass or circulate. (*ATP* 4)

Art then might make use of the components of cliché in order to resist cliché. It undoes the triple organisation of affections, perceptions and opinion – that is to say our habitual mode of being – and substitutes something else, a different organisation or assemblage, a different 'take' on the world, in fact a different world in itself. We might say then that art's power to deterritorialise, its affective dimension, is actually produced through 'history', through the utilisation and mixture of past forms, past affective assemblages. This is often what makes a successful work of art: it utilises the stuff of the world to go beyond that world (again, it operates on a number of different registers, signifying and asignifying). We might say then that the apparent simplicity of the 'aesthetic moment' is a result of an overall historical complexity. Indeed art is the name for this simple yet complex object.

In fact, this signifying or conceptual function of art is not really separate from its affective function. Both are involved in a circular causality (returning to Spinoza, we might understand concepts as themselves the result of affects, just as they 'cause' new affects to arise). History itself, as it is encapsulated in bodies and in art objects is a history of affects (a history of becomings). Art is then like a platform of sorts that produces the means to experience that which lies 'outside' history (what Deleuze, following Nietzsche, names the 'Untimely') (*WP* 111). Art always looks two ways in this sense: towards the world (we might say towards the forms instantiated by capitalism), and towards the universe (a line of flight from these forms into a realm of potentiality).

The novelty of art, its constitution of new complexes, will often appear strange and unfamiliar. It may even be that it surprises its producer (it speaks back to the artist as it were, or appears to come from 'somewhere else'). This in itself means that art is ontologically difficult. It is not made for an already constituted audience but in fact calls its audience into being. It is through the extraction of 'new harmonies, new plastic or melodic landscapes, and new rhythmic characters' that art summons forth this new people (*WP* 176). In presenting us with a new composite, art encourages us to feel and reason in new ways. Indeed, it is in this sense that contemporary art – and that which is contemporary in all art – holds a particular power, for although it might utilise previous form it does so in a new way and with an eye to that which has not yet been realised. Such art produces a line of flight from within already constituted territories so as to produce new modes of becoming and new worlds for a people yet to come. As we shall see in the next chapter this means art has a prophetic function; it is always future-orientated.

3
Art and the Political
Minor Literature, the War Machine and the Production of Subjectivity

In this chapter I want to think through the possibilities of utilising Deleuze and Guattari's writings for theorising what we might call the political effectivity of art, and specifically that of contemporary practices. The chapter is broken down into three self-contained sections. In the first I address Deleuze and Guattari's important concept of the *minor*, understood as a kind of operational tool, a way of thinking through what political or artistic strategy might involve. The concept of the minor has been touched on in the previous two chapters (albeit generally without naming it) in terms of the way in which art can produce a break with habitual formations and dominant signifying regimes. Here I want to attend to the actual mechanisms involved in such a break, and also to the way in which such a break involves the concomitant affirmation of something new. This first section then involves a working through of the characteristics of a 'minor literature' as laid out in Deleuze and Guattari's book on Kafka, and some thoughts on how these might be usefully brought to bear on art practice and art theory. In general what I have to offer are notes towards such a minor practice, although I do make some reference to actual art collectives, especially in the footnotes. In this first section I also make a brief detour into Michael Hardt and Antonio Negri's *Empire*, a book which involves an 'application' of many aspects of the Deleuzoguattarian project to the realm of contemporary geopolitics.[1] The second section involves a shift in terrain, and indeed a turn from art altogether. It involves a further deployment of the minor, but this time in relation to guerrilla political organisation. I am interested here in what lessons might be learnt for an artistic 'war machine' from apparently non-artistic and politically engaged collectivities. We might say that this is a case of looking at an extreme example of a radical practice that foregrounds certain logics and procedures. In particular, I am interested in how such practices produce, or call into being, a specifically collective subjectivity. This will involve attending to the creative and affirmative aspects of a politically engaged practice, or at least these two as accompaniments to those more dissenting and critical aspects. I do not make any easy connections to art practice as such here, but leave it to the reader to draw their own implications. The third and final section of the chapter involves a reading of two texts by Deleuze and Guattari respectively, specifically on this production of subjectivity and also on a kind of production that goes beyond this.

Minor literature

In their book on Kafka Deleuze and Guattari give three determining characteristics of a minor literature, or, which is to say the same thing, of the conditions in which a literature becomes revolutionary:

*1. That a minor literature should deterritorialise the major language (*K 16*).* Such a deterritorialisation involves the neutralisation of sense, or the signifying aspects of language, and a foregrounding of the latter's asignifying, intensive aspects. This involves a kind of stammering and stuttering – or 'becoming a stranger' – in ones own tongue. Deleuze and Guattari give the example of Black Americans 'use' of English (as well, of course, as Kafka's own 'use' of German). We might think of the ongoing creolisation of the English language in general. A side effect of this is that a minor literature operates to counteract the transmission of 'order words', and the exercise of power this entails ('To hate all languages of masters' as Deleuze and Guattari remark (*K* 26)).

*2. That in a minor literature everything is political (*K 17*).* Political here means that the lives and individual concerns of the characters in a minor literature are always linked to the larger social, and indeed *a*social, milieu (and not, for example, fixated on the familial, domestic unit). It is in this sense that a becoming animal is always political, a line of escape (for Kafka's Gregor, for example) from conjugality and the nuclear family. This links up with point 1: the animal cry – as sound, as deterritorialised noise – operates to neutralise sense, we might say to neutralise the habits of representation, of 'being human'. Asignification here takes on an explicitly political function; it disrupts dominant systems of signification and representation. In fact, the relationship between asignification and signification, and between literary–linguistic systems in general is itself a 'political situation', expressing as it does relations of power (relations of domination and resistance). Deleuze and Guattari, following Henri Gobard, provide a tentative matrix for these relations, in fact a four-way model: vernacular language (local and territorial), vehicular language (international, a deterritorialisation of the former), referential (the language of sense and culture, a cultural reterritorialisation) and mythic. This last is positioned 'on the horizons of cultures, caught up in a spiritual or religious reterritorialisation' (*K* 23).[2] This schema can only be provisional. The relationships between, and functions of, different languages will always vary depending on the specifics of space and time, which is to say a definition of the minor will depend on a definition of the major.

3. *That a minor literature is always collective (K 17).* Collective in the sense that a minor literature works as a collective enunciation. There is less emphasis on individual authors and talents, which are at any rate scarce within a minor literature, and more on the collective production of work (its always already collaborative status). It is in this sense that we can see the artistic production of statements as a kind of precursor of a community (and often a nation) still in formation.[3] This is the utopian function, specifically *immanent*, of a minor literature. A minor literary machine then prepares the way, in fact in many senses calls into being, the revolutionary machine yet-to-come ('We might as well say that minor no longer designates specific literatures but the revolutionary conditions for every literature' (*K* 18)).

It is this last point especially, it seems to me, that gives us a framework for thinking many recent contemporary art practices which might be seen to be involved with precisely this utopian pursuit: the collectivisation of subjectivity and the calling forth of new kinds of community that this implies. Before I go on to consider this I want to briefly think through points 1 and 2 also in relation to contemporary practice.

First point 1, the deterritorialisation of a major language. Deleuze and Guattari point out that a minor literature does not occur 'elsewhere' or 'apart from' a major literature (this is not a dialectic) but on the contrary operates from within, using the same elements as it were but in a different manner. In fact, it is not so much a question of the minor or of the major but of a *becoming* minor in the sense of producing movement from 'within' the major (if the minor names this movement – these 'crystals of becoming' – then the major is the name for their immobilisation).[4] What then might we understand as the major, and thus the minor, language(s) of contemporary art practice? Here are five suggestions.

First, we might think of the major and relatively recent tradition of Western art, that is to say modernism, and thus identify practices that are specifically minor to this. Both feminist and post colonial art practices and art histories might be seen as minor in this sense, involving as they do a kind of deterritorialisation, or stammering, in the 'international language' of modernism. We might take this further and identify practices of art and indeed art history that deterritorialise legitimate critiques of modernism,[5] and indeed other 'legitimate' postmodern practices (and this might well involve a return to previously evacuated terrain).[6] Indeed, minor practices will emerge wherever and whenever a priest and a party line emerge and order words are given.

Second, we might also think of those marginal and dissonant practices that were themselves part of modernity but which also in some senses turned against it; modernity's 'other voice' as it were. Dada, for example, which was nothing if not the making stammer, the stuttering, of language and art. We might note here the Dada manifestos, and indeed the other dissident manifestos of modernity (from Futurism to the Situationists) all of which would precisely fit our above three criteria of a minor literature.[7] Here the question of how, when and why a minor literature – or any minor practice in general – becomes major (the apparatus of capture) will be particularly pertinent. In fact, artistic strategy might well involve a 'return' to some of these practices that have retained a deterritorialising function, for it might be the case that a minor practice does not necessarily become major but is simply passed over by the major.

Third, leading on from the above, we might alter our focus slightly and think about the major media of art, specifically painting, and thus characterise those practices as minor which abandoned the canvas (happenings, performance and so on) or otherwise deterritorialise the figure.[8] We might begin to identify a general 'becoming minor' in art here. Art begins with a deterritorialisation of forms that have become fixed. The expanded practices of today would be but the latest moment in this genealogy of a minor art positioned explicitly outside the gallery and indeed 'outside' typical and traditional definitions of art.

Fourth, it is also important to recognise that contemporary art increasingly has itself a form derived from the international art market (and in particular the increasing presence of international biennales) – a kind of vehicular-referential 'global' language. A minor practice might then involve itself in 'stammering' the global language of contemporary art production, for example, in a focus on the local (a turn to the vernacular) or in the use of specifically non-artistic materials. Thomas Hirschorn's 'monuments' to various philosophers would be a case in point, although we might want to ask whether a practice commissioned by Documenta can ever really be positioned as minor in this sense.[9] A better example might be 'Outsider Art', although this category would itself need to be broken down and specific practices looked at on their own terms, and an account would have to be given of the increasing commodification of many examples. A key question here is the relationship of the minor to capitalism. On the one hand we might identify the minor as operating at the sharp end of capital's expansion; the minor involving the production of new forms. On the other hand, a minor practice will precisely stammer and stutter the commodity form, disassembling those already existing forms of capital and indeed moving beyond the latter's very logic.

Fifth, in each case this deterritorialisation of the major will to some extent involve the neutralisation of sense and the foregrounding of art's intensive, affective quality. Here art '*stops being representative in order to now move towards its extremities or its limits*' (*K* 23). A minor art pushes up against the edges of representation; it bends it, forces it to the limits and often to a certain absurdity. This is not to say that a minor art cannot itself work through representation (or at least through fragments of representation). Indeed, affective ruptures – which themselves utilise existing materials – are the fertile ground for new forms of representation, new signifying regimes. Deterritorialisation is always accompanied by reterritorialisation in this sense. A minor practice must then be understood as always in process, as always becoming – as generating new forms through a break with, but also a utilisation of, the old. It is also in this sense that the argument might be made that a practice can still be 'activated', or become minor, even if it is located 'within' a major institution, or has otherwise 'become major'. Here the question of the spectator's investment in, and participation with, a particular practice becomes crucial, which is to say, his or her specific production of subjectivity and propensity for deterritorialisation.

As a brief aside we might point to the use of humour in such a deterritorialisation of language. Humour can operate as a strategy of dissent – but also of affirmation. In fact, we might see humour as a form of affirmative violence; a violence against typical signifying formations.[10] Humour here is not the irony of postmodern practice, but something more affirmative, celebratory even, and something that works on an intensive rather than a signifying register.

Point 2, the political. A minor art will connect different regimes together, and in particular will connect art to the wider social milieu. This is to return to the terrain of Chapter 1 and to restate the importance of rhizomatics, or simply a general principle of connectivity. Again, we might think here of the artistic avant-garde groupings of modernity and beyond, those that seek to 'bring art back down' to life (which we might rephrase here as a desire to connect art to life). Even more pertinent are those recent collectives and groups that interact, and indeed position themselves as part of, the wider social and economic fabric. The socially engaged projects of groups such as *Superflex* or *n55* would be a case in point (although this does not necessarily mean such practices will fit our other criteria of a minor practice).[11] This turn away from a certain kind of autonomy (from art about art, or art about the art world) also involves a turn away from typical forms of political and social engagement. A minor art practice is not political in the usual sense. It does not involve itself necessarily with political – or what we might call molar – organisations, rather it works to connect up the different aspects of life, be they individual or social (or indeed non-human) so as to produce new lines of causality and new pathways of experimentation, precisely the production of what Guattari once called 'molecular revolutions'.[12] If a minor practice is always political then it is because it is always opening itself up to an outside in this sense. It is in this sense also that the minor produces a different kind of relative autonomy, for example, an association of individuals who have 'being against' the major in common. We might add here that a minor practice will also often look to 'popular', or what we might call immanent cultures (those that are self-organising as it were). Graffiti for example would be a paradigmatic example of a minor literature, as would so called underground forms of music, such as punk,[13] and more recently dance.[14] Again, attention would need to be given to the specific apparatus of capture of these minor forms.

Finally point 3, the collective character of minor literature and its 'futurity', or what we might call its prophetic function. A minor art will involve a collective enunciation, the production of collaborations and indeed the calling forth of new kinds of collectivities.[15] Here a minor practice joins forces with what Deleuze and Guattari call philosophy, that practice which in itself calls forth 'a new earth, a new people' (*WP* 99). Philosophy, for Deleuze and Guattari, involves a resistance to the present in its specifically future orientation (it creates concepts *for* a new earth and a new people). We might say that a minor art practice parallels philosophy's more abstract (and absolute) deterritorialisations in offering a resistance to the present in the form of its imagined communities and prototype subjectivities.[16] Indeed, we might say that minor practices, like philosophy, involve a 'diagramming of becoming', the invention of new modes of existence.[17] A minor art in this sense summons its audience into being.

It is worth a digression to Deleuze's *Cinema 2* here, to note the comments made about this future orientation in relation to modern political cinema:

> This acknowledgement of a people who are missing is not a renunciation of political cinema, but on the contrary the new basis on which it is founded, in the third world and for minorities. Art, and especially cinematographic art must take part in this task: *not that of addressing a people, which is presupposed already there, but of contributing to the invention of a people* [my italics]. (*C2* 217)[18]

It is this utopian calling that differentiates modern political cinema from classical political cinema, both Soviet and American. In the latter (for example Eisenstein) 'the people are already there', in fact, are the *subject* of film (*C2* 216). 'Hence the idea that the cinema, as art of the masses, could be the supreme revolutionary or democratic art, which makes the masses a true subject' (*C2* 216). For Deleuze this belief was compromised specifically with the rise of Hitler, Stalin and the Party, and with the break-up of the American people, hence Deleuze's comment that: 'if there were a modern political cinema, it would be on this basis: the people no longer exist, or not yet ... *the people are missing*' (*C2* 216).[19]

The 'third world film-maker', as Deleuze calls him, in particular follows this path of the minor:

> Sometimes, the third world film-maker finds himself before an illiterate public, swamped by American, Egyptian or Indian serials, and karate films, and he has to go through all this, it is this material he has to work on, to extract from it the elements of a people who are still missing. (*C2* 217)

We might say then that the third world film-maker often lacks an audience, and as such must call his or her audience into being *through* his or her films. Importantly, this minor practice is produced through a manipulation of the elements of the major. To return briefly to the terrain of the previous chapter, we might say that this is the use of cliché in order to disrupt cliché. We might add that this minor cinema is of course not just apparent in what Deleuze terms the 'third world', but in any and all practices that somehow deterritorialise – stutter and stammer – the major language of film, or indeed any major representational tropes (we might think of the films made by Goddard, as well as those more recent ones made under the Dogma rubric). In fact, we might recognise such minor practices as being very much part of the expanded field of contemporary art as it exists today: the so-called documentary turn in art practice (the increasing presence of video art). The development of hand held camcorders, as well as the ongoing development of digital technology in general, although it can operate in the service of the major, allows the production of different forms of 'minor cinema' in this sense.

In this respect, we need also note, as Deleuze reminds us, that: 'the difference between minorities and majorities isn't their size. A minority may be bigger than a majority. What defines majority is a model you have to conform to ... A minority, on the other hand, has no model, it's a becoming, a process' (*N* 173). Furthermore, this missing people is not necessarily someone else (or not just someone else) but ourselves too, 'for, if the people are missing, if they are breaking up into minorities, it is I who am first of all a people, the people of my atoms' (*C2* 220). It is then not a question of waiting for the missing people (there is no hanging around in messianic time), for these people are in a sense already here, albeit masked, obscured by habitual modes of representation and commodified productions of subjectivity, precisely, the major.

All of this gives the minor an affirmative function. To refuse, or somehow negate, the existing language (and thus the existing major forms) is important, but a minor art must do more than this. It must also involve creation. It is also this that gives the stuttering and stammering of a minor practice such an inspirational, we might even say hopeful, tenor. A minor art is involved in the invention and imagining of new subjectivities as well as turning away from those already in place.[20] A minor art then does not just orientate itself against, or position itself in, an 'outside'. Rather it operates at a more oblique angle (it looks for other entry points). It is at once inside and outside the major, *in* the 'world' but not quite *of* it.[21]

Interlude 1: *Empire* and affirmation

A political art, a *politics*, of dissent but also of affirmation. Such is the rational of Hardt and Negri's *Empire*. In fact *Empire* clearly and persuasively delimits two moments or movements of modernity: the production of new forms of life (the activation of the plane of immanence) and then their 'capture' by an apparatus of control and classification (the instalment of a regime of transcendence).[22] We might see this as a relation between the minor and the major, hence the powerful insight of Deleuze, his reversal of typical left-wing understanding: resistance, or the minor, is primary. For Hardt and Negri, following Deleuze, it is likewise the production of life that is primary. Empire acts as a parasite on this fundamentally affirmative and creative production.[23] Usefully, Hardt and Negri point out that the strategy of deconstruction merely attacks the second moment, but remains more or less oblivious to the first (once more deconstruction might be figured here as a form of expanded ideological critique). The same can be said of a politically engaged art practice that contents itself solely with refusal and dissent. It is blind to the very ontological force that exists prior to that which it seeks to negate. Such critiques, although important as an entry point, can become caught in what we might call a melancholic echo chamber of negative critique. They remain reactive rather than creative. We might say that this latter attitude is to do with a certain *style* of thought; for those who think resistance as secondary (in a sense produced *by* a repressive state), political art practice will always be reactive and involved in negative critique and in fact determined by that which it critiques. In this place political art practice will be involved in a continuous struggle against the 'ideological veils' of the state. If on the other hand one sees resistance as primary, and the state apparatus as secondary (as capturing this 'life'), then one becomes involved in affirming this ontologically prior moment. This is the move from critique to creativity, or in fact the location of critique from within creativity.

Nevertheless dissent is important. A simple celebration of the world can be nothing more than an acceptance of the status quo and an abdication of any critical position. Dissent is crucial, and indeed can itself, in some cases, produce new kinds of thought and new modes of subjectivity. It is then as if there must be two moments or movements to a minor practice. One of dissent (either a strategic withdrawal as a form of engagement, or strategic engagement itself), and one of creativity (the production of new forms). We might say that art is a name for both of these strategies. We might reformulate this as a question of moving at different speeds to the institutional apparatus of capture, of moving faster, but also, if we take Henri Bergson's thesis into account, of sometimes moving slower (and sometimes even standing still).[24]

The minor then operates to upset any simple affirmation of a new people, or logic of an already constituted movement that is already here, indeed the minor is always a 'movement in becoming' in this sense. We might say then that the minor sits between Derrida's politics, his attention to the mechanisms and politics of exclusion (the limitations of any given system, or sovereignty), and Negri's 'logic of gathering', which can sometimes read as too celebratory (and thus in fact exclusionary). Indeed, if there is an affirmation of a new community, it is precisely of the always already excluded, a bastard community of the sick and the frail, a mutant community always in progress, always open to any and everyone.[25] If there is a gathering of the new people, then what they will have in common is their stuttering and stammering, their failure (intentional or otherwise) to 'live up' to the models offered (in fact forced upon them) by the major – and these major models might well operate within those formations that apparently orientate themselves against any given state formation.

Interlude 2: back to Spinoza

An affirmation of the 'first moment' of modernity is then an affirmation of the multitude, or of what Alain Badiou simply calls, in a return to Marx, the 'proletariat', as a name for the people-yet-to-come.[26] This multitude, or, more accurately, this productive activity (or 'biopower') is 'beyond measure' in the sense that ultimately it is beyond the mechanisms of measure at the disposal of any state or indeed supra-state apparatus (i.e. Empire). Indeed, it is akin, philosophically, to what Deleuze and Guattari in *What is Philosophy?* call, following Nietzsche, the 'Untimely', that which takes place in spite of history (and in so doing produces history) (*WP* 111–13). Another name for this moment or movement is becoming ('Becoming isn't part of history; history amounts only to the set of preconditions, however recent, that one leaves behind in order to "become", that is, to create something new' (*N* 171)). We might note here the specifically aesthetic character of this politics: it is involved in the production of new forms of life.

For Hardt and Negri it is important to explore how this virtual potentiality of the multitude might become possible, and ultimately real. Indeed this might be characterised as political strategy. These terms are used in a different way to Deleuze and Guattari but the point seems to be the same: it is the *edge*, where potential becomes realised, that is crucial. One way of accessing this virtual power of the multitude, as we saw in Chapter 2, is through 'organising good encounters, composing actual relations, forming powers, experimenting' (*PP* 119). This is the production of joyful encounters that increase our capacity to act in the world.[27] This is an affirmative and celebratory politics of friendship, of collaboration and collectivity.[28] In fact, it is here that politics and art practice meet, for a minor art practice might be seen as the production of productive encounters in this Spinozist sense.

Indeed, it is precisely when Spinoza's ethics is extended out into the supra-individual domain that we begin to see the latter's political importance and relevance. Here is Deleuze commenting on this move:

> Heretofore it was only a question of how a particular thing can decompose other things by giving them a relation that is consistent with one of its own, or, on the contrary, how it risks being decomposed by other things. But now it is a question of knowing whether relations (and which ones?) can compound directly to form a new, more 'extensive' relation, or whether capacities can compound directly to constitute a more 'intense' capacity or power. It is no longer a matter of utilisations or captures, but of sociabilities and communities. How do individuals enter into composition with one another in order to form a higher individual, *ad infinitum*? How can a being take another being into its world, but while preserving or respecting the other's own relations and world? And in this regard, what are the different types of sociabilities for example? (*PP* 126)

In Deleuze's reading of Spinoza there are in fact two distinct forms of modern human sociability. The first is one in which control and organisation are imposed from an outside, precisely the civic state in which men are ruled by their hopes and fears (following *Empire*, we might call this a transcendent formation – a projection *onto* man); and the second, what Deleuze following Spinoza calls the state of reason, in which men freely unite and are joined together through nothing other than their own will. This specifically immanent formation is a community produced on the basis of active feeling – and on the common notions (the commonality of man) that arise from this.[29] In the best cases the first, specifically when it is a democracy, prepares the grounds for the latter, although, I would argue, at some point a radical reorientation is needed – an upheaval – to switch from a transcendent formation to an immanent one (the change cannot be gradual in this sense). Although this immanent formation is ontologically prior to its transcendent organisation, it might nevertheless be the latter (the state machine) that prepares the way for the former (the war machine). In terms of actual temporal sequencing neither form has priority.

And so from within the major the minor can appear. Indeed the minor is a precursor of Spinoza's (and Hardt and Negri's) multitude (and in fact operates as a corrective, a stuttering fringe, to that very multitude). A minor art practice works as the relay for a people – or a revolution – yet-to-come (it is on the edge between potential and its realisation). Revolution is to be understood here as that moment which allows all of us to form new alliances, new relations, and produce new joyful subjectivities. This then is a minor art's future call. It might well speak to an already constituted audience (no doubt a small one) but at the same time it speaks from a future place in order to draw forth from its audience a subjectivity still-to-come (a subjectivity in progress as it were).[30] This is why often with art practice, as with jokes, it is a question, of 'getting it'. That is to say, not necessarily of understanding (what is there to 'understand' anyway?) but of being in a certain mode so that the practice 'works', something is activated by it. To paraphrase Jean-François Lyotard we might say that this is why an art work has the character of an event that always arrives too soon (Lyotard 1984, 71–84). It is also why so many attempts to interpret art are reductive, clumsy and/or redundant. Art outruns any interpretive discourse on it, and a minor art in particular (including sometimes an art scene) always moves at a different speed to those discourses or disciplines that attempt to track it.

The war machine

Definitions

In *A Thousand Plateaus* the question of the minor becomes also the question of the war machine, understood as that form of organisation that opposes the dominant state form (or simply the major). At stake here is the formation of a group or collectivity, or simply a practice, that does not become merely a smaller state machine, but also that does not dissipate (become chaotic). This is the production of a machine that can follow the vectors of deterritorialisation, can operate on the line of flight, but does not become a line of abolition or disappear into a black hole. In terms of *Anti-Oedipus* we might call this war machine a collection of desiring-machines. In terms of *What is Philosophy?* we might call it simply creative thought. In each case it is the production of an assemblage, a practice, or simply a *life*, that operates with different spatial and temporal coordination points to the state, we might even say operates in a different reality. In terms of another plateau from *A Thousand Plateaus* we might also characterise it as the formation of a passional regime of signs from within the despotic.[31]

The war machine is then defined less by warfare then by the space it occupies and in fact generates: the production of a smooth space from within the striated. As Paul Patton remarks: 'Smooth space is a rhizomatic or "patchwork" space in which local regions are juxtaposed without reference to an overarching metric principle or directionality' (2000, 112). This kind of nomadic space, a space of fluidity and connectivity, is always at odds with state, or striated space, the space of numbering, of representation. As such:

> an 'ideological', scientific, or artistic movement can be a potential war machine, to the precise extent to which it draws, in relation to a *phylum*, a plane of consistency, a creative line of flight, a smooth space of displacement. It is not the nomad who defines this constellation of characteristics; it is this constellation that defines the nomad, and at the same time the essence of the war machine. (*ATP* 422–3)

Importantly, this war machine is not to be understood as simply 'anticapitalist', at least in the typical left wing sense (in fact left wing parties are often precisely mini state machines in this sense). Indeed, capitalism is the smooth space of our time. Rather, the war machine is anti the blockages of desire, the reterritorialisations that occur on the deterritorialised flows. As such the war machine, or war *machines*, are similar to probe-heads as mapped out in the previous chapter – forms of organisation at odds with the dominant, but made out of the same stuff as it were, and in a sense always ahead of the apparatus of capture that tracks them. It is in this sense also that the war machine is avant-garde rather than democratic, at least in as far as democracy is the rule of the majority as in the West.

As Deleuze and Guattari point out in the plateau on Nomadology there can be a variety of relationships between the state and the war machine, not least the employment, always uneasy, of a war machine by the state (*ATP* 351–6). *War* is in fact the specific result of the states' confrontation with the war machine, a confrontation that to all extents and purposes is inevitable given the two machines opposing functionalities.[32] Violence against the state then, though it might appear as an isolated, random, and unprovoked attack, might be reconfigured as the inevitable result of the state machine's striation of space in political, social and economic terms. What appears – or is presented – as unpredictable and unjustified is then just the surfacing once more of the war between two kinds of machine, or simply between desire and its repression:[33]

> And each time there is an operation against the state – insubordination, rioting, guerrilla warfare, or revolution as act – it can be sad that a war

> machine has revived, that a new nomadic potential has appeared, accompanied by the reconstitution of a smooth space or a manner of being in space as though it were smooth. (*ATP* 386)

For Deleuze then the war machine is a 'particular way of occupying, taking up, space-time, or inventing new space-times', and as such 'revolutionary movements' and 'artistic movements too, are war machines in this sense' (*N* 172). In the interview from where these last few comments are taken, Deleuze remarks that people 'don't take enough account, for instance, of how the PLO has had to invent a space-time in the Arab world' (*N* 172). In the spirit of such a enquiry, and as a kind of case study of the above (and despite Guattari's own comments (see note 38)), I want now to turn away from art and give my attention to a revolutionary guerrilla organisation specifically to see what lessons might be learnt from this guerrilla war machine for an artistic war machine.

Case Study: the Red Army Faction

> Man and woman in the Guerrilla are the new people for a new society, of which the guerrilla is the 'Breeding cell' because of its identity of power, subjectivity, a constant process of learning and action (as opposed to theory). Guerrilla stands for a collective process of learning with the aim to 'collectivise' the individual so that he will keep up collective learning. Politics and strategy live within each individual of the Guerrilla. (Meinhof 2001a, 63)

The guerrilla organisation, in this case the Red Army Faction (RAF), has both a centrifugal and a centripetal force.[34] On the one hand its activities are obviously directed to an outside, indeed, it is this that defines the guerrilla. It is directed against and in opposition to that which surrounds and paradoxically produces it. The guerrilla is in this sense essentially *parasitic*. The RAF saw themselves in this light, as conducting a war on capitalism–imperialism (which amongst other things had produced the nightmare of Vietnam) from behind enemy lines.[35]

However, there is also a force directed within the guerrilla, a force that operates on the members of the guerrilla group themselves. We might call this force a kind of alternative production of subjectivity. Put simply, the guerrilla, in the relations and alliances it produces, and in its relative isolation from 'the world', produces a 'becoming political' (a politicisation) of the individual. As well as being parasitical the guerrilla might then also be thought of as having a *germinal* function, as being involved in the production of something 'new'.[36] We might also position this latter function as a becoming minor, in fact the guerrilla cell as a form of minor literature. A productive exercise might then be to apply our three criteria for a minor literature to the RAF. This is not to diffuse or efface the avowed centrifugal intent of the RAF (its force directed against the state) nor to make an apology for the fear generated by their actions. Rather, it is to see whether there is something we can take, something productive (for a politically engaged art practice perhaps?) from this particular history of guerrilla warfare, so that a group such as the RAF is not merely identified with the black hole of terrorism that their practice, at least for some, inevitably announced and still announces.

1. A deterritorialisation, a stammering, from within the major language. The slogans, proclamations and manifestos of the RAF have often been highlighted as a key characteristic of the group and, on a literal level, such communiqués did involve a kind of stammering. In fact, their literary output had the character, as Thomas Elsaesser has pointed out, of a kind of 'literary *avant-garde*' (1999, 290). Elsaesser quotes Dietrich Diedrichsen who wonders:

> where are we to locate the symbolic rupture between the early enthusiasm of Ensslin or Vesper for modern poetry, and the full-blown RAF diction, present in the lower-case type written messages, influenced by sub-culture colloquialisms, shaped by decisionist rhetoric, and celebrating orgies of one-line sententiousness? (Elsasser 1999, 290)

The language between members of the group might also be seen as a becoming minor of typical bourgeois strategies of avoidance, involving as it did a directness and apparent political incorrectness: the RAF were it seems well aware, intuitively, of the inherently political nature of language.[37] We might note here the general predicament and thus general strategy of those who must use a language that is not their own: they must use it in such a way as to make it their own.

In fact the RAF's deterritorialisation of the major language went further. Their very actions and modes of interaction involved and 'effected an aesthetic break' with previous 'political' action and organisation, belonging as it did to the emergent 'culture of the happening, to graffiti art and fluxus events, to street theatre and the Living theatre' (Elsaesser 1999, 284). We might also note here the RAF's utilisation of that other aspect of a minor language, its intensive or affective quality ('Oppose a purely intensive usage of language to all symbolic or even significant or simply signifying usages of it') (*K* 19). Here is Elsaesser again, this time quoting Michael Dreyer:

> For Dreyer, the RAF's street violence was not only street theatre, it was a kind of 'music' ('no more/mere words'). He felt their political violence as a percussion cutting into the monotone of his everyday, a form of 'bodily' sensation which, rather like rock music, delivered non-verbal expression and opened up a new subjective space'. (1999, 289)

Of course, the RAF cannot be passed off as a purely aesthetic movement, after all their notoriety arose from their acts of violence. We might, however, want to enquire into what this violence entailed. Was there a sense in which the violence was itself a deterritorialisation of the major language of the state, premised as the latter was on violence? The RAF might be seen as twisting and folding – stuttering – the major language back on itself.[38] A terror turned against the terror of the state, and specifically the state sponsored terrorism of Vietnam (seen as yet another genocide performed by the parent generation).[39] We might want to go further than this and note the specificity of the RAF targets; their actions were directed not only against a US-dominated military complex, but also against those who had risen to power during the Nazi era.[40] The RAF might then be seen as attempting to make manifest the violence that lay beneath the apparent luxuries – and 'peace' – of a US consumerist hegemony. As the RAF themselves remarked: 'These are the strategic dialectics of anti-imperialist struggle: through the defensive reactions of the system, the escalation of counterrevolution, the transformation of the political martial law into military martial law, the enemy betrays himself, becomes visible' (Meinhof 2000b, 279).

We might also want to approach this issue of violence in a different, even more *affirmative* manner; violence as an inevitable factor of breaking with mainstream society and typical subjectivity (the bourgeois individual). This is a form of violence at once removed from 'state' violence, in fact a violence aimed at undercutting the premises of the state.[41] We might call this the violence of collectivity, or of fraternity – a violence specifically orientated against notions of individualism.[42] This amounts to saying that the RAF was nothing other than the sharp end of a war machine, the latter understood here as the specifically collective uprisings of the 1960s and 1970s.[43]

2. A becoming political. As Ulrike Meinhof remarks in the quote that begins this section of the chapter, the guerrilla was the site of the 'becoming political', of the individual. Meinhof herself might be seen as a case study of this, turning her back as she did on her family and her bourgeois upbringing and hence precipitating a process of politicisation and a kind of collectivisation of her identity. This disavowal of amongst other things the nuclear domestic set up invariably involved the affirmation of other types of alliance, other modes of being (and other types of sexuality), as well as announcing a break in certain signifying and subjectifying regimes – specifically those regarding women. Indeed Meinhof's 'becoming guerrilla' operated as a rupture in typical narratives of capitalist subjectivity (girl, wife, mother etc.). The media at the time picked up on this but also, and at the same time, reterritorialised Meinhof around the sign 'terrorist'.[44] This collectivisation/politicisation of the individual continued in Stammheim prison via letters surreptitiously passed between the members of the group. This was carried out against the backdrop of what we might see as the prison's major function in relation to the RAF: the interruption in the continuing collectivisation of their subjectivities, hence the prisoners' constant complaints about their isolation.[45]

3. A future orientation. The RAF was a practice of dissent, of refusal, but it also inevitably involved a celebration of spontaneity, of action, of life (the centripetal, *affirmative* aspect of the cell accompanying the latter's centrifugal *negative* critique of the state).[46] In this it called to a future and to a people-yet-to-come. In a sense all guerrilla warfare involves this double aspect: the violence is a means to an end, a precursor to a something that is yet-to-come (this is the guerrilla's prophetic aspect). We might also say that the very form of the organisation of the group cannot but help foreshadow what is being hoped and fought for. Indeed, the cell operates as a fragment of the future society projected backwards into the current state of affairs – although the cell is also prone to the very fascism, in a concentrated sense, that it orientates itself against. Hence, in a band without leaders, Andreas Baader seems to emerge as the charismatic leader of the group. We might also note here the power of the Baader–Ensslin couple that did so much to attract Meinhof to begin with. How to understand this apparent charisma and leadership, particularly of Baader? Was it indeed a micro-fascism within the group (indeed, did the group at times operate as a mini state machine?), or was it the projection of an anxious state? Certainly the RAF trial at Stammheim foregrounded the latter's desire to identify and isolate the 'ringleaders' (if only to produce individual subjects under the law, which is to say, a criminal conviction), and no doubt the media did much to effectuate the fascination and seductive power of Baader, Meinhof, Ensslin and the rest).[47]

However, we might also think of Baader as a kind of *exemplar* (a forerunner of the people-yet-to-come). Hence Meinhof's comments:

> The function of leadership in the guerrilla, the function of Andreas Baader in the RAF is orientation: not just to distinguish the main points from the minor ones in each situation but also to remain with the entire political context in all situations; to never lose sight, among technical and logistic details and problems, of the aim, which is the revolution. (2000b, 276)

We need also add here that there is often, *on the face of it*, a very thin line between this affirmative, productive leadership and something more negative, more destructive. In other words, there is a million miles but at the same time just a hair's breadth between fascism and a genuinely new people.[48] It goes without saying that being able to tell the two apart is as crucial as it can be difficult. Certainly the RAF, its organisation and its 'leadership', involve a complex and grey history. It is certainly not clear whether Baader, and the RAF in general, were fascist *or* revolutionary. Perhaps one is always between the two? Certainly a minor practice will always involve mistakes, and indeed run the risk of flipping over into that very form it organises itself against.

Thinking art practice through guerrilla organisation, in turn thought through Deleuze and Guattari's notion of a minor literature, is to think about art practice in terms not usually associated with art. It is also to reconfigure what an engaged politics might involve, particularly as regards what Guattari calls the 'production of subjectivity' (*S* 1996). The latter, a call for us to become involved in our own processual self-creation through interaction with one another and our world, changes the terms (and the stakes) of a 'political art'. Today, what constitutes an effective political practice is uncertain and may well involve strategies that hitherto were the sole remit of the guerrilla cell – precisely in its relative autonomy and affirmation of another way of life. We might say that this is an explicitly ethical and aesthetic project, as well as a political one.

A final word of caution however. As we have seen there are two moments in radical collectivities: one of dissent and one of affirmation. In a sense each begs the other (the dichotomy is false). To dissent means invariably to affirm other modes of life. In affirming these one cannot but help dissenting from the norm. However dissent in itself can operate as a purely reactive mechanism, here dissent is a form of resentment. Indeed, it is this kind of resentment that produces violence as a reactive end in itself (a resenting subject will always blame and attack anything and everything). Nothing creative can come from this (as the saying goes there is no way that an angry man can be happy). In such a subject it is always others who are to blame, always others who are responsible *for* the world.

Important then is what Deleuze, following Nietzsche and Spinoza, might call one's *style* of life, one's way of operating in, and attitude to, the world. This is prior to any political strategy. It is in this sense that it is important to disentangle the different forms of guerrilla organisation, or simply terrorisms, that are often grouped together and also the rhetoric of terrorism as deployed by the legal system and the media. Equally important, though not within the scope of this book, would be to construct a topology of different collectivities, those other urban guerrilla groups of the 1960s and 1970s such as the Red Brigades in Italy, or even the Angry Brigade in the UK. Attention would also need to be given to the larger non-violent experiments in collective action (*Autonomia* for example), and of course this topology would need to include non Euro-American revolutionary groups also: the African and Arab liberation movements and the movements in South America for example.[49] We would need also to map out the relevance these radical and guerrilla groupings have today in the increasing 'democratisation' of the world (and indeed to democracy in its ideal sense). And then there are the apparently non-political groupings: the communes of the 1960s through to the punk collectivities of the 1980s and sound system collectives of the 1990s. Which are negative formations (the product of a destructive resentment) and which positive (involved in dissent but also in the production of something new)? At stake in such a mapping, I would argue, are not just the possibilities for an engaged political art practice today but also the possibilities for an effective politics of resistance in general.[50]

The production of subjectivity

In a world variously called postmodern, late capitalist, the 'new world order' or simply Empire, a world in which power has been decentred, virtual centres of power exist everywhere. We might say that these *virtual* centres are our own subjectivities, and thus that the battleground against this power is in some sense ourselves. Hence the importance in understanding politics, as well as political art practice, as not just being about institutional and ideological critique, but also as involving the active production of our own subjectivity. As regards this I want now to switch my attention to two texts by Deleuze and Guattari respectively, each of which concerns itself with our capacity for self-creation. Taken together, they read as a powerful manifesto for a serious consideration of subjectivity as itself a political field, as well as for a more fluid and complex notion of subjectivity in general. Both also draw our attention to the material nature of subjectivity (it is never just a question of saying 'I'), as well as providing some pointers for thinking subjectivity beyond what we might consider its typical articulations.

Guattari's essay 'Subjectivities: For Better or Worse', emerges from his pragmatic involvement in psychoanalytical practice (and especially *La Borde* clinic in France), although it contains lines of flight into other areas, for example, the aesthetic theories of Mikhail Bahktin.[51] Deleuze's text, 'Michel Tournier and the World without Others', although not exactly philosophy, is not exactly literary criticism either.[52] In fact in it, and through it, literature becomes a kind of philosophy. In this latter text we see manifest Deleuze's interest in other modes of being beyond the human (the essay is very much Nietzschean in this sense), and in a world of forces and cosmic energies beyond that which is usually perceptible. Nevertheless, both essays deal with the same subject matter: subjectivity. The text by Guattari deals specifically with the latter's production, whereas Deleuze's essay operates as a counterbalance to Guattari's, addressing as it does the production of a kind of *post* subjectivity (the possibilities of non-alienated living, of life beyond the subject/object split).

Both essays are also about art and creativity. In fact, each might be read as precisely a call to creativity, a call to become involved in various strategies and practices that might allow us to produce or transform, and perhaps even go beyond, our habitual selves. As Guattari remarks elsewhere: 'through interacting with one another, with other objects and with other "means of expression" ' we create new possibilities of life just as an 'artist creates from colours on his palette' (*C* 7). The production of subjectivity, and of anything 'beyond' subjectivity, is then precisely an aesthetic business.

Guattari's ecology of subjectivity

For Guattari subjectivity is multivalent and polyphonic; there is no one dominating factor, for example the economic, which determines our social being (*S* 193).[53] Indeed, and as Guattari points out, subjective factors often interact back, which is to say, themselves determine larger economic movements (for example, psychological factors producing stock market crashes) (*S* 193). Hence the importance in thinking through the complexity of processes that form subjectivity, the mental and social ecologies that produce us as subjects.[54] In this particular essay Guattari is interested in three aspects of this production, and of its subsequent increase in relevance for us today. First, that subjectivity in general is having an increased centrality, and visibility, on the world stage. Guattari gives us the example of the Chinese students in Tianamen Square, although he also gives us the contrary example of the 'subjective revolution of Iran' and the subsequent mistreatment of women (*S* 193–4). This amounts to saying that the processes of emergent subjectivations can go backwards as well as forwards (put simply, they can be reactionary). Indeed, we are all familiar with this in the West with the emergence of nascent nationalisms within Europe, and the resultant suffering. We might also position here the apparently extreme opposing subjectivities of the West and the East, which is to say of Euroamericanism and Islam. This is not to revive an Orientalism, but it is to note that what we have here are two distinct regimes, two different productions of subjectivity. In fact, it is worth considering whether the conflicts between these two – so-called terrorism and the so-called war on terrorism – can ever really be resolved until this question of the production of subjectivity is addressed. Certainly, subjective factors, and in particular, religion, are playing their part in the ongoing business of terrorist and counter-terrorist strikes. Religion here is not necessarily a veil hiding deeper economic issues, but rather part and parcel of the whole complexity of factors, of which the economic is but one. Whether the 'universalist representation of subjectivity' embodied by capitalism, and the capitalist colonisation of the East, is increasingly bankrupt as Guattari remarks, is open to question (*S* 194).[55] What is not is that many see this particular production of subjectivity in a very poor light, linked as it is to larger historical issues of dominance and exploitation.[56] For Guattari, we are at present unable to measure the consequences of this. Of course it might be argued that we are no longer in this state of ignorant innocence.

Guattari's second aspect is the importance that new technology, and in particular new machines of communication and information (from television to the omnipresence of the World Wide Web) are now playing in the production of subjectivity, on a signifying register and also on an affective one (*S* 194).[57] Is the production of subjectivity different for a generation brought up with the ubiquitous personal computer? This is an important question in terms of thinking through the massive subjective revolution taking part in Asia and on the Indian sub-continent in particular (the nationwide implementation of computer training and computer industries (spearheaded by *Microsoft*)). There are also newer technologies to consider – Virtual Reality and emergent AI, for example. One can only speculate on the strange and novel subjectivities that will be produced by these technologies (I will be returning to this briefly towards the end of Chapter 5). Again, this can have positive results, the production of new means of expression, the opening up of what Guattari calls 'new universes of reference' (for example with the World Wide Web), but also negative results, most obvious in the top-down programming of the mass media.[58] Art practices that utilise and experiment with these new technologies might be seen to be at the 'sharp end' of this technological production of subjectivity. We might say further that the new universes of reference opened up by these technologies will also have a less obvious, more oblique impact on art practice, and on subjectivity in general, which is to say that technological developments will have an impact on contemporary productions of subjectivity whether or not particular subjects are PC users.

Guattari's third observation is the importance of ethological and ecological factors in the production of subjectivity, that, for example, it might not be the case that we go through various stages of mental life as we mature (as for example psychoanalysis suggests: an Oedipal stage, a mirror stage and so on), but that each of these states exist in parallel with one another and can be 'accessed' whatever one's 'stage of life' (*S* 195–6). Thus we have Deleuze and Guattari's mobilisation elsewhere of the notion of 'blocs of childhood', precisely a 'becoming child', understood as a spontaneous and creative state of being (and having nothing to do with regression, with a nostalgic 'return to childhood') (*ATP* 256–8). Guattari writes also of the possibility and potentiality of trans-subjective states (love for example – a molecular love like that between the wasp and the orchid) that effectively tears down the ontological curtain between self and other (*S* 195). The plateau 'November 28, 1947: How Do You Build Yourself a Body without Organs?' might be positioned as precisely a series of strategies to produce trans-subjective states such as these (*ATP* 149–66).

Thinking ecologically we might see subjectivity in terms of a multiplicity: a complex aggregate of heterogeneous elements. Important here will be decentred relationships (i.e. no specialists, no priests and no transcendent principle) and also relationships with architecture, with the group (however this is thought), with economic factors and always with an outside to whichever institutions the individual happens to be part of. Indeed, an ecology of subjectivity will emphasise this contact and communication with an outside (there are in this sense no closed systems, no completely isolated individuals).[59] Importantly, this ecology and ethology of subjectivity implies a kind of self-construction or self-organisation, a certain auto-cohesiveness, or what Guattari calls, following Francisco Varela, an autopoiesis (*S* 195). Thus we have Guattari's notion of subjectivity as an 'existential territory', sometimes formed predominantly by an individual in the world and sometimes, as we saw in the case study of the previous section, the result of group formation (*S* 196).

This is to go against Freudians, or rather, it is to see the Freudian model as just one regime of the production of subjectivity (others might be Christianity, Courtly love, Bolshevism and so on). For Guattari, Freud himself was in fact a prodigious inventor of concepts with which to think, and to organise subjectivity, rather than a discoverer of some kind of truth about the latter (*S* 196). The point to be emphasised is that one can invent new ways to live and to love – new cartographies of subjectivity – and that perhaps 'Freudianism' with its phallocentrism, its obsession with domestic representations and face turned to the past, is not necessarily the most relevant or productive for us today (*S* 197). Hence, again, the work Guattari carried out with Deleuze to produce a 'looser' notion of subjectivity, as that which is made up of multiple strata – a schizoanalytic cartography to replace the psychoanalytical (*S* 197). As Guattari remarks, this is to move from a scientific paradigm, where subjectivity is the 'object' of 'study', towards an ethicoaesthetic one, where subjectivity is always in process (*S* 197). It is also to invite us to become involved in our own production of subjectivity, to move from passive spectators to become active participants, to take what we need from Guattari, or indeed from elsewhere, in our own project of 'processual creativity', precisely to treat our lives as a work of art.

In fact, Guattari looks to Kant's aesthetic here, and to the notion of the disinterested response (*S* 198). For Guattari the latter might be a kind of model, or strategy, for the production of alternative subjectivities. Indeed, Guattari claims Bahktin moves in this direction in his suggestion that with art we form a relationship with a part that detaches itself from the object – especially in terms of rhythm and movement (*S* 198). This aesthetic response itself involves a kind of atypical desire, a break with the norm, a break with already existing 'reality' (and particularly with an already existing temporality) (*S* 199): 'A singularity, a rupture in a sense, a cut, the detachment of semiotic content – for example, in a Dadaist or surrealist fashion' (*S* 200). Following on from this 'event' will be the production of a new kind of rhythm, or what Guattari calls the production of 'mutant centres of subjectivation' (*S* 200).[60] Guattari consistently returns to this notion of art as a break, but also as the germ for a new synthesis.[61] In the final chapter of *Chaosmosis* for example, Guattari comments on arts:

> function of rupturing with forms and significations circulating trivially in the social field. The artist – and more generally aesthetic perception – detach and deterritorialise a segment of the real in such a way as to make it play the role of a partial enunciator. Art confers a function of sense and alterity to a subset of the perceived world ... The work of art, for those who use it, is an activity of unframing, of rupturing sense, of baroque proliferation or extreme impoverishment, which leads to a recreation and a reinvention of the subject itself. (*C* 131)

We might emphasise here that any real rupture in habit must indeed involve a disinterestedness on some level, more often than not a 'non-reaction' to pleasure and pain. It is also important to point out that breaking with habit requires first and foremost that one becomes aware of such habits, which is to say one must attend to one's already existing reactions and responses. It is in this sense that the making of connections, the production of encounters, must be paralleled by a vigilance of the body–mind.[62] Guattari does not attend to this, but I think it follows from his argument (indeed how else can one break habits?). In relation to this we might argue that the predominant production of subjectivity today is based on fear. A fear that is often exaggerated and played upon by the mass media.[63] Hence there is an intrinsic fear of the other – and of difference generally – within typical subjectivity. Such a mechanism – that operates on what we might call a microphysical level – has to be sorted out before progress can be made on a macro-level (after all fascism arises precisely from this fear). This is not to completely turn inwards (or to reinstall an inner/outer binary), nor is it to suggest that attending to ourselves and the production of our own subjectivity can solve all the world's problems, but it is to say that such attention must always and everywhere accompany any obvious political strategy.

For Guattari then subjectivity is made up from a multiplicity of refrains. Indeed, we are, in this sense, all musical beings (*S* 199). Guattari gives us the example of the multiple refrains involved when we watch television – the kettle is boiling, the baby is crying, the phone is ringing, and then there is the television itself, which has a narrative refrain, but also affective ones (*S* 200). For the time I am 'hooked' into the screen the latter operates as the dominant refrain (this is the point around which my subjectivity is organised). A simpler example is bird song, understood as a territorialising refrain, producing a kind of home and thus a kind of 'subjectivity' for the bird (*S* 200). We might also think about the use of music to create a territory in this sense, as for example in the simple humming of a tune when one is scared, or indeed when one is safely in one's own territory. In each case the tune operates as a territory-building technology. The plateau '1837: Of the Refrain' in *A Thousand Plateaus* deals specifically with these multiple modalities of the refrain (*ATP* 310–50). We might position art practice as a particular type of refrain in this sense – the production of a particular kind of subjective territory (and also, as we shall see below, the production of a more cosmic refrain of deterritorialisation). Indeed, for Guattari all human societies, modern and premodern, have these refrains, for example, the rituals and practices of archaic societies or the refrains of Greek Tragedy (*S* 201). In this latter case we can see quite clearly the existence of purely affective refrains – the production of a module of sound or rhythm that produces an affective response (*S* 198). Again, these affective refrains are 'mutant centres of subjectivation'; they are a rupture that throws us off onto another path, allowing us to break with old habits and perhaps form new ones (*S* 200).

We have here a kind of chemistry of subjectivity – the extraction and separation of different elements as precisely the exercise that might allow for other recombinations (*S* 200). As Guattari remarks:

> Just as chemistry had to begin by purifying complex mixtures in order to extract homogeneous atomic and molecular matter, and then to create from them an infinite array of chemical entities that had not existed previously, the 'extraction' and 'separation' of aesthetic subjectivities or partial objects, in the psychoanalytic sense, facilitates an immense complexification of subjectivity, of new and unprecedented existential harmonies, polyphonies, rhythms and orchestration. (*S* 200)

It is here, once again, that Guattari positions art or the 'poetic function' as that which can produce these ruptures in the dominant *and* produce new refrains which themselves hold together the heterogeneous in new ways (*S* 201). We return here to the war machine, and to the importance of new forms of organisation (we might even say new habits) as well as of breaking with the old. As with Spinoza then, the business of life involves going beyond appearances and 'felt affections' to their causes, thus producing the knowledge to alter our make up. Again, for Guattari, it is the encounter, with other things as well as with other beings, that accompanies and in some senses produces this chemical 'knowledge' of subjectivity. Hence again the importance of *La Borde* clinic, which as we saw in Chapter 1, might be understood as precisely an arena of encounter. In such a place individuals are given access to 'new materials of expression' as well as to the 'individual-group-machine' which allow them access to hitherto unknown 'universes of reference' which further allows them to resingularise themselves (*C* 7).

In passing, it is worth noting again Negri's work, and his attention to the specific importance of experienced time in the constitution of our subjectivities (Negri 2003). For Negri we live in a time of the total subsumption of capital, it penetrates every aspect of our lives, including our experience of time. Thus, I would argue, the importance of exploring different temporalities – of daydreaming, of being with friends, of being creative (but not necessarily for a specific end and certainly not for the market). This is a kind of non-productivity in capitalist terms, but it is precisely productive in a more Spinozist sense. Art practice might be a name for the exploration of some of these different temporalities, not just in film, and the other arts of the moving image, but the time of painting for example, or the time of sculpture (the time we spend with art). I shall be thinking about this in more detail in the next chapter.

Again, these questions of the production of subjectivity might involve us in a rethinking of political strategy. For example, it might not necessarily be a question of 'resisting', of 'slowing down' capitalism at least in one sense. Indeed, we might say that we need more and not less – more mutations, more lines of flight, more alternative temporalities. We need more experimentation and expression and not the proliferation of controls on the latter. This will involve always being alert to the apparatus of capture that blocks this expression. Indeed the business of demarcating the two is crucial and calls for scrupulous attention (and flexibility). After all art, as well as being a name for this experimentation, can also be the name for just such apparatuses of capture. It is in this sense that we need also to demarcate those productive and creative subjectivities from the production of other apparently 'free' subjectivities (for example, the production of liberal tolerating subjects in the Western liberal democracies that masks a deeper intolerance to non-Western subjectivities).

Indeed, we need to ask ourselves the fundamental political question: where are the dissenting/creative subjects of today? And how are they being produced? In both cases, I would argue, the answer must involve a serious consideration of the role of art, and of the aesthetic dimension in general, in the production of subjectivity.

Deleuze's becoming-world

I want now to turn from Guattari to Deleuze, for whom the question of the production of subjectivity is equally crucial. However, with Deleuze's essay we get something more elemental, we might even say something more cosmic. For what Deleuze finds in Michel Tournier's retelling of the Robinson Crusoe story in his novel *Friday* is an account of an overcoming of subjectivity, at least of a certain kind (the kind that is produced through 'others'). We might call this a 'becoming-world'. Indeed, and as Deleuze points out, Tournier's novel differs from Defoe's on precisely this point. It is not a novel of origins, the origins of modern (one might say capitalist) man, but rather a meditation on ends, on what man might become (*LS* 302–3). Like the novels of Carlos Castaneda that are 'utilised' in *A Thousand Plateaus*, Tournier's book can then be characterised as a programmatic work. We might further characterise this programme, these strange experiments and becomings, as involving precisely adventures beyond representation.

Robinson's adventure on the island is then a narrative about what happens to a man who is forced to dwell in a world without others, and thus in a world without a certain kind of subject-production, for it is Deleuze's reading of Tournier that it is others that precisely produce typical subjectivity. In a world *with* others, in our world, we might say that nothing much happens. We are surrounded by a kind of benevolent murmuring. My marginal world, that which lies outside my perception, poses no threat as I assume it exists as a world for others. Others precisely assure the margins and transitions of the world I inhabit. Indeed, the other expresses other possible worlds, and as such it is through the other that I come to 'know' the world (*LS* 304–5). Furthermore, all my desires pass through these others; I desire what I perceive others as having. In this sense even my very desires are produced by, and pass through, others (*LS* 306).

Importantly, it is not necessarily concrete others that perform this function, rather it is the structural other, or the perceptual field organised by the other, that operates to produce a certain subjectivity (*LS* 307). The other is then not an object in my perceptual field, although it is that too, but is in fact that which constitutes the field itself. This perceptual field operates then as a mechanism – or a *pattern* – to produce a certain kind of ordering and configuration, precisely my subjectivity. Robinson's adventure is then the experience of a world in which this mechanism breaks down. In fact, when Robinson first arrives on the island the perceptual field still operates, despite there being no actual others, and Robinson goes through a neurotic stage of peopling his island with (imaginary) people (*LS* 309). We might remind ourselves here that solitude does not necessarily produce an alternative production of subjectivity. For Robinson however the structural other does in fact gradually disappear, and thus begins Robinson's transformation, terrifying yet exhilarating.

Perhaps the key production of the structural other is to separate consciousness from its object. Thus, in the world without others Robinson gradually merges with, *becomes*, the island; the splitting of the subject and object is gradually healed. In this sense it is others who in fact *disturb* the world. Thus, in the world without others, we have a liberation of desires, a liberation of a more elemental consciousness (*LS* 312–13). This is the 'great health', that necessarily involves a restructuring of the self and world (*LS* 315).

When Friday, an actual other, does make an appearance, the structural other, for Robinson, has already ceased to function. Friday then operates less as an other than as a expression of this new world. Indeed, Friday becomes an ally in the continuing transformation of Robinson. We might say that he indicates another mode of being (*LS* 315–16). Robinson then has moved beyond the world structured by the a priori other into a world with a more perverse structure. In fact, for Deleuze, this is what produces Robinson's very particular behaviour – a certain sexuality not orientated towards others (*LS* 319). Thus, we have the various rituals and practices that Robinson involves himself in, for it is Deleuze's argument that the world of the pervert is precisely a world beyond subjects, a world in which others do not structure the possibilities of life.

Is this anything more than a kind of fantasy story? Well there are certainly those who seek out a world without others, precisely in order to overcome a certain subject/object split, to access a different state of consciousness, a different space-time. However, Tournier's Robinson, in the various practices he involves himself in, also gives as another way of thinking art: as the production of situations, of rituals, which allow us to access states beyond the everyday and beyond habitual subjectivity. We saw this in the previous chapter with Bataille writing about the Lascaux cave paintings operating as part of a ritual to take us out of mundane time into sacred, cosmic time. We saw it as well with Kristeva writing about installation as a multi-sensory space of encounter whose *modus operandi* is transformation. In each case art operates to open up other possible worlds. This is precisely what happens with Tournier's Robinson. He organises certain situations, and goes through various experiences, all of which are involved in opening up a world hitherto invisible. This is not a regression for, as Guattari also points out, these states coexist throughout our lives. Crucial in all these practices is also a *performative* aspect: the production of different kinds of subjectivity, or even of a beyond to subjectivity, involves actions and practices in the world. We might add further that this production will need to be processual – habits of being are not broken in a day – and indeed that any new kind of subjectivity will require new habits, new ways of thinking and feeling in order to produce a certain cohesiveness or consistency.[64]

So in these two texts by Deleuze and by Guattari we have two treatise on subjectivity. In both, subjectivity is something that is produced through a variety of practices. It is not merely something given, something determined and fixed by principles outside our control. Rather, for both Deleuze and Guattari there is an emphasis on our pragmatic involvement in the material production of our own subjectivities. Is this perhaps a call for an expanded notion of what art practice is? Certainly, it is to realise that one of the roles of art – understood as an activity of creatively interacting with the world – is precisely the production of subjectivity. We might even say a *minor* subjectivity orientated as it is against the subjectivity produced by the major (and in particular by the 'mass media'). This might well involve the use of the stuff of the world in the construction of new stuttering and stammering languages, new affective assemblages – it will also involve attention being given to our own subjectivities as they exist now. Indeed, the latter are themselves assemblages, and as such can be reordered and reconfigured. In such an understanding of the ethicoaesthetics of subjectivity, art history might become replaced by a kind of art chemistry and art cartography; the mapping out of new complexes and of the possibilities of life that these new complexes allow.

4

From Geophilosophy to Geoaesthetics

The Virtual and the Plane of Immanence versus Mirror-Travel and the *Spiral Jetty*

In this chapter I want again to switch the ontological categories for thinking art away from a certain representational register. In particular, I want to explore other ways of thinking the ethical and 'political' effectivity of art, and specifically its 'other worldliness' (its resistance to the present milieu), away from a horizon of transcendence and a logic of the possible. I propose to do this in a slightly different manner to previous chapters, by adopting a double pronged and somewhat experimental approach. The chapter then involves two philosophical discussions or two philosophical encounters with Deleuze, and at the same time a non-philosophical encounter with an art practice that mirrors the philosophy, and in some senses 'grounds' it. To a certain extent I might be accused of deliberately misreading Deleuze here insofar as I utilise his ideas on philosophy, rather than on sensation and affect, to think these practices. The chapter is then an experiment in taking Deleuze's philosophical concepts into other milieus (and in allowing the latter to feed back on Deleuze). It is in this sense that the artistic 'case studies' are meant not as illustrations but as parallels to, and in some senses deviations from, the conceptual work. They also serve to demonstrate that art is a form of thought in and of itself.

The first philosophical discussion, which begins with another brief contrasting of Deleuze with Theodor Adorno, is on the notion of the virtual.[1] It is here that I track through Deleuze's Bergsonism, and think about the application and implication of the latter for art. The second philosophical discussion is on immanence, and specifically the *plane of immanence*, the latter understood as a kind of non-philosophical but founding moment of philosophy. I also make a detour to Deleuze and Guattari's important notion of the *Body without Organs*. The other two sections, or excurses, concern the practice of the artist Robert Smithson, who, in his earthworks, 'non-sites' and sculptures, and in his copious writings, presents us, I would argue, with what Deleuze might call a new 'image of thought'.[2] As we shall see, we might also characterise Smithson's works as the construction of a Body without Organs.

Although Smithson died young, he was nevertheless one of the most influential (and least containable) artists of the late 1960s/early 1970s. This was a time when artists were radically questioning accepted assumptions about art and involving themselves in practices that located themselves outside of the gallery (and indeed beyond the remit of art altogether).[3] We might say that these expanded and conceptual practices are the precursors of those more relational practices pointed to in Chapter 1. Smithson, like Donald Judd, Robert Morris and others, took the break with representation to its most extreme edge, in Judd's case expunging any reference to anything outside of the object.[4] Like Judd, Smithson's practice involved objects in the world rather than pictures of the world, although his work also had a certain 'mythic' quality to it. Indeed, as we shall see, a notion of narrative, albeit a kind of posthuman geological narrative, is a consistent element in Smithson's art. As such, and although he can be grouped with other artists of his generation, Smithson stands out as somewhat singular and atypical. The art works themselves also draw attention to the always partial and occasionally reductive readings that are given to minimalism when it ignores these more fantastical (we might even say more psychedelic) elements. This chapter focuses on the more fantastical aspect of Smithson's practice, and on just two of Smithson's projects: the *Yucatan Mirror Displacements* and the *Spiral Jetty*, both of which are, in their own way, exemplary of Smithson's attitude and style as an artist.[5] Although I attend to the actual works, I am also interested in Smithson's own writings on the latter, and how such writings encapsulate a certain style of thought in themselves.

The late 1960s were of course also a time of wider political unrest and ethical experimentation. Indeed, for Michael Hardt and Antonio Negri, the plane of immanence, understood by them in a geopolitical sense, was itself being activated once more in a new revolutionary energy; new non-traditional modes of being and new non-formalised practices of life and art were both being experimented with (*E* 260–79). It is the same moment that Deleuze's philosophy comes into its own, the publication of *Difference and Repetition* announcing the project of constructing an 'image of thought' beyond representation. This fourth chapter then marks a moment in which a philosophy of difference and an art practice of immanence are both being constructed (what we might call in each case a move towards abstraction). This is not the first time that such a philosophy is produced (one need only think of Spinoza), but it might be argued that at this moment philosophy and art so closely follow one another that they become two forks of the same serpent's tongue.

The virtual (or Deleuze's Bergsonism)

In a difficult passage from *Bergsonism* Deleuze outlines what for him, as for Henri Bergson before him, is the important, in fact crucial, difference between the ontological couplings of the actual and the virtual, as opposed to those of the real and the possible. This difference, as Deleuze remarks elsewhere, is not simply a question of terminology, but rather 'of existence itself' (*DR* 211). Here is the passage in full:

> The possible has no reality (although it may have an actuality); conversely, the virtual is not actual, but *as such possesses a reality* ... On the other hand, or from another point of view, the possible is that which is 'realized' (or is not realized). Now the process of realization is subject to two essential rules, one of resemblance and another of limitation. For the real is supposed to be in the image of the possible that it realizes. (It simply has existence or reality added to it, which is translated by saying that, from the point of view of the concept there is no difference between the possible and the real.) And, every possible is not realized, realization involves a limitation by which some possibles are supposed to be repulsed or thwarted, while others 'pass' into the real. The virtual on the other hand, does not have to be realized, but rather actualized; and the rules of actualization are not those of resemblance and limitation, but those of difference or divergence and of creation. (*B* 96–7)

The possible then is realised through resemblance and limitation whereas the virtual is actualised through difference and creation. Indeed, the key issue with the possible, which is implied above and pursued by Deleuze in *Difference and Repetition*, is that it is 'retroactively fabricated in the image of what resembles it' (*DR* 212). Put simply, the possible is always already a kind of representation of the real that appears to pre-exist it. We might say then that the possible becomes as such by a sleight of hand. It is in fact merely an isotope of the real inasmuch as it only lacks reality (it merely 'doubles like with like') (*DR* 212). The possible then operates as a mirror image of reality, but one that sets itself up as if it offered a 'real' alternative. This is the illusionistic moment, the *camera obscura* of the possible, which appears to offer something 'new' but in fact only offers more of the same. Indeed, we might rename this logic of the possible a logic of utopia, inasmuch as utopian thinking (and this includes representations of utopia) is often locked into this double movement. Utopia, we might say, can be nothing more than a reflection (however distorted) of the real, although as we shall see it need not necessarily operate in this manner.

As a contrast to Deleuze we might look briefly at how Adorno deploys a notion of utopian thought, specifically in relation to art. Here are his words from *Aesthetic Theory*:

> Art's utopia, the counter-factual yet-to-come is draped in Black, it goes on being a recollection of the possible with a critical edge against the real ... It is the possible, as promised by its impossibility. Art is the promise of happiness, a promise that is constantly being broken. (1984, 196)

For Adorno art operates as a kind of 'utopian blink'; it presents the possible through its apparent difference to the existent. Indeed, for Adorno, art is not really 'of' this world at all, it prefigures and promises a world yet-to-come. Art, if you like, operates within messianic time. And yet such art is inevitably doomed to frustration: the promise (of this other world, of reconciliation) is constantly being broken. Art is positioned within this melancholy field, this always already defeated logic. In fact, it is worth noting that philosophy, for Adorno, operates on this register also: 'The only philosophy which can be reasonably practised in the face of despair is the attempt to contemplate all things as they would present themselves from the standpoint of redemption' (Adorno 1978, 247). In a sense then Adorno has abandoned the existent. Indeed, this is what gives his work its particular tenor.

On one level this is certainly different to Deleuze's position inasmuch as the possible seems to involve a form of transcendent criticism (that is to say, criticism made from the standpoint of redemption). If, however, we were to position Adorno's broken promise as a form of immanent criticism, that which seeks to grasp the contradictions inherent in the existent by presenting, via art, something 'different', then we might be able to stake out some common territory between Adorno and Deleuze.[6] In fact, there seem to be many points of connection between Frankfurt School Critical Theory and the later writings of Deleuze and Guattari. Indeed, in their last work together, Deleuze and Guattari themselves attend to a notion of utopia, and to a notion of what they call immanent, revolutionary, utopias (as opposed to authoritarian, transcendent ones).[7] Such utopias are synonymous with what they call political philosophy: 'that conjunction of philosophy, or of the concept, with the present milieu' (*WP* 100). For Deleuze and Guattari this utopian impulse in philosophy (which in fact *is* philosophy) involves a resistance to the present, 'the creation of concepts [which] in itself calls for a future form, for a new earth and people that do not yet exist' (*WP* 108) That is, precisely, revolution, understood as the affirmation of a 'people-yet-to-come'.

Can Adorno be brought into this fundamentally affirmative and creative project? To a certain extent, after all, both Adorno and Deleuze articulate a resistance to the present and in so doing make a call to the future. However it is really Adorno's philosophical attitude, his style of thought as perhaps Deleuze would say, which is the stumbling block. To generalise, we might say that Adorno, as a thinker, is trapped in a form of negativity (as are all proponents of negative critique). For Adorno then, art, that very autonomous of objects, must operate in/as a negative dialectic (it is the 'impossible possible'). Art must be involved in a critique of what 'is' (specifically the alienation of the modern world). We can return to Deleuze here and remind ourselves that his issue with the possible is that it is never a genuinely creative category (even if it may seem so) but is in fact always already limited by the real that it resembles and cannot help but resemble. This is the case even, and perhaps especially, when it seeks to negate this real. This is not to disavow the criticality of art works but it is to say that this criticality must be accompanied by creativity (and in fact we might say that the former, when it really is criticism, is only ever really produced by the latter).

Back to Deleuze then, who in his discussion of the possible is keen to demarcate a notion of difference that does not imply a negativity and indeed that escapes 'identity thinking' altogether. He will do this not through recourse to a negative dialectic but through recourse to a notion of the virtual. First though, back to the possible once more, whose characteristic, for Deleuze, is that it 'refers to the form of identity in the concept' (*DR* 211). Difference here is nothing but the 'negative determined by the concept' (*DR* 211). Another way of saying this is that the possible, in order to be realised, merely has existence added to it, but an existence which is already determined by the concept albeit as a kind of 'outside'. Here then the possible operates as a point of transcendence, but, as with all transcendence, is in fact a product of immanence which has been abstracted out and then 'projected' back onto the plane of immanence as if it came from an 'elsewhere'.[8]

The virtual on the other hand names a field of difference that is not, and cannot be, subsumed by the concept. The virtual 'designates a pure multiplicity' which as such 'radically excludes the identical as a prior condition' (*DR* 211–12). The virtual then names a real place but one which has yet to be actualised. Whereas the real and the possible instigate a philosophy of transcendence, the virtual and the actual affirm immanence. We might rephrase this and say that whereas the possible names a logic of Being (ontology of stasis), the virtual affirms a logic of becoming (ontology of process). Indeed, it is only with, and within, the virtual that we have pure difference in and of itself (we might call this anoriginal complexity,[9] pure multiplicity, aliquid being,[10] or simply the realm of the undifferentiated). The virtual, or rather the actualisation of the virtual, is then the creative act – precisely the production, or actualisation, of difference and thus diversity from a pre-existing field of potentialities.

Another way of thinking this process of actualisation is as problem solving. To quote Deleuze: 'the virtual possesses the reality of a task to be performed or a problem to be solved. It is the problem which orientates, conditions and engenders solutions, but these do not resemble the conditions of the problem' (*DR* 212). It is in this sense, thinking biologically, that the organism is the solution to a problem: the eye as a solution to the specific 'problem' of light, the claw as a solution to the need for food and so on. Art can also be seen as a 'solution' in this sense, as part of a general, creative evolution, the forms of art precisely providing 'solutions' to 'problems' of space and time, perception and memory (problems of human existence).[11]

One way to think this virtual multiplicity, as we saw briefly in Chapter 2, is as the 'pure memory' of Bergson's thesis. As such the virtual can be understood as a temporal dimension of the object. The virtual is 'a part of the real object – as though the object had one part of itself in the virtual into which it plunged as though into an objective dimension' (*DR* 209). We might say then that the virtual is a kind of fractal realm. The virtual would always be 'contained' within the actual as it were, though in an ever more condensed state as it approaches the present. In fact, the same might be said of perception; the closer one is, the more apparently simple forms become complex, which is to say the realms of space and time are both fractal in character.[12]

It is here that the differences between Deleuze's notion of the virtual and its more common usage within technological discourses (Virtual Reality, Cyber theory and the like) become clear. In these latter places and spaces the virtual is understood as a property of matter, albeit matter interpenetrated by information.[13] With Deleuze however the virtual differs in kind from the actual. It is not 'of' matter but 'of' spirit as Bergson might say (as Deleuze remarks, Bergson reserves the use of the possible only in relation to matter, i.e., to a closed system) (*B* 43). In a sense the realm of pure perception ('before' any selection on the basis of needs and interests has been made) *is* a virtual realm, but this 'pure perception' is not the same kind of virtuality as that of pure memory. It exists, as Bergson demonstrates, on a different axis; it is spatial rather than temporal.[14] In fact, both pure perception (matter or, in Deleuze's terms the 'movement-image') and pure memory (time or, in Deleuze's terms again, the 'time-image') are intuitive abstractions from what, in experience, is a mixed state of affairs (our habits of representation and of representational thought). Pure memory ('identical to the totality of the past') is then like pure perception ('identical to the whole of matter'), an inhuman, super objective state which can only be accessed intuitively – we might even say imaginatively. Put bluntly, it is difficult, given the present human configuration, to access this pure perception and pure memory which is nevertheless a kind of 'background' to our experience. We live in a state in which differences in kind (between matter and memory) are mixed. We are 'badly analysed composites' 'that arbitrarily group things that *differ in kind*' (*B* 18). Deleuze's transcendental empiricism is then as such because it involves intuitively going beyond experience towards the conditions of experience (and not the conditions of possible experience (Kant) but the conditions of real experience).[15] This implies an ethical imperative, the latter understood as a pragmatic enquiry into our particular space–time coordinates (or simply our consciousness). We must divide these mixed composites along lines that differ in kind, and then follow these lines to their pure states, before returning back, armed with a kind of Spinozist 'knowledge', to the mixtures.

When it comes to actually actualising different spatialities and temporalities then technology has a crucial role to play. For Deleuze this is paradigmatically the case with the movie camera. In *Cinema 1* and *Cinema 2* this machine-eye-consciousness is portrayed as a kind of 'actualising machine'. It opens up perception and memory to a world beyond the strictly human (its mechanical eye moves towards a state of pure perception in the movement-image and towards a state of pure recollection in the time-image). For Deleuze, following Bergson, this gets to the very heart of philosophy's role, to think beyond the human (beyond representation). We might say then that the camera, and in fact all 'visualising' technologies, continue Bergson's intuitive method 'outside' of philosophy. We might also say that the actualisations these technologies perform and produce are specifically non-human, or machinic modes of consciousness.

Equally important is that we look to the field of that which has already been actualised. Again, we must ask the fundamentally ethical questions of how and why such and such becomes actual (how and why are we the mixtures that we are, perceiving the mixtures that we do?) Indeed, following Brian Massumi, it might be argued that it is not the actual that should hold our attention, nor in fact the virtual, but rather the processes of actualisation (the processes of selection if you like). We need to attend to that border, or 'seeping edge' as Massumi calls it, between the actual and the virtual, for, as Massumi also remarks, it is precisely at this edge that the potential for transformation is found.[16]

We might say then, again following Massumi, that the world of things (the object world) is but that which has been extracted or has emerged from the realm of relations, or conditions.[17] It is the body–brain complex that actualises these 'things', although this actualisation is not uniform, for different subjectivities exist in different worlds, these worlds being determined by the various 'technologies' at each individual's disposal. Technology here is then the name for that which enables, but also controls and manipulates actualisation/emergence. Capitalism's most sinister aspect, in this respect, is that it 'controls' many if not all of these matrices of emergence, that is to say, determines what becomes actual. Art practice might have a role to play in reversing this process, in reconnecting us with pre-objective relations/conditions and allowing a different combination, a different set of modulations as it were, to emerge. Art practice might then, like philosophy, involve intuition, an intuition incarnated in materials that takes us 'beyond' the actual, plunges us deep into the virtual, before returning with new actualisations. Indeed, art practice can be positioned at that 'seeping edge' between the existing state of affairs and a world 'yet-to-come.'[18] Again, this is not to position art as transcendent, for as we have seen the ontological coordinates of the actual and the virtual operate 'within' immanence (within this world). The virtual does not lack a reality, but is merely that which has yet to be actualised.

Excursus 1: mirror-travel

In his essay 'Entropy and the New Monuments' Robert Smithson writes about those artists who are his contemporaries (and as such he is also writing about himself) precisely in terms of pure matter and pure memory. The 'New Monuments', the emerging minimalist objects and expanded practices of the late 1960s, are here described as crystal objects with a face turned to the actual, and a face plunging deep into the virtual.[19] Indeed, for Smithson, this is what characterises the 'New Monuments'; they present a different view of matter and a different conception of time:

> Instead of causing us to remember the past like the old monuments, the new monuments seem to cause us to forget the future. Instead of being made of natural materials, such as marble, granite, or other kinds of rock, the new monuments are made of artificial materials, plastic, chrome and electric light. They are not built for the ages but against the ages. They are involved in a systematic reduction of time down to fractions of seconds, rather than in representing the long spaces of centuries. Both past and future are placed into an objective present. This kind of time has little or no space in it; it is stationary and without movement, it is going nowhere, it is anti-Newtonian, as well as being instant, and it is against the wheels of the time-clock ... [The] destruction of classical time and space is based on an entirely new notion of the structure of matter. (*CW* 11)

This 'new' image of time is then one in which the past is coextensive with the present, which itself is coextensive with the future. This is an image of time in which the latter is no longer determined by movement.[20] A stationary time, the time of *cronos*. As Smithson remarks this also involves the production of a 'new' image of matter. Indeed, we might say, following Deleuze-Bergson, that it is a kind of 'pure perception' of matter, produced by new synthetic materials. We might then characterise these 'New Monuments', following Deleuze, as involving the production of a specifically Bergsonian image of thought. To quote Deleuze:

> Bergson's major theses on time are as follows: the past coexists with the present that it has been; the past is preserved in itself, as past in general (non-chronological); at each moment time splits itself into present and past, present that passes and past which is preserved. (*C2* 82)

It is this preservation of the past in the present that Smithson sees in the 'New Monuments' (a kind of 'freezing' of time).[21] In fact, for Smithson the 'New Monuments' go one step further in also actualising a kind of future within the present (we might say that this is their future orientation or prophetic function).

Smithson calls this 'backward looking future', and sees it as a characteristic of many of the 'New Monuments' in which there is the conjunction of an 'extreme past' with a science fiction future (*CW* 15). Put simply, for Smithson, the 'New Monuments' activate a different, non-human, inorganic and what we might call geological duration. This becomes paradigmatic in Smithson's own work, and especially with the later and larger earthworks that Smithson completed, for example *Broken Circle, Spiral Hill* or the *Spiral Jetty* (both of which one had to enter into). Indeed, Smithson's large earthworks, as well as involving a manipulation of matter, might also be seen as involving a manipulation of time; the mobilisation of different temporalities. As Paul Wood has pointed out in relation to *Broken Circle, Spiral Hill*, there is certainly a kind of geological time at play. Smithson referred to the block of stone located in the middle of the broken circle, which he originally wanted to move but was unable to, as a 'warning from the ice age'. There is also the time of the seasons, the time of day and the 'time' of the weather, all of which are crucial to the experience of the earthwork (Wood 1976). Finally, of course, there is human time – the time it takes for us, for our body, to move around, to experience, the monument (Wood 1976). We might add here that there is the time of construction too, the time taken to build the earthwork. Indeed, the earthwork is a sedimentation of 'time' in this sense; it has its own 'self-contained' duration as it were. Following Bergson then, we might say that *Broken Circle, Spiral Hill* involves a foregrounding of different durations but also our own duration in relation to these, allowing a reflection on our particular temporal relation to the world. Wood, following Smithson's own thoughts, also refers to *Broken Circle, Spiral Hill* as being a place in which the 'remote future meets the remote past'. Indeed, the entropic quality of the monument – it is slowly returning to its 'natural' state – seems to point towards a future that it in fact encapsulates. As Wood remarks, the earthwork operates then as a kind of *vanitas*, a *memento mori*. We might say it is a monument to a future in which it no long 'exists'.

With Smithson's smaller works, his crystal and mirrored objects, time also becomes a material to play with. Indeed, as Smithson remarks in another essay, 'A Sedimentation of the Mind: Earth Projects', and in very much a Bergsonian vein:

> When a *thing* is seen through the consciousness of temporality, it is changed into something that is nothing. This all-engulfing sense provides the mental ground for the object, so that it ceases being a mere object and becomes art. The object gets to be less and less but exists

> as something clearer. Every object, if it is art, is charged with the rush of time even though it is static, but all this depends on the viewer. Not everyone sees the art in the same way, only an artist viewing art knows the ecstasy or dread, and this viewing takes place in time. (*CW* 112)

It is then as much the viewer (a specific kind of viewer) as the object that produces art in this sense (we might say that actualises the virtualities of the 'object'). For Smithson art is the name for this encounter in which an object rejoins the flow of time it was always already a part of (but had been extracted from). Indeed, all these objects and practices, these 'New Monuments', might be located on that 'seeping edge' between the actual and the virtual, which we might rephrase here as the coexistence of the pure past (and future) with the present, or simply a seeing of the object *as* object, and a seeing of the object *in* process, *as* duration.

In the earlier quote, and in Smithson's essay on the 'New Monuments' in general, there is, I would argue, a kind of philosophy going on, inasmuch as there is the deployment of certain concepts (for example of a 'time' no longer determined by movement) in order to 'think' a new kind of art. Indeed, Smithson's writings, in their use of an idiosyncratic archive (from science fiction novels and films to geological maps and other printed matter) produce a different conceptual system for understanding the world – and for making connections, suggesting compatibilities, in that world.[22] Like Deleuze and Guattari's own writing, there is a fundamentally creative and affirmative aspect to Smithson's essay in this sense that is also produced by a certain energy and speed of writing and indeed humour. Smithson, an autodidact, mobilises a variety of resources not normally associated with art; he offers a 'reinterpretation' of things in the world via a different framework to that found elsewhere.[23]

In the essay on 'New Monuments' there is then a description of how these minimalist practices actualise the virtual, but not the performance of this actualisation itself. Indeed, for this we have to actually experience Smithson's works (walk around *Broken Circle, Spiral Hill* for example). But we can also turn to another of Smithson practices, and in fact need not necessarily leave the realm of words (after all, for Smithson, these are as much the matter of art as any geological material). Here, we turn to a different kind of writing, a programmatic text, 'Incidents of Mirror-travel in the Yucatan', in which Smithson reflects on the construction of his *Yucatan Mirror Displacements*.

The *Yucatan Displacements* involved the positioning of eleven or twelve small square mirrors in nine different constellations within the South American desert landscape that Smithson and his fellow travellers were driving through. Each *Displacement* has a peculiar quality to it that comes down to the specifics of the context in which it was placed (geology, flora, weather and so on). Each *Displacement* then extracts and pictures a particular set of durations. The remarkable essay that accompanies the *Displacements* is, however, not just a record of Smithson's journey, but also operates as a set of pragmatics on how to access, or actualise, these other virtual dimensions. Indeed, the essay records what 'happens' with each *Displacement*, a disruption of time and space (precisely mirror-travel), but also, and I think more importantly, the essay contains instructions on how to conduct the *Displacements* again. Here for example is an extract from *The Third Mirror Displacement*:

> In the side of a heap of crushed limestone the twelve mirrors were cantilevered in the midst of large clusters of butterflies that had landed on the limestone. For brief moments flying butterflies were reflected; they seemed to fly through a sky of gravel. Shadows cast by the mirrors contrasted with those seconds of colour. A scale in terms of 'time' rather than 'space' took place. The mirror itself is not subject to duration, because it is an ongoing abstraction that is always available and timeless. The reflections on the other hand, are fleeting instances that evade measure. (*CW* 122)

In each of the *Displacements* Smithson inserts the mirrors into the earth. The mirrors then become *a part of the* landscape placed as they are in the geological ground zero of the desert. And yet the mirrors are also *a part from* the earth inasmuch as they reflect the sky (and other flora and fauna) and in so doing actualise other durations of organic and inorganic life. In fact, the mirror, in Smithson's hands, becomes a device for 'erasing' typical duration, or simply human, linear time. For flattening it out, precisely for making time into a multiplicity: 'but if one wishes to be ingenious enough to erase time one requires mirrors, not rocks. A strange thing, this branching mode of travel: one perceives in every past moment a parting of ways, a highway spreads into a bifurcating and trifurcating region of zigzags' (*CW* 131).[24]

This 'switching' of registers via the *Mirror Displacements* (for Deleuze it would be the crystal) occurs in space as well as time inasmuch as they involve the actualisation of micro-universes that are usually imperceptible. Here for example is Smithson again, this time from *The Fifth Mirror Displacement*:

> On the outskirts of the ruins of Palenque or in the skirts of Coatlicue, rocks were overturned; first the rock was photographed, then the pit

> that remained. 'Under each rock is an orgy of scale,' said Coatlicue … Each pit contained miniature earthworks – tracks and traces of insects and other sundry small creatures. In some beetle dung, cobwebs, and nameless slime. In others cocoons, tiny ant nests and raw roots. If an artist could see the world through the eyes of a caterpillar he might be able to make some fascinating art. Each of these secret dens was also the entrance to the abyss. (*CW* 126)

For Smithson each of the *Displacements* operates further to 'summon forth' a Mayan God from the Mexican desert who then articulates the workings of that specific *Displacement*. Here art practice has left the realms of representation and become an incarnation of sorts, each God 'coming forth' to embody a certain Mayan understanding of the world. Are these figures of Gods projected onto the plane of immanence (figures of transcendence)? Perhaps, but they can also be understood as Smithson's *conceptual personae*, 'future-people' that embody a certain mode of being, a certain style of life. For example, Quetzalcoatl from *The Ninth Mirror Displacement*:

> The double aspect of Quetzalcoatl is less a person than an operation of totemic perception. Quetzalcoatl becomes one half of an enantiomorph (*coatl* means twin) in search of the other half. A mirror looking for its reflection but never quite finding it … By travelling with Quetzalcoatl one becomes aware of primordial time or final time – The Tree of Rocks. (*CW* 131)

Smithson's essay is then a work of imagination, a kind of creative fabulation, and yet the essay also works as a manual of sorts. It offers a series of notes on 'mirror-travel', an undertaking we might recast in Deleuzian terms as 'travel' 'into' the virtual. Importantly, this mirror-travel must be performed, the instructions must be followed. Smithson gives us an account of his own journey, and in doing so informs us how we might repeat the experiment. What we have here then is an example of a pragmatic and practical philosophy (philosophy as a way of life as it were). After all we can read, and understand, the concepts of the actual and the virtual but in order to actualise the virtual these 'concepts' need to be incarnated in other materials and via other practices. We might say that this is the ritualistic function of an art practice such as Smithson's which endeavours to take us out of our usual space/time coordinates, precisely to produce a reconfiguration of our habitual mode of being.

The plane of immanence (or the non-philosophical moment of philosophy)

> In short, the first philosophers are those who institute a plane of immanence like a sieve stretched over chaos. In this sense they contrast with sages, who are religious personae, priests, because they conceive of the institution of an always transcendent order imposed from outside ... Whenever there is transcendence, vertical being, imperial State in the sky or on earth, there is religion; and there is philosophy whenever there is immanence. (*WP* 43)

For Deleuze and Guattari philosophy *is* thinking immanence. Philosophy operates on the plane of immanence and through 'forms' that are themselves immanent to the plane (they do not 'arrive' from 'elsewhere'). In this sense philosophy is radically opposed to religion that projects its figures onto the plane of immanence from a transcendent point. In *What is Philosophy?* Deleuze and Guattari write about Chinese hexagrams, Hindu mandelas, Jewish Sephiroth, Islamic 'Imaginals' and Christian icons all as being projections from a kind of vertical being, precisely a populating of the plane with figures (*WP* 89). Philosophy, on the other hand, populates its plane with concepts that are intimately connected to one another and to the plane from which, in some senses, they emerge.

But philosophy is only one form of thought amongst others, each with their own specificity. Indeed, *What is Philosophy?* demarcates what Deleuze and Guattari see as the three great forms of thought, that is, philosophy, but also science and art, each of which throws a 'plane over chaos' and has its own particular milieu and rules of invention (*WP* 197). In fact, in *What is Philosophy?*, notions of the virtual are only really relevant to the first two forms of thought: philosophy actualises the virtual in an event by means of the concept (Deleuze's famous example, from Lewis Carroll, being 'the smile without the cat'). Science, on the other hand actualises the virtual in 'states of affairs' on a plane of reference, by a process of 'slowing down' and the positioning of 'partial observers' (we might say simply 'a cat') (*WP* 197). Art, in *What is Philosophy?* anyway, and despite what Deleuze and Guattari say elsewhere (and as I have argued above), is more involved in notions of the possible. The aesthetic figures with which it populates its plane of composition express 'possible worlds'. I have dealt with what *What is Philosophy?* has to say about the workings of art in Chapter 2, and the notion of art expressing possible worlds will be looked at further in the next chapter. Here I want to continue paying attention to philosophy, and more specifically to what appears to be the *non-philosophical* moment of philosophy, and which in a sense grounds the philosophical enterprise. In fact, we might say that this moment lies at the very heart of all creative thought.

Before moving on however, it is important, in fact, it is one of the avowed purposes of *What is Philosophy?*, to distinguish these three forms of thought from mere opinion. Whereas opinion reproduces the present milieu, forms of thought such as art and philosophy are rather future-orientated. In their construction they 'summon forth a new earth, a new people' (*WP* 99). Indeed this, for Deleuze and Guattari, as we have seen, is what makes philosophy political, if not revolutionary. Philosophy's absolute deterritorialisation (of the concept on the plane of immanence) conjoins with the present milieu in a resistance to the present (the relative deterritorialisation of capital and the accompanying domination of opinion). At stake here are new becomings that are always minor in nature.[25] Opinion then might be characterised as the *quasi* thought of the majority, the *doxa* of any particular time. The latter works by proposing:

> a particular relationship between an external perception as state of a subject and an internal affection as passage from one state to another (exo- and endoreference). We pick out a quality supposedly common to several objects that we perceive, and an affection supposedly common to several subjects who experience it and who, along with us, grasp that quality. (*WP* 144)

When philosophy becomes confused with opinion (which, when it is called 'theory', it so often does), thought itself suffers and becomes little more than the confrontation of rival opinions, or, as Deleuze and Guattari remark, little more than 'pleasant or aggressive dinner conversations at Mr. Rorty's' (*WP* 144).

For Deleuze and Guattari doing philosophy involves something a good deal more precise, and we might say a good deal more radical. Indeed, it involves three interconnected operations: the creation of concepts, the construction of *conceptual personae*, and the 'throwing down' of a plane of immanence. Each in some senses relies on the others. The plane of immanence is the philosopher's point of view or attitude. It is the laying out of a ground, or terrain, on which concepts (themselves territories) can be constructed. Concepts are constructed through the combination of various components (which are invariably 'borrowed' from other concepts) and which are then given a certain consistency. This latter procedure itself involves a further invention of *conceptual personae* that 'live' these concepts (these characters are kind of philosophical avatars of the philosopher himself: Descartes' idiot, or Nietzsche's Zarathustra, for example). It is the last however, the laying down of the plane of immanence, understood as the philosopher's particular style (what Deleuze in *Difference and Repetition* calls an 'image of thought') which procedurally comes first. It is the laying out of a plane as the conditions of a problem, the concepts that populate it being the case of a solution. Importantly, it is a non-philosophical undertaking. It is in fact the non-philosophical moment of philosophy. Deleuze and Guattari's project here, as is Deleuze's in *Difference and Repetition*, is to excavate and map out the modern 'image of thought' and specifically that of Kant. How the latter always returns to resemblance, to recognition (to representation) and ultimately to an unquestioned assumption of common (read good) sense. However, it follows from this that other images of thought, other planes of immanence can be instituted. Indeed, as Deleuze and Guattari say: 'those who do not renew the image of thought are not philosophers but functionaries who, enjoying a ready-made thought, are not even conscious of the problem and are unaware even of the efforts of those they claim to take as their models' (*WP* 51). This is why the encounter, the non-philosophical encounter, is of such importance to the philosopher: it can bring about the destruction of a previous image of thought. Here then are Deleuze and Guattari writing about this encounter with the 'outside' of thought:

> Precisely because the plane of immanence is prephilosophical and does not immediately take effect with concepts, it implies a sort of groping experimentation and its layout resorts to measures that are not very respectable, rational or reasonable. These measures belong to the order of dreams, of pathological processes, esoteric experiences, drunkenness, and excess ... To think is always to follow the witch's flight. (*WP* 141)

The plane of immanence is then precisely a form of experimentation and implies a certain experimental mode of being. It is a 'sieve stretched over chaos', in fact an attempt to give consistency to chaos ('to give consistency without losing anything of the infinite') (*WP* 141). This is opposed to science which 'seeks to provide chaos with reference points' thus abandoning infinite movement in a general limitation of speed (the slowing down that science, to be as such, must perform) (*WP* 42). It is also, as we have seen, opposed to religion, which installs a transcendent order from above, by the projection of figures onto the plane.

This non-philosophical moment of philosophy (that in turn renews philosophy) can only proceed by intuition and by a certain amount of 'losing-one's-self'. Deleuze and Guattari cite the example of Henri Michaux and the notion that one only really thinks by 'becoming something else, something that does not think – an animal, a molecule, a particle – that comes back to thought and revives it' (*WP* 42). Deleuze and Guattari are not referring to Michaux's art works here ('usually these measures do not appear in the result, which must be grasped solely in itself and calmly') but rather, it seems to me, are referring to the journeys, the adventures (whether drug influenced or not), which in some senses allow for, and perhaps provoke, such and such a concept, or indeed such and such an art work, to be made (*WP* 41–2). It is at this place that we move away from the three forms of thought to something wilder, something more chaotic. Indeed, later in *What is Philosophy?* art, science and philosophy are characterised as 'chaoids', forms of thought which refer back to chaos, and are in fact *of* chaos (a chaos given consistency) (*WP* 208). However, before this consistency is achieved there is the moment of the encounter with chaos, the confrontation with non-thought. It is in this place, at this moment, that the plane of immanence is instituted, almost as a survival mechanism, but also as that which will allow thought and creativity to unfurl.

It might be useful to turn here from *What is Philosophy?* back to *A Thousand Plateaus*, the latter being very much a book about the non-philosophical adventures of philosophy. In this earlier, and in many senses more experimental work, we have, as might be expected, a series of strategies for 'accessing' immanence, which is here described in more concrete terms. The plane of immanence in *A Thousand Plateaus* is a more slippery, we might even say more liquid 'place'. It is Spinoza's God/Nature/substance, but the latter stretched, a place in which

> There are no longer any forms or developments of forms; nor are there subjects or the formation of subjects. There is no structure, any more than there is genesis. There are only relations of movement and rest, speed and slowness between unformed elements, or at least between elements that are relatively unformed, molecules and particles of all kinds. There are only haecceities, affects, subjectless individuations that constitute collective enunciations. (*ATP* 266)

Here the plane of immanence is opposed to the plane of transcendence (also called the plane of organisation and development). It is the realm of the molecular – or simply inorganic 'life' – from which molar aggregates such as our subjectivity and identity are formed.[26] It is, on, and across, this plane that the 'Body without Organs' (BwO) moves, the latter understood, at this point anyway, as itself a kind of surface upon which the 'I' is a mere striation. It is in this sense that the BwO is a mechanism, a procedure, for undoing the strata that binds us:[27]

> Let us consider the three great strata concerning us, in other words, the ones that most directly bind us: the organism, signifiance, and subjectification. The surface of the organism, the angle of signifiance and interpretation, and the point of subjectification or subjection. You will be organized, you will be an organism, you will articulate your body – otherwise you're just depraved. You will be signifier and signified, interpreter and interpreted – otherwise you're just a deviant. You will be a subject, nailed down as one, a subject of the enunciation recoiled into a subject of the statement – otherwise you're just a tramp. To the strata as a whole, the BwO opposes disarticulation (or *n* articulations) as the property of the plane of consistency, experimentation as the operation on that plane (no signifier, never interpret!), and nomadism as the movement (keep moving even in place, never stop moving, motionless voyage, desubjectification). (*ATP* 159)

The BwO is then a kind of aesthetic machine, but its operating field is immanence rather than transcendence. It breaks down the subject/object boundary, tears apart, to use the quote from Guattari again, the 'ontological iron curtain between being and things' (*OM* 8). It is always *a* BwO, never mine, or yours, or his or hers. It is constituted solely by *a*personal affects, by intense thresholds and differential gradients of speed and slowness. It has a relation with the strata that it is in some senses a part of, but it is also that which sets the strata free, that which allows for the possibility of destratification.

Of course, the point is to build yourself a BwO, and as such the BwO is a technique of construction as well as the production of intensities: 'But what comes to pass on the BwO is not exactly the same as how you make yourself one ... One phase is for the fabrication of the BwO, the other to make something circulate on it or pass across it' (*ATP* 152). In *A Thousand Plateaus* Deleuze and Guattari offer us a whole selection of constructed BwO's, some of which are botched (simply do not 'work'), some of which are cancerous (producing a proliferation of strata, that is, fascism) and others of which are destructive (e.g., the drug addict producing a hollowed out and ultimately nihilistic BwO, or the masochist who might build a BwO but then find no intensities come to pass). Perhaps the most 'successful' BwO's are those that can be repeated, those that can be 'reused'. Art might be a name for these experimental modes of being, these strange and exciting (and sometimes frightening) 'new' images of thought, although art can also be, and often is, the name for those BwO's which have precisely been blocked, botched or otherwise broken. This amounts to saying that the dangers of transcendence, everywhere and always, accompany experiments and adventures in thinking immanence.

Excursus 2: the *Spiral Jetty*

In his essay 'A Sedimentation of the Mind: Earth Projects' Smithson lays out his project of 'abstract geology' understood as a general 'slowing down' of thought.[28] This is how the essay begins:

> The earth's surface and the figments of the mind have a way of disintegrating into discrete regions of art. Various agents both fictional and real, somehow trade places with each other – one cannot avoid muddy thinking when it comes to earth projects, or what I will call 'abstract geology'. One's mind and the earth are in a constant state of erosion, mental rivers wear away abstract banks, brain waves undermine cliffs of thought, ideas decompose into stones of unknowing, and conceptual crystallisation break apart into deposits of gritty reason. Vast moving faculties occur in this geological miasma, and they move in the most physical way. This movement seems motionless, yet it crushes the landscape of logic under glacial reveries. This slow flowage makes one conscious of the turbidity of thinking. Slump, debris slides, avalanches all take place within the cracking limits of the brain. The entire body is pulled into the cerebral sediment, where particles and fragments make themselves known as solid consciousness. A bleached and fractured world surrounds the artist. To organise this mess of corrosion into patterns, grids, and subdivisions is an esthetic (sic.) process that has scarcely been touched. (*CW* 100)

Here the artist confronts chaos or as Smithson calls it, the 'undifferentiated', in front of which he organises grids and patterns, his 'abstract geology', as the precondition for thought and creativity.[29] This is the 'primary process' of 'making contact with matter', a process that Smithson feels is often overlooked in favour of the 'finished' piece (*CW* 103). Indeed, according to Smithson, critics such as Michael Fried disparage the encounter (the 'abyss' fills them with fear) choosing instead to cast their gaze at the second moment, the construction of that which 'fences in' the abyss (that which halts becomings) (*CW* 103–4). Smithson is not nihilistic, he does not plunge into the abyss, but like Deleuze he favours that art which has something of the abyss, of chaos, about it.[30] Hence his preference for material and for forms which arise from the earth itself.

As a case study of this process we might take Smithson's most well-known earthwork, the *Spiral Jetty*, and also Smithson's own essay on the latter that records and recounts the selection, construction, and 'activation' of the earthwork via words. Like 'Incidents of Mirror Travel in the Yucatan', 'The Spiral Jetty' essay is also a kind of philosophy, a practical philosophy, in the sense that it draws concepts (the 'spiral' or the 'helicopter', for example) across an already constituted plane of immanence, understood here as both Smithson's attitude to the salt lake *and* the salt lake itself.

The first stage then, as the essay tells us, is the search for the 'site' (we might say the location of a construction site for a BwO). The search is careful, not just any place will do, but somewhere which 'grabs' Smithson (which selects him as it were). It is in fact the site that will determine the earthwork. Eventually Smithson locates it:

> About one mile north of the oil seeps I selected my site. Irregular beds of limestone dip gently eastward, massive deposits of black basalt are broken over the peninsula, giving the region a shattered appearance. It is one of the few places on the lake where the water comes right up to the mainland. Under shallow pinkish water is a network of mud cracks supporting the jig-saw puzzle that composes the salt flats. As I looked at the site, it reverberated out to the horizons only to suggest an immobile cyclone while flickering light make the whole landscape appear to quake. A dormant earthquake spread into the fluttering stillness, into a spinning sensation without movement. This site was a rotary that enclosed itself in an immense roundness. From that gyrating space emerged the possibility of the Spiral Jetty. No ideas, no concepts, no systems, no structures, no abstractions could hold themselves together in the actuality of that evidence ... No sense wondering about classifications and categories, there were none. (*CW* 146)

For Smithson then there is not so much a before to the selection, an idea that might be *re*presented in a given site. In fact the site itself functions to suggest the work, and as such might be said to already hold within it a potentiality (precisely the *Spiral Jetty*), which is then brought out in the resulting construction.[31]

The second moment commences with the construction of the jetty itself. The tail and spiral are staked out and then the machines – two dump trucks, a tractor and a front loader – move the earth and fill the jetty in. Smithson's use of machines is important; this is not a return to some kind of primitive pre-modern practice, or rather it is not just this. Indeed, the *Spiral Jetty* involves a mobilisation of the technology of modernity but precisely in order to produce something *different* (a new assemblage). The landscape Smithson works on is likewise less a raw 'nature' than an always already 'contaminated' terrain, a terrain moulded as much by modern man as by elemental forces. Indeed, it is particularly these industrial wastelands that attracted Smithson and which provided the ground for his constructions. Again, we might say that these kinds of terrains are already overflowing with potentialities of which the work actualises just a selection.

Then comes the third moment. In standing on the jetty and indeed seeing it from the shore, there is a switching of registers, the switching of what Smithson calls 'scale' ('To be in the scale of the Spiral Jetty is to be out of it. On eye level, the tail leads one into an undifferentiated state of matter') (*CW* 147). This involves a further activation of the earthwork, the passing of intensities across the body-without-organs, understood here as a body-brain-earth assemblage:

> On the slopes of Rozel Point I closed my eyes, and the sun burned crimson through the lids. I opened them up and the Great Salt Lake was bleeding scarlet streaks. My sight was saturated by the colour of red algae circulating in the heart of the lake, pumping into ruby currents, no they were veins and arteries sucking up the obscure sediment. My eyes became combustion chambers churning orbs of blood blazing by the light of the sun. All was enveloped in a flaming chromosphere. (*CW* 148)

Finally, in the helicopter ride over the jetty the earthwork is further activated. Scale is again introduced (registers are switched). Questions of natural versus artificial become redundant here as Smithson reaches degree 0, *the* plane of immanence understood here as precisely a state of non-organic life:[32]

> The helicopter manoeuvred the sun's reflections through the Spiral Jetty until it reached the centre. The water functioned as a vast thermal mirror. From that position the flaming reflection suggested the ion source of a cyclotron that extended into a spiral of collapsed matter. All sense of energy accelerated expired into a rippling stillness of reflected heat. A withering light swallowed the rocky particles of the spiral, as the helicopter gained altitude. All existence seemed tentative and stagnant. The sound of the helicopter motor became a primal groan echoing the tenuous aerial views ... I was slipping out of myself again, dissolving into a unicellular beginning, trying to locate the nucleus at the end of the spiral. All that blood stirring makes one aware of protoplasmic solutions, the essential matter between the formed and the unformed, masses of cells consisting largely of water, proteins, lipoids, carbohydrates, and inorganic salts. (*CW* 149)

We might say that the above narrative is merely a fiction, after all the *Spiral Jetty*, at least on one level, is just earth and rocks deposited in a lake. But the *Spiral Jetty* is also a machine that produces a different experience of the world – a new myth – and thus a different, we might say altered, consciousness. The jetty's disappearance relatively soon after it was built also lends it this mythic quality – its very invisibility giving it a further future-orientated-event quality.[33] This quality has also to do with certain questions and problems that the jetty poses. Who is it built for? What cargo might be unloaded here?[34] The answers to these questions move us beyond our habitual world, beyond our familiar space–time. The jetty has recently emerged, encrusted with white salt crystals. Again, a certain temporality is at play here – not a human temporality, but a solar temporality (the jetty re-emerged because of the prolonged drought in Utah).[35] Once again then the jetty demands participation, demands that we walk along it and enter into its mythic temporality, its geological and inhuman duration.

It is in this sense of opening up non-human worlds that the film of *Spiral Jetty* is as important as the essay. The film – a kind of geo-cinema – is in fact a construction just as the essay and the jetty themselves are (all involve the manipulation of matter). Through the use of montage, close-ups and stills (for example, of maps and charts, of the ripples of the lake and of the sunlight), as well as the different 'view points' of the car speeding through the desert towards the lake, the slow motion and low camera angle of the dump trucks constructing the jetty, and the helicopter's birds eye view over the jetty itself, the film actualises the different durations and different scales at stake in the experience of the jetty, and written about in the essay. The camera then operates here as a machine eye opening us up to worlds beyond the human.[36] The soundtrack of the film also works to produce different and fractured temporalities, from Smithson's mantra-like reading of the directions of the compass to the sound of the helicopter's blades and indeed the silences of the National History Museum. We might say then that the film parallels the work of the essay, which itself parallels the construction and the experience of the jetty itself. Each is a component of the *Spiral Jetty machine* whose operative field we might give here a new name: *geoaesthetics*.

5
From Possible Worlds to Future Folds
Abstracts, Situationist Cities and the Baroque in Art

In the previous chapter art was configured as a kind of practical philosophy. Whether it was in the actualisation of the virtual, the generation of planes of immanence or the construction of local BwOs that dismantle the strata that binds us, art named a process of experimentation and ultimately one of transformation. However, if we are to follow Deleuze closely then we must also return to the notion of the possible that we distanced ourselves from in Chapter 4, for as Deleuze remarks throughout his writings, art must also be thought as the expression of *possible worlds*. In fact this notion was present in Chapter 2. Art, as a bloc of sensations, expresses a particular and different world-view (and not necessarily that of its artist). In this final chapter I want to think through the notion of possible worlds as developed in Deleuze's book on Proust and, more significantly, his book on Leibniz. I also want to look briefly at an essay by Jean-François Lyotard on contemporary art that in many respects parallels Deleuze's own thoughts.

In particular, and as with Chapter 4, I want to produce an encounter between certain philosophical concepts, such as the *monad* and the *fold*, and a specific art practice, in this case the paintings of the German contemporary artist Gerhard Richter. Richter's practice involves a variety of different components, from the so-called Photo Paintings, through the Colour Charts, Townscapes and Monochromes to the more recent Abstracts. It is the latter that this chapter deals with, and more particularly the work produced in the 1980s.[1] Again, the art practice is meant not as an illustration of the philosophy, nor is the philosophy intended as a kind of 'Deleuzian take over' of the paintings. In fact, the chapter attempts to think a Deleuze–Richter conjunction, to set each alongside the other and in so doing to produce a new kind of assemblage between the two.[2] Indeed, the chapter is an experiment in this sense, an exploration of the resonances between two kinds of thought which although logically distinct seem to parallel one another in their creative and affirmative character.

Leading on from this conjunction I want to think a little about the 'new' or expanded Baroque as Deleuze understood it, and which might be characterised by the city, and especially the Situationist city as it was theorised in the writings of Ivan Chtcheglov. We might say that this fictionalised and utopian city is an example of the Deleuze–Leibniz monad being opened out onto an expanded field of inter-connectivity (and as such we return to the terrain of Chapter 1). We might also characterise this new Baroque as the introduction of a logic of participation into art practice. I also make some very brief comments here on the relation of this 'New Baroque' to new technologies. At stake in each of these moments is again a turn from the linguistic turn of much art theory towards the actual matter of art and to the latter's expressive character. As regards Richter, the chapter also intends a different, more affirmative reading of the paintings than those that tend towards a deconstructive, melancholy and mournful 'interpretation'.

Different worlds

From Proust to Leibniz

The essence of art for Deleuze's Proust is difference, understood here as the different viewpoint (that is, different from our own) expressed by the work of art. Art allows us access to other worlds, allows us to experience another's world that would otherwise remain closed to us: 'only art gives us what we vainly sort from a friend, what we would have vainly expected from a beloved' (*P* 42).[3] It follows, as Proust himself remarks, that 'as many original artists as there are, so many worlds will we have at our disposal' (*P* 42). Further, these viewpoints, ostensibly on the same world, are in fact 'as different as the most remote worlds' (*P* 42). Indeed, it is this irreducible difference, this distinct viewpoint, that expresses the world (and, as such, constitutes art) (*P* 41). The essence of art is then a kind of country or landscape, a region of being (*P* 43).[4] Essence in this sense does not name some mysterious, transcendent quality of art, but rather its internal consistency, or what we might call its 'world-building' character. Indeed, essence is not explained by subjects, but rather itself constitutes distinct artistic subjectivities. As Deleuze remarks: 'Essence is not only individual, it *individuates*' (*P* 43).[5]

For Deleuze's Leibniz, this individuation is accomplished by the monad and by relations between monads, in fact between a kind of hierarchy of monads. Deleuze writes about this in his last major philosophical work, *The Fold,* foregrounding Leibniz's diagrammatic notion of the *dominata* and the *dominated,* an account of how, in a superabundant, fractal universe the 'stuff' that makes up our world, and ourselves 'sticks' together (*F* 110–11). On this level then we have the Baroque conception of matter: a world of material fabric, composed of smaller and smaller parts and of relationships of capture between these parts. We might call this a general *texturology* of the world. However, monads consist of two floors, or two regimes. The world of matter, open to the universe (exteriority), and the world of the soul, closed in on itself and without windows or doors (interiority). The monad, on its lower floor is in and of the world, connected as a body, to all other bodies (receiving their 'imprint' as Henri Bergson might say).[6] On its upper floor however there are no such connections and there is no such communication. The upper floor of distinct monads are like private apartments, although each involves 'variants of the same interior decoration', variations on the same dark background (*F* 100). For Leibniz the upper floor is the soul, or what we might call, following Guattari, the incorporeal aspect of subjectivity. As Deleuze remarks in an interview:

> Leibniz's most famous proposition is that every soul or subject (monad) is completely closed, windowless and doorless, and contains the whole world in its darkest depths, while also illuminating some little portion of that world, each monad, a different portion. So the world is enfolded in each soul, but differently, because each illuminates only one little aspect of the overall folding. (*N* 157)

It is in this sense that the monad can be understood as a kind of ego, involving as it does a 'sphere of appurtenance', a clear zone, or again in Bergson's terms, a 'zone of perception' ('containing' only that which is 'of interest' to that specific monad).[7] Everything outside of this zone constitutes the larger dark background, the obscure, the imperceptible, which itself will constitute the clear zone of other monads. A monad then is *determined* by its clear zone (and by the relation of differences therein).[8] The clear zone of the tick, for example, is smaller than that of man, involving as it does a smaller zone of clarity (perception of light, smell of prey, tactile sense of surface (or where best to burrow)) although each expresses the whole world for its respective being.[9]

We can reconfigure this notion of perception as a kind of ownership. That which is 'in' my 'clear zone' is *my* world. It is in this sense that Deleuze reads Leibniz as setting forth an ontology of having over being.[10]

Life becomes a question of ownership and of its crisis (a crisis in property that links Leibniz to capitalism),[11] for parts are constantly leaving, more often than not captured by other monads.[12] As Deleuze remarks, this is why 'Nietzsche felt himself so close to Leibniz', for ownership – one's domination over the dominated – is a question of power and of one's personal power to dominate what we might call the 'swarm' of one's being (*F* 110). This notion of ownership might itself be reconfigured as a question of folding: to have is always to fold. We *fold* that which is outside, inside.[13]

For Deleuze–Leibniz it is the convergence of the two levels, of 'vertical immanent causality' (impression) and of 'transitive horizontal causality' (expression), of the world folded in the monad and the world creased in matter, which constitutes beings (*F* 100). Individual beings, or souls in Leibniz's terms, are those reasonable monads not content with mere functioning but which are of a sufficient complexity, have a sufficiently large 'clear zone', to allow reflection on, and an overview of, the world. These monads are then similar to Bergson's complex centres of indetermination; in both a kind of self-awareness and self-reflexivity is achieved through increasing perceptual apparatus and overall brain–body complexity.[14]

These individuals, or 'true forms', 'actualise a virtuality or a potential' (*F* 110).[15] Put simply, each monad brings its own world into being. Importantly, and perhaps surprisingly, this is not necessarily a question of the organic versus the inorganic, for true or 'genuine forms' are in fact primary forces which 'do not only apply to living organisms, but to physical and chemical particles, to molecules, atoms and photons' (*F* 103). Here there is no difference in kind between the organic and the inorganic, which is to say there is no clear boundary between the two. As we shall see paintings might be understood as individual beings in this sense, as having two levels: of collective or mass phenomena and of individual form (the primary forces) that in some senses organises or folds this matter. These two regimes are then folded over/into one another. They resonate together forming a harmony. We might say that this harmony, or larger fold, is like the style of beings in the world (the production of specific subjectivities), or indeed the style of art works.

Leibniz's monad then parallels Proust's essence. In both, communication is not the issue, but is replaced by another operation: *interpretation* (*P* 23).[16] But this is not the interpretation of signifying regimes (in the Saussurean and post-Saussurean sense), rather it is the *explication* of signs, the unfolding of that which is implicated. Art, we might say, is that which is folded. Art is a possible world folded, by means of the artist's style, in substance. We are forced to unfold these worlds, that is, to think, when we encounter the work of art. Thought here is that process which comes after the encounter (thought is the ripples produced by this meeting).[17] We might say then that art is like a 'cut'; it shakes us out of our habitual modes of being and puts other conditions into play (indeed this is its aesthetic power).[18] This is the 'violent effect' produced by the sign, not thought itself but the 'food of thought' (*P* 23). Of course, and as Proust suggests, this forcing of thought, this desire for interpretation, is also produced when we fall in love (in Leibniz's terms, when we encounter another monad). At first we think it is the object of our love that forces us to think (precisely to interpret), then we move from the object to the subject, locating the origin of this force within ourselves. In fact, it is both and neither. It is only when we move from our apprenticeship in love towards our encounter with art that we understand the difference, the difference of another's world, which has forced us to thought. Art then offers us a new image of thought (a new *folding*), one in which recognition (and resemblance) is less important than the encounter. One in which violence replaces 'good will' (hence Proust's elevation of love, or rather 'falling in love', over friendship).[19] In this new image of thought it is difference, and the embracing of difference, that replaces representation and recognition. We might say simply that it is this difference that constitutes art's force and power to move us.

Interlude: Lyotard and multiplicity

As a brief digression, and before turning to Richter, it is instructive to look at Lyotard's writings on contemporary art for a kind of parallel thesis to Deleuze's. In his essay 'Philosophy and Painting in the Age of their Experimentation' Lyotard maps out a flat plane, or what we might call a plane of immanence, for contemporary art. In such an expanded field art becomes inherently satirical; it will adopt any genre to put over its 'point of view'. This 'immense diversity', or multiplicity, of genres involves 'exploring things unsayable and things invisible', and as such, 'strange machines are assembled, where what we didn't have the idea of saying or the matter to feel can make itself heard and experienced' (*LYO* 190). Lyotard continues:

> the whole point is always to try out whether that situation, that event, that hole in the ground, that wrapping of a building, those pebbles placed on the ground, that cut made on the body, that illustrated diary of a schizophrenic, those *trompe l'oeil* sculptures, and all

> the rest – whether they too say something to us. The powers of sensing and phrasing are being probed on the limits of what is possible, and thus the domain of the perceptible-sensing and the speakable-speaking is being extended. (*LYO* 190)

For Lyotard these artistic adventures are not subjective perspectives on being, rather they 'are made "within being" and not before its eyes' (*LYO* 190).[20] Each work then presents a micro-universe (or a *micrologie*). Each time Being is nothing but one of these specifically different presentations; a series of thought experiments that 'babble, huff and puff and are envious of one another' (*LYO* 191). As with Deleuze, so for Lyotard: each work of art encapsulates a universe, a world unto itself.[21] Indeed, art is precisely anti-systematic in this sense. In fact, in this essay, as elsewhere, Lyotard orientates himself against those philosophers (and their arrogance) who claim to identify a single voice of Being. As Lyotard remarks 'No one knows what "language" Being understands, which it speaks, or to which it can be referred. No one even knows whether there is only one Being or many, and whether there is only one language of Being or Many' (*LYO* 190). For Lyotard, it is of course precisely different art works that 'present' different beings, or, we might say different becomings.

Like Lyotard, Deleuze is a philosopher of becoming, a thinker of multiplicity. Nevertheless, commentators have often positioned him as a philosopher of Being, a philosopher of a kind of reversed Platonism. Alain Badiou, one of the most astute readers of Deleuze gives an account of Deleuze's philosophy, specifically as it appears in *Difference and Repetition*, as precisely a philosophy of the One (encapsulated in the quote from Deleuze 'There has only ever been one ontological proposition: Being is Univocal' (*DR* 35)).[22] In a sense Badiou is correct. Deleuze's philosophical position on Being can be understood, albeit somewhat reductively, as univocal. Indeed, those philosophers he takes as his precursors are also univocal in this sense. For example Leibniz's (and indeed Spinoza's) 'belief' in, and centrally positioning of, 'God' make them univocal (with Leibniz, the monads, ultimately, are expressions of, and determined by, the divine), and Deleuze, when he writes on them (or with them) is likewise univocal. However, things are more complex than this, for Deleuze, like Leibniz is a philosopher of the one *and* the multiple. Indeed, how these relate is one of the key questions of his philosophical *oeuvre*. For Deleuze, it is then always the One in the Many and the Many in the One. I will be returning to this point.

We might however also want to look at this ontological problem from another perspective. For, as Lyotard remarks above, no one can know if there is one or more beings or how many languages of being there might be. We might then want to ask how productive the debate about Deleuze's univocity actually is. Badiou's discussion in his book on Deleuze about a (false) organic/vitalist multiplicity (Deleuze's) versus a (true) mathematical one (Badiou's) is compelling, but in some senses misses the point. Indeed, perhaps this question of Being, the question really of our 'origin', needs to be replaced by something more pragmatic: how to live (that is, where we are going).[23] Deleuze's books, his meditations on different philosophers, as well as his own philosophy, might then be understood as explorations of other's worlds, and specifically the different worlds of univocal philosophers, but less for 'answers' to the question of origins and more in terms of strategies, or precisely ethics, on how to live (on how to move 'beyond' our limited human condition). Pragmatically speaking it might well make sense to take strategies and concepts from one's friends or enemies, or to tactically inhabit another's image of thought. Indeed, in Leibniz's terms we might see Deleuze as precisely exploring different foldings of thought. It is in this sense that Deleuze's collaborations with Guattari are amongst his most important works involving as they do a two-fold thought that itself explores other folds, other kinds of thought.

We might want to continue Deleuze's enquiry by reading his writings on philosophers, in this case Leibniz, alongside other practices. What might Deleuze–Leibniz open up in our encounter with art (and vice versa)? Art is to be understood here less as the *re*presentation of Being (the representation of a world already existent) or, indeed, as the representation of a philosophical treatise already written, but rather as the production of worlds in process, the production of different kinds of fold.

Richter's Abstracts

Monadic painting

> The invention of the readymade seems to me the invention of reality, in other words the radical discovery that reality in contrast with the view of the world image is the only important thing. Since then painting no longer represents reality but is itself reality (produced by itself). And sometime or other it will again be a question of denying the value of this reality in order to produce pictures of a better world (as before). (*RIC* 124)

In an interview with the art critic Benjamin Buchloh the painter Gerhard Richter remarks, in riposte to Buchloh's observation that

Richter's Abstracts are kind of staged, 'second-order' paintings, that in fact they evoke 'moods' and indeed have something 'anticipatory' about them (1992, 1042). They are not merely a 'perversion of gestural abstraction', 'not ironic', but, for Richter, 'express some kind of yearning' for a 'better world' (Richter 1992, 1042). Does this make them melancholy? Are they to be positioned in messianic time, as the frustrated hope, the broken promise of a longed for but endlessly deferred redemption?[24] Are they defeated allegories?[25] In fact, they seem to operate in a much more affirmative space.[26] The paintings seem to celebrate and express a certain other worldliness. They are, I would argue, creative or world creating in their very being. This notion of expression is tricky, for the paintings are not expressions of Richter's subjectivity (there is no return here to the artist-centred models of traditional art history, and thus no turn to the deconstruction of such models).[27] Rather the expression is, as we shall see, precisely *not* of Richter's subjectivity.

As abstract paintings then they are certainly not representations of the world as we experience it, but rather they are pictures of other, we might say possible worlds. Indeed, this is perhaps their essential nature. Are they then utopian in the sense Theodor Adorno might use the term? That is to say do they offer a kind of preview of redemption (of reconciliation), which although a lie (i.e. ideological) is also a lie that contains a truth – that things might be as they are portrayed in the painting? Again, this is certainly one way of taking them, as 'utopian blinks'. However, I would argue, it is not necessarily the most productive, for Richter's Abstracts seem to offer something different, something equally utopian, but from a different perspective. For this utopia is not a promised but deferred possibility (a world that is always beyond our grasp) but is in fact a possibility in the world as it is here and now. In Deleuze–Leibniz's terms we might say that a Richter Abstract is the actualisation of a set of virtualities resulting in the specific *content* of a specific painting (its organisation), and on the other hand, a realisation of a set of possibilities in the actual *matter* of the painting (the paint, canvas, etc.). The Abstracts then might be understood as monads, as instances of Deleuze–Leibniz's two-floored Baroque house.[28] Let us look at the mechanics of this complex operation.

As Deleuze remarks other worlds may have an actuality in the monads that express them, an actuality that remains possible, but which has not yet been made forcibly real (a world in which 'Adam does not sin or Sextus who does not rape Lucretia' (*F* 104)). We might call this an actuality that has yet to be realised, precisely a world to come. Hence, the problem of realisation is added to the problem of actualisation.

We might say then that Richter's paintings are indeed the *actualisation* of certain virtualities. However, we need also to consider to what extent they are *realisations*. In fact, I think we can posit two levels of realisation and non-realisation with Richter's paintings. On the one hand, as paintings, they are already realised actualisations; they are after all objects in the world (they are objective, concrete reality). On the other hand, again as paintings, they are *pictures* of something/somewhere else. They express a world as yet unrealised. *This* is their utopian character.

Importantly, the processes of actualisation and realisation differ in character. The former operating through distribution (difference) the latter through resemblance (representation) (*F* 105). We have here a formula for Richter's practice: the paintings perform difference within repetition. Indeed, it is this that constitutes Richter's style as a painter, precisely the production of difference from 'within' painting, and more specifically from within the different series of Richter's practice.

> What should I paint, how should I paint. The 'what' is the most difficult, as it is the most essential. By comparison, the 'how' is simple. Beginning with the 'how' is frivolous, but legitimate. To apply the 'how', namely the conditions of technique, of the material, as with those of the physical possibilities – in relation to the intention. (*RIC* 118)

Painting, for Richter means paradoxically beginning with the realisation (the 'how') rather than with the actualisation (the 'what'). In this sense the paintings are, at least philosophically, counter-intuitive. We might note here the reverse strategy as found in pure maths, fractal equations, for example, which have an actuality but which are not realised in images.[29] Maths here is diametrically opposed to painting, at least as Richter pursues it. Richter then begins with the lower level, the how rather then the what, a strategy of allowing the painting to emerge from an always already constituted background. This technique, that involves a continuous layering and scraping of paint, again constitutes Richter's style and we might say characterises him as a specifically Baroque painter. As Deleuze remarks:

> Baroque is abstract art par excellence: on the lower floor, flush with the ground, within reach, the art comprehends the textures of matter ... But abstraction is not a negation of form: it posits form as folded, existing only as a 'mental landscape' in the soul or in the mind, in upper altitudes; hence it also includes immaterial folds.

> Material matter makes up the bottom, but folded forms are styles or manners. (*F* 35)

Ultimately, in a painting that 'works' a harmony is produced between the material of the painting and the picture that emerges. It is the discovery of this harmony, or resonance, of force operating on matter, that constitutes abstract art. Here 'we go from matter to manner, from earth and ground to habitat and salons', to what we might call the production of territories (*F* 35).[30] We might move from here back to *What is Philosophy?* where style (the production of a harmony in the above sense) is, as we have seen, portrayed as the very thing that constitutes art. As we noted in Chapter 2, and as Deleuze and Guattari remark, when this 'style' is thought in relation to painting it amounts precisely to the 'portrayal' or *capture* of forces.[31]

The art object, in this case a Richter Abstract, might then be seen to have the character of an event.[32] An event that actualises a set of virtualities and in so doing *expresses* a possible world. An event drawn from the pure reserve of events, the pure virtuality of an ideal pre-existing world (the 'silent and shaded part of the event' (*F* 106)). The Abstracts are, in Deleuze–Leibniz's terms, *compossibles* that have been 'sifted through' the great screen. They are abstractions, we might even say extractions, from a chaotic multiplicity, itself understood as the sum total of all possibilities. Painting then is not painting onto the blank canvas *à la* Clement Greenberg *et al*. Indeed the canvas is never blank, or empty in this sense, but rather is always already 'full' of potentialities. Painting then becomes a process of subtraction from Leibniz's 'dark background', the black dust of the imperceptible. Indeed, this is a distinctive feature of Deleuze's and Leibniz's ontology. An ontology of fullness, of plenitude, of which 'the world' as we 'see' it is an abstraction/subtraction. For Deleuze–Leibniz it is differential relations (and their reciprocal determination) that operate as the 'filter' for this field of potentialities. Here the perceptible emerges from, and merges with, the imperceptible. Clarity emerges from, and merges with, obscurity, just as sense emerges from, and merges with, nonsense. We might compare this complex and superabundant ontology *and* the differentials that organise it, with what Richter says about the motivation behind his early Abstracts:

> The pictures are related to the more recent Colour Charts, above all to the ones in preparation, where a few examples of an infinite variety of mixtures and possible arrangements represent the infinite number

> of never-to-be-realised possibilities, the boundlessness and complete meaninglessness that I consider hopeful, not as a slogan: 'everything is nonsense', not as an ideology ... But from the point of view a picture by Mondrian is not constructivist, but political ... (*RIC* 110)

The Colour Charts, and the Abstracts that follow immediately on from them, express worlds 'produced' by simple differential equations (yes/no decisions).[33] Likewise, and in the same note, Richter remarks that his 'jungle' Abstracts are called as such because they operate under similar conditions to organic jungles: 'There everything grows as it grows, not planned, not meaningful, not asked for or necessary but because certain conditions, space, nutrition, etc. are there by chance, therefore neither good nor bad, nor free, nor intended for a particular end or purpose' (*RIC* 110). These paintings – we might call them simply *in*organic jungles – are made up from just three primary colours, which, through combination and recombination, produce 'pictures' in the same way in which life produces the forms it does in a kind of purposelessness purposiveness:[34]

> The 'jungle' pictures in the [Venice] biennale use nature's colours; I took a long time to consider my materials, with which I can manufacture everything, red-blue-yellow (and light white), pictures that emerge from a process. Three primary colours as a starting point for an endless chain of colour tones ... Pictures that emerge, grow from the making, not creations, not creative in the sense of that mendacious word ... but certainly creaturely. (*RIC* 123)

We might say that the paintings are creaturely in the sense that Bergson's ontology of creative evolution is creaturely; the endless production of new and diverse forms (life's actualisation) (Bergson 1998). The Abstract's utopian and indeed political aspect then comes from the fact that they express a different world, a different *combination*, from the one we experience/inhabit everyday.[35] Although it is conjoined to the world, made out of the same materials if you like, it does not 'appear' from 'some other place' or promise to take us there. Of course, with Richter's Abstracts it is not just the combination or differential relation of colours but also the different sizes of brush and spatula's used and the different speeds or intensity of the painting.[36] Once more, this is part of Richter's style. In this sense the Abstracts introduce a new element to the Colour Charts that we might name here as Richter's particular technique of *blurring* his canvases.[37]

It is productive here to look at the similarities between Richter's technique and that 'second' type of oil painting that Deleuze and Guattari write about in *What is Philosophy?*, what we might call a kind of 'bottom up' immanent painting. Indeed, for Deleuze and Guattari it is precisely the relationship between the 'how' and the 'what', the technical plane (or what we might call the painting's realisation) *and* the aesthetic plane of composition (the actualisation) that produces different kinds of painting. The history of art, for Deleuze and Guattari, can in fact be configured as an account of this interrelationship, and particularly of an oscillation between two types of the latter:

> Take two states of oil painting that can be opposed to each other: in the first case, the picture is prepared with a white chalk background on which the outline is drawn and washed in (sketch), and finally colour, light, and shade are put down. In the other case, the background becomes increasingly thick, opaque, and absorbent, so that it takes on a tinge with the wash and the work becomes impasted on a brown range, 'reworkings' [*repentirs*] taking the place of the sketch: the painter paints on colour, then colour alongside colour, increasingly the colours become accents, the architecture being assured by 'the contrast of complementaries and the agreement of analogues' (van Gogh); it is through and in colour that the architecture will be found, even if the accents must be given up in order to constitute large colouring units. (*WP* 192)

Deleuze and Guattari go on to remark: 'In the first case *sensation is realized in the material* and does not exist outside of this realization. It could be said that sensation (the compound of sensation) is projected onto the well prepared technical plane of composition, in such a way that the aesthetic plane of composition covers it up' (*WP* 193). Here 'art enjoys a semblance of transcendence that is expressed not in a thing to be represented but in the paradigmatic character of projection and in the "symbolic" character of perspective' (*WP* 193). We might note that this kind of painting has the character of those projections – specifically theological – from which Deleuze differentiates philosophy (*WP* 88–90). This is painting as representational, as always already 'thought out', predetermined before it is even begun.

> In the second case it is no longer sensation that is realized in the material *but the material that passes into sensation* ... It is at this moment that the figures of art free themselves from an apparent transcendence

> or paradigmatic model and avow their innocent atheism, their paganism ... One no longer covers over; one raises, accumulates, piles up, goes through, stirs up, folds. (*WP* 194)[38]

We might position Richter's Abstracts as precisely pagan in this sense, as militant strikes against transcendence. Indeed, we might characterise Richter's paintings as involving the paradoxical notion of an immanent aesthetic, or a kind of ground level, Baroque aesthetic. When this is combined with what has already been said about Richter's combinations of colours, and the production of difference this allows, it amounts to positioning the paintings as kind of 'immanent utopias'. Here is Richter saying something remarkably similar about his specifically materialist attitude and also utopian impulse in 1986:

> Fundamentally I am a materialist. Spirit, soul, wanting, feeling, sensing, etc. have material causes (mechanical, chemical, electronic, etc.) ... Art is based on these material conditions. It is a particular mode of our daily dealings with appearance, in which we recognise ourselves and everything that surrounds us. Thus, art is the desire in the manufacture of appearances that are comparable with those of reality, because they are more or less similar to them. Thus, art is a possibility of thinking about everything differently, of recognising appearance as fundamentally inadequate; thus it is an instrument, a method of approaching things closed and inaccessible to us (banal future as well as things fundamentally unrecognisable, metaphysical). Because of that, art has an educative and therapeutic, comforting and enlightening, exploratory and speculative function, thus it is not just existential pleasure, but utopia. (*RIC* 118)

From difference to repetition. Richter's series, the ongoing production of Photo Paintings and Abstracts (what Richter calls his 'worklist'), as well as the smaller series within these, are precisely repetitions.[39] Each painting has the character of a moment in an ongoing process, almost a kind of working through of the same problematic (what is it to paint?). This pushes the paintings, particularly the Abstracts, towards a certain absurdity. Many commentators see Richter's paintings as deadly serious, as involved in the business of irony, but they also have this lightness, we might even say a certain humour. A humour – endlessly affirmative in character – that derives from an obsessive but playful repetition of difference.

Repetition, as Deleuze makes clear in *Difference and Repetition*, can be of two kinds: the repetition of the same (i.e. representation and resemblance), and the repetition of difference, of that which cannot be represented but only repeated.[40] A repetition *but with* difference; the repetition of the singular. It is precisely in this sense that Richter's paintings are repetitions. Indeed, each time, with each painting, Richter begins anew (this is the daily practice of painting). Clare Colebrook's thoughts on Deleuze's notion of repetition are then equally applicable to Richter's practice:

> We need to *repeat* difference and thinking; the minute we feel we have grasped what thinking and difference *are* then we have lost the very power of difference. Repetition is not the reoccurrence of the same old thing over and over again; to repeat something is to begin again, to renew, to question, and to refuse remaining the same. (Colebrook, 2002, 7–8)

Colebrook, following Deleuze, also draws attention to the way in which repetition is always the repetition of an event's 'untimely power', that is a *reactivation* rather than a representation. This is, of course, the secret repetition of revolution and of all *calls* to revolt. In passing, and in a return to Chapter 3, we might say that this is also the power and remaining impact that the various manifestos of modernity have still today (from the Futurists and Vorticists through to Dada and the Situationists); each time we read them they are reactivated (they precisely 'echo forwards' repeating all future activations).[41] Their future orientation, or call to a 'future world', is perhaps their defining quality.

Deleuze refers to this strange and secret operation of repetition right at the beginning of *Difference and Repetition*. In the following passage he also demonstrates that this power of repetition is the same in revolution as it is in painting (for Monet's water lilies we need only read Richter's Abstracts):

> To repeat is to behave in a certain manner, but in relation to something unique or singular which has no equal or equivalent. And perhaps this repetition at the level of external conduct echoes, for its own part, a more secret vibration which animates it, a more profound, internal repetition within the singular. This is the apparent paradox of festivals: they repeat an 'unrepeatable'. They do not add a second and a third time to the first, but carry the first to the 'nth' power. With respect to this power, repetition interiorises and thereby reverses itself: as Péguy says, it is not Federation Day which commemorates the fall of the Bastille, but the fall of the Bastille which

> celebrates and repeats in advance all the Federation Days; or Monet's first water lily which repeats all others. (DR 1)[42]

We might say then that Richter's first painting repeats in advance the paintings still to come. Hence the importance of beginnings.[43] Repetition here has the character of a celebration, an affirmation of the energy of creation. In Nietzsche's terms we might say that Richter's paintings are an affirmation of the eternal return; each painting a new dice throw. In more prosaic terms we might say simply that each of the paintings offer up a different combination, a different selection of elements to those with which we are familiar. This also implies a different temporality of painting, in fact an understanding of painting *as* an event. Indeed, *this* is the time of painting (just as it is the time of revolution).

Richter's paintings may be the production of possible, even utopian worlds, but they are *not* Richter's worlds. It will be remembered that for Deleuze's Proust it is the characters of the novels who express different worlds, but if Richter's paintings have, or are, characters in this sense they are not characters 'invented' by Richter[44] (although he did of course 'make' them).[45] For Richter's 'intention' has always been, whether it be in the Photo Paintings or the Abstracts, to extract himself from his work (himself understood here as the system of beliefs, attitudes – habits of being or clichés – which make up one's character).[46] The paintings are not expressions 'of' Richter then, or rather they are not expressive of Richter. Indeed, Richter's technique of painting militates against this, perhaps most obviously in his use of photography (often found images) in the Photo Paintings.[47] With the Abstracts this involves the continuous painting over of an already laid out pictorial organisation. A method of obliteration then but also, in the 'new' picture that emerges, of revelation. This involves the productive utilisation of chance, albeit within boundaries (the rectangle of the painting, Richter's skill with the brush and spatula and so on). We might also call this, in a return to Chapter 2, and following Deleuze's book on Bacon, the painting of a *diagram* over the top of a planned and already painted structure/surface:

> (Everything that one can think out for oneself in this way, all this idiocy, these foolish things, cheap constructions and speculations, amazing inventions, harsh, surprising juxtapositions, which one is of course also forced to see a million times a day in and day out, this mentally deficient misery, the whole stupidly bold botch) – All this I paint away, clear out of my head when I start a picture, that is my ground, which I deal with in the first few layers, which I destroy layer

> by layer, until all the frivolous rubbish is destroyed. Thus what I ultimately have is a work of destruction. It goes without saying that I cannot do without these detours, thus that I cannot begin with the final state. (*RIC* 121)

We might say then that Richter's paintings involve at one and the same time an actualisation of certain virtualities (and consequently, as paintings, the realisation of possible worlds) *and* a *de*actualisation of a certain reality, in this case Richter's subjectivity (or at least certain aspects of it). The same operation happens, ideally, when we encounter a Richter Abstract, especially if we can approach the latter away from our typical 'habits of seeing', or, which is to say the same thing, away from the clichés of art (and indeed of consumer culture in general).[48] The paintings then produce/perform a different combination, a different *extraction*, from all the possibilities. It is this that gives them their political but also their ethical and aesthetic character. It is this that makes them endlessly affirming of life and not just acts of negation.

The new baroque

From monads to nomads

We might say that Richter's Abstracts are an example of what Deleuze sees as characteristic of modern painting: the '*all-over* fold' (*F* 123). As such they show us a different kind of folding to those found elsewhere, a different way of folding in and of the world. Richter's paintings, as possible worlds, are then *not* the monads of a typical and habitual subjectivity (i.e. his or ours) but something more non-human. We might even say that they are a form of non-organic life. The paintings can also be understood as atypical forms of thought in this sense, or, as atypical forms that produce atypical thought. Another way of saying this is that the paintings operate as future orientated monads that call their audience, understood here as new kinds of subjectivity, into being (we might ask ourselves what kinds of subjectivity Richter's art invokes? Who are its 'missing people'?).

But this is not the end of the story, for Richter's Abstracts remain paintings and as such do not express the limit of the Baroque within art. For, as Deleuze remarks, a further characteristic of the Baroque is a certain 'over spilling', a blurring or smearing of boundaries. As such, painting becomes Baroque when it 'exceeds its frame', bleeds into sculpture, which itself bleeds into architecture and city planning (*F* 123). The Baroque then names that which is 'between' the different arts, which allows, or forces, their deterritorialisation:

> Perhaps we rediscover in modern abstract art a similar taste or a setting 'between' two arts, between painting and sculpture, between sculpture and architecture, that seeks to attain a unity of arts as 'performance', and to draw the spectator into this very performance (*minimal* art is appropriately named following a law of extremum). Folding and unfolding, wrapping and unwrapping are the constants of this operation, as much now as in the period of the Baroque. This theatre of the arts is a living machine of the 'new system' as Leibniz describes it, an infinite machine of which every part is a machine, 'folded differently and more or less developed'. (*F* 124)

This is not however a system, or universe, without a kind of centre. For the Baroque names not just the 'broadest unity of extension' but also the 'highest inner unity' (*F* 124). If the lower floor is a rippling multiplicity – the world, the *city* – this is still from the point of view of the upper floor. The Baroque is then like a cone, its base the seething world of yet-to-be actualised virtualities, but only from the point of view of its summit which surveys this terrain, and indeed actualises the latter. It is in this sense that the Baroque is at one and the same time the multiple *and* the One, a constant interplay, or resonance, between the two – the two floors of the Baroque house. We might say that the Baroque world *is* then without centre (that is to say it is *post*-structural) but that it is always 'seen' from a certain perspective. For Deleuze this is why the Baroque world is allegorical in nature, containing as it does a multiplicity of individual 'points of view' (*F* 125–6). To return briefly to Richter we might say that the extractions the Abstracts perform can then also be understood as specific points of view onto a field of pre-existing virtualities.

This perspective or projected unity, although not altogether disappearing is however changing. It is no longer the unity of a singular monad but rather the paradoxical unity of a kind of divergent series, or trajectory, which in the arts Deleuze names 'performance'. Although this is not a new term in terms of art history, what we have with Deleuze's use of it is a specifically philosophical description of the 'new' expanded practices of the 1960s and onwards. A description of that art which includes its audience, and the wider world, in its being as art (which is incomplete without this participation).[49] Something is happening here to the closed monad, almost as if part of its upper chamber is being ripped or prized open on to other monads, other worlds.

Indeed, Deleuze refers to the road trip of Tony Smith, the 'sealed car speeding down the dark highway' (*F* 137), as a new kind of model, involving as it does new kinds of technology and new relations of speed.[50] These new worlds are the expression of a different kind of harmony, a 'new harmony', between the two floors of the Baroque house. We might note here Michael Fried's refusal, or inability, to engage with this form of practice that he names as not art but theatre. Deleuze also footnotes Gysin and Burroughs as exponents of this new kind of folding or 'fold-in' with their practice of cut-ups (precisely the production of an open text) (*F* 164, n 37). We are moving from the autonomy of the Baroque house and of the art object to something more open, something more complex. The Baroque house has been opened out, at least in part, and this will have a profound effect on the subjectivities that these new kinds of monads express.

Chtcheglov's city

We might characterise this change as the opening out of the Baroque house onto the Baroque city. Here 'the painter has become an urban designer' (*F* 123). We might move here from the utopian paintings of Richter to the earlier utopian urban 'plans' of the Situationists: the 'city models' of Constant, or the larger city paintings of Asger Jorn (both of whom specifically made the move from easel painting to urban planning). Even more pertinent are the writings of that early psycogeographer Ivan Chtcheglov. In fact, Deleuze's formulation of this 'New Baroque' reads like a parallel manifesto to the 'new' psycogeographical practices called for by Chtcheglov. Here is Deleuze:

> This extensive unity of the arts forms a universal theatre that includes air and earth, and even fire and water. In it sculptures play the role of real characters, and the city a decor in which spectators are themselves painted images or figurines. The sum of the arts becomes the Socius, the public social space inhabited by baroque dancers. (*F* 123)

Compare this to Chtcheglov's manifesto for a 'New Urbanism', in which the city becomes a site for, and the very means of, expressing one's subjectivity:

> Architecture is the simplest means of *articulating* time and space, of *modulating* reality, of engendering dreams. It is a matter not only of plastic articulation and modulation expressing an ephemeral beauty, but of a modulation producing influences in accordance with the

> eternal spectrum of human desires and the progress in realising them. The architecture of tomorrow will be a means of modifying present conceptions of time and space. It will be a means of *knowledge* and a *means of action*. The architectural complex will be modifiable. Its aspect will change totally or partially in accordance with the will of its inhabitants. (Chtcheglov 1989, 24)[51]

Cities, for both Deleuze and Chtcheglov, are stages for experimentation and play, for the actualisation of different virtualities and the performance of different possibilities.[52] And for both writers, these cities are yet to be made, or rather, the people for them are yet to arrive (Deleuze shares with the Situationists this prophetic orientation).[53] Formulated in this way, the city, or what we might call the expanded field of architecture, is a field of folding; a folding that takes place in matter but also in the soul (the desires) of those who produce and are produced by their surroundings. As Deleuze remarks elsewhere:

> Architecture has always been a political activity, and any new architecture depends on revolutionary forces, you can find architecture saying 'We need a people', even though the architect isn't himself revolutionary ... A people is always a new wave, a new fold in the social fabric; any creative work is a new way of folding adapted to new materials. (*N* 158)

The city as a new kind of fold *and* as a platform for new kinds of folding then. In many ways this is a description of modernity, but it also takes us beyond the modern conception of the city. Indeed, Baudelaire's *flâneur* might be seen as an exemplar of the isolated yet connected two-floored monad (at once *a part of* and *apart from* the crowd/the world). The new *flâneur* of the new Baroque has perhaps lost that detachment that characterised Baudelaire, Poe *et al*.[54] The new *flâneur* thoroughly participates in (is immanent to) the city, we might even say is an expression of the city.[55] Inevitably this new city (and new city inhabitant) is future orientated. Chtcheglov's city *is* utopian, but it is a utopia firmly attached to the present, specifically in its utilisation of the already existing city albeit in a different way: the practice of the *Continuous Dérive*:

> This new vision of time and space, which will be the theoretical basis of future constructions, is still imprecise and will remain so until experimentation and patterns of behaviour have taken place in cities

> specifically established for this purpose ... buildings charged with evocative power, symbolic edifices representing desires, forces, events past, present and to come ... Everyone will live in his own personal 'cathedral' so to speak. There will be rooms more conducive to dreams than any drug, and houses where one cannot help but love. Others will be irresistibly alluring to travellers ... The principal activity of the inhabitants will be the *Continuous Dérive*. The changing of landscapes from one hour to the next will result in complete disorientation. (Chtcheglov 1989, 25)

In passing it is worth noting that for that other Situationist, Guy Debord, the *Dérive* is not just an architectural deterritorialisation, but also a way of modifying actual human relations, precisely an 'opening up' of that which is closed, a breaking out of alienation:[56]

> A rough experimentation toward a new mode of behaviour has already been made with what we have termed the *dérive*, which is the practice of a passional journey out of the ordinary through rabid changes of ambiances, as well as means of study of psycogeography and situationist psychology. But the application of this will to playful creation must be extended to all known forms of human relationships, so as to influence, for example, the historical evolution of sentiments like friendship and love. (Debord 1989, 27)

Leibniz's house has here been multiplied and opened up in a new form of urbanism which in fact Chtcheglov names, in an echo of Leibniz himself, its specifically 'baroque stage' (1989, 25).[57]

Future folds

So, the old fold, in art as in the city, has been overtaken by new and different kinds of folds. Folds that have less to do with the isolated monad and more to do with open monads *and* with the relationships between monads. How has this new harmony come about? Deleuze reminds us that Leibniz's monads 'submit to two conditions, one of closure and the other of selection' (*F* 137):

> On the one hand, they [monads] include an entire world that does not exist outside of them; on the other, this world takes for granted a first selection of convergence, since it is distinguished from other possible but divergent worlds, excluded by the monad in question. (*F* 137)

Furthermore 'it carries with it a second selection of consonance, because each monad in question will fashion itself a clear zone of expression in the world that it includes (those parts excluded precisely forming the clear zone of other monads)' (*F* 137). This second selection, a selection made on the basis of a certain harmony, the production of a certain unity, is the operation that is under alteration. The old kind of harmony, the old kind of folding, is losing its privileged position: 'dissonances' are 'excused from being "resolved", and consequently divergences can be affirmed' (*F* 137).[58] This in turn works back on the first condition; the isolated, autonomous monad bleeds over into its fellow monads.

In this strange world, in fact our world, differences between outside and inside, between public and private, are increasingly irrelevant, and instead are replaced by relations of variation and trajectory. This world or *chaosmos* is made up of 'divergent series', of pure difference, and, as such, 'the monad is now unable to contain the entire world as if in a closed circle' (*F* 137). 'It now opens up on a trajectory ... a vertical harmonic [the summit of the cone or point of view] can no longer be distinguished from a horizontal harmonic'; the line between the private condition of a dominant monad and the public condition of monads in a crowd becomes blurred or rather 'fuse' in a system of interpenetration and transitory moments of capture (*F* 137). Deleuze footnotes the 'planar sculptures' of Carl Andre that no longer contain a volume (express a singular world) but embrace a limitless space in all directions (*F* 160, n 4). Again, we might add that such sculptures precisely require *participation*, an opening up along the horizontal plane, in order that they be activated.

So, monads, or *nomads*, now express a different point of view on a different ground (or cityscape). As I suggested above, this is the new kind of foldings that emerge in the 1960s, not only in the expanded performative art practices or the psycogeography of the Situationists, but also simply in the wider experiments and explorations in drug use/sexuality/communal living, and so forth (the opening-up of the 'closed house'). This is the actualisation and activation of the plane of immanence discussed by Hardt and Negri in *Empire* (*E* 260–4). Indeed, at this point history, itself a kind of background – a 'scene' of the event of art – can be brought back in. The geopolitical conditions (economic and social, but also environmental and ecological) which, although not 'of' the event, provide its ground. In this light we might see the development of new technologies as playing a part in the emergence of this new fold. As we have seen the speeding car of Tony Smith for example. Or, we might add, cinema, which as Deleuze demonstrates in the Cinema books offers up a new image of thought, precisely a reconfiguration of space and time (a new folding) and an opening up the closed monad of our subjectivity to other non-human worlds (a camera-machine consciousness). The same could be said of the incorporeal universes opened up by even newer visualising and communications technology, VR and the World Wide Web, the latter being an almost literal instance of the 'New Baroque' (and involving the concomitant production of a nomadic subjectivity). Parallel to this is the ongoing production of robotic monads whose foldings are even further removed and stranger than our own (moving as they do to different spatial and temporal rhythms). In fact, as Donna Haraway, amongst others, has pointed out, we are already part of this new folding inasmuch as these new prosthetic technologies involve the folding of silicon assemblages 'into' our own carbon ones. We might add here the experiments in tissue engineering and molecular biology in general, all sorts of genetic foldings producing all sorts of strange beings, and the even stranger worlds they express (and we would have to also include here the ubiquitous medical and 'recreational' drug use of today or indeed any other personal and intentional molecular alteration). It is in all these new formations that, as Deleuze remarks, monadology is overtaken by nomadology, understood here as the production of new and different kinds of folding, in new and different kinds of worlds.[59]

The superfold

In the final couple of pages of his book on Foucault Deleuze likewise considers these new or future kinds of folds. The 'superfold' as Deleuze calls it will be the result of three folds. First, what we might call the fold of molecular biology, the discovery of the genetic code. Second, the fold of silicon with carbon and the emergence of 'third generation machines', cybernetics and information technology. And third, the folding of language, the uncovering of a 'strange language within language' – an 'atypical form of expression that marks the end of language as such' (*FO* 131). As with the other two this is a fold that opens man out to that which is non-human, which puts him in contact with forces that can then be folded back 'into' himself. For Deleuze (as for Foucault) this superfold is synonymous with the superman or with that which 'frees life' from within man:

> The superman, in accordance with Rimbaud's formula, is the man who is even in charge of the animals (a code that can capture fragments from other codes, as in the new schemata of lateral or retrograde). It is a man in charge of the very rocks, or inorganic matter (the domain of

> silicon). It is a man in charge of the being of language (that formless, 'mute, unsignifying region where language can finds its freedom' even from whatever it has to say). (*FO* 132)

The first of these folds is the remit of science (although there might be art that 'pictures' this fold).[60] The second, although also science, bleeds into art (a contemporary example is the performance artist Stelarc).[61] It is the third however, as we saw in Chapter 3, that is properly the terrain of art, the latter understood here as a kind of becoming minoritarian. Art stammers and stutters the materials available to it and in doing so produces new ways of folding the world 'into' the self, or, more simply, new kinds of subjectivity. We can return here to Richter's Abstracts, and indeed to the more creative experiments of the Situationists; both involve this manipulation of matter, the production of these new kinds of fold.

Of course there may be other foldings still. The Oriental fold for example, which, as Deleuze remarks, is perhaps not a fold at all and consequently not a process of subjectivation (*F* 36). As Deleuze remarks in relation to this 'it may be that the Baroque will have to confront the Orient profoundly' (*F* 36). It might be argued that the relation of art to this non-fold is one of *ritual*. Which is to say not the production of possible worlds (fabulation), and not the production of subjectivity, or rather both of these but only insofar as they allow access to something else, the void, the 'ground' from which these worlds, these subjects had emerged.[62] An *un*folding then as that which always accompanies the fold, producing new folds but also opening us out to that which is yet to be folded.

Conclusion
Three Endings

In place of a conclusion I want to offer three different endings.

Fabulation: myth-science

Myth-critique and mythopoesis

Throughout the chapters of this book I have been attempting to outline a way of thinking art beyond representation via what might be termed a Deleuzoguattarian optic. In general, this has involved the foregrounding of art's affective and asignifying potential as against its signifying content. To a certain extent this manoeuvre has been strategic, operating as a corrective to much recent art history that positions, and interprets, art as 'signifier'. Nevertheless, and as I pointed out at the end of Chapter 2, contemporary art does of course often involve a narrative content. In fact, these signifying elements can never really be divorced from art's more affective register, each operating as a platform for the other. Indeed, we might return to Henri Bergson here and note once more his observation that there are two kinds or two functions of art: one of story telling, or fabulation, the other of genuine creativity.[1] Is Deleuze less useful for this former kind of art, focusing as he does on the figural and abstract, specifically as it occurs in painting? To a certain extent this is indeed a limit to Deleuze's actual writings on art. In fact, Deleuze can be seen, at least at first glance, as quite conservative in his choice of art and objects. However, as we have seen, there is no reason we cannot look to Deleuze's other writings, on cinema and literature for example, and creatively apply concepts from these different mediums and milieus to the field of expanded visual art as it exists today. The same is true for Deleuze's writings on philosophy. They exist as a rich conceptual vein that we can use to think art's complex operating terrain. Indeed, if we do not do conduct this specifically transversal operation then we will dramatically reduce the relevance of Deleuze's writings for art, and indeed the art that might be explored via the Deleuzian optic.

As a first ending then I want to continue exploring the creative and ontological productivity of art by returning to a notion of narrative and to what might be called the *mythopoetic* character of specifically contemporary art. In a sense this has been very much part of the subject matter of the various art practices looked at so far, inasmuch as mythopoesis, as I am using the term, names the *imaginative transformation of the world via fiction*. We saw this with Robert Smithson who utilises a specifically mythical language in telling the story of his experimental *Yucatan Mirror Displacements*. Likewise with the *Spiral Jetty* – the essay and film operate as a kind of 'myth-machine' situating the jetty itself in what we might call a mythic context. These myths are not metaphors and certainly not regressions, rather they are the creative construction of new narratives for new, and we might say future, subjectivities. We saw a similar constructive attitude with Gerhard Richter's Abstracts which, although not narrative in themselves, might nevertheless be understood as having a mythic 'world-building' character. The paintings picture worlds-in-progress; they diagram future subjectivities. The Situationists too, especially in their artistic fringes, might also be portrayed as myth-makers. Here myth-construction is a form of 'counter-knowledge' to that propagated by the Spectacle.[2] We also saw this mythopoesis in Chapter 2; art, as a bloc of percept and affects, offers up a different world to the one we typically perceive. Finally, in Chapter 3, art's 'political' function, its call to a future people, might also be characterised as its mythic quality.

Indeed, to a large extent, it is this future orientation that seems to define modern and contemporary art, almost as if such art is a fragment of a future world projected backwards in order to call that world into being. It is in this sense that art is always calling its audience into being (even if such an audience is already partly constituted, art will still draw forth something new from within any specified context). In fact, art, as mythopoesis, does not so much create a people as *invoke* them. As Deleuze remarks in interview:

> It's the greatest artists (rather than populist artists) who invoke a people, and find they 'lack a people' ... Artists can only invoke a people, their need for one goes to the very heart of what they're doing, it's not their job to create one, and they can't: Art is resistance: it resists death, slavery, infamy, shame. But a people can't worry about art.

> How is a people created, it's through its own resources, but in a way that links up with something in art ... or links up art to what it lacked. (*N* 174)

And so there is something similar about the construction of a people, an explicitly political practice but also an *aesthetic* act, and the work of art, a specifically aesthetic practice, but also a *political* act. Although it is not as simple as saying that art is ahead of a people who come after, there is a sense in which art's operating field is the future, whereas the construction of a people must always begin in the present.[3] We might say then that art's peculiarity is that it utilises the stuff of the present in order to move beyond that present. Put simply, art involves a new combination, a new dice throw as perhaps Deleuze would say. Such art does not so much offer up a set of knowledges as set up the conditions, the contours, for future knowledges still to come. It is in this sense also that art involves the posing of new questions and as such will always make demands on any already existing audience.

It is precisely the imagination, or simply the ability to 'go beyond' what appears to be reality (that is, our habitual perceptions and practices), that constitutes this fundamental power of innovation and invention. As Deleuze remarks: 'Utopia isn't the right concept: it's more a question of "fabulation" in which a people and art both share' (*N* 174). This fabulation, or the production of fictions, is the mythopoetic character of art. We might say then that myth offers an alternative point of view, a different perspective, from another place, another time.

It is crucial here to note that there are different kinds of myth, and equally crucial to demarcate those myths that might be fascistic, which we might say are exclusive, from those that are inclusive. The former includes the 'blood and fire' mythology of the Nazis (the 'master-race') or indeed any mythology premised on exclusion (a 'them and us' logic). The latter includes the stuttering and stammering minorities of Chapter 3 (here the people-to-come 'belong' together precisely because they do not belong anywhere else). It is of course the job of myth-critique (of ideology critique), whether it be Roland Barthes' *Mythologies* or Theodor Adorno's *The Jargon of Authenticity* to critique these pretensions to 'truth' and 'authenticity' that can often become powerful protofascist myths. This myth-breaking involves the scrambling of codes that we looked at in Chapter 1 (and the concomitant invention of new autonomous codes). We might note here as well the crucial importance of being historically specific when it comes to myth-analysis. The Nazi mythology for example cannot be divorced from its context, the fertile ground of

1930s and 1940s Germany. Likewise, attention needs to be paid to the components of a myth system and to how it functions. In the case of Nazi Germany this seemed to involve a peculiar combination of pre-modern (and in fact often non-Western) characters and archetypes alongside certain myths of technological progress and continuous machinic warfare.

As we saw in Chapter 4, Deleuze and Guattari are also keen to demarcate these potentially fascistic myths from more libertarian enterprises. This is the demarcation of transcendent utopias from those more immanent and revolutionary ones – a demarcation that can be difficult in that it is not always entirely clear where one ends and the other begins. As Deleuze and Guattari remark, in relation to Heidegger, perhaps: 'all concepts include this grey zone and indiscernability where for a moment the combatants on the ground are confused, and the thinkers tired eyes mistakes the one for the other – not only the German for a Greek but the fascist for a creator of existence and freedom' (*WP* 109). Heidegger's philosophy would be a case in point of this 'wrong turn'. For Deleuze and Guattari: 'He got the wrong people, earth, and blood. For the race summoned forth by art or philosophy is not the one that claims to be pure but rather an oppressed, bastard, lower, anarchical, nomadic and irremediably minor race' (*WP* 109).

Here then an immanent utopia (or what we might call a communist myth) is not necessarily a regression but is in fact a progression of sorts. This is then not a return to those always already determined and constituted stories (myths of the nuclear family, of Oedipal sexuality, of an idyllic past, of the Nation state, of a 'glorious death', of nine-to-five careerism and commodity obsession) but the invention of new stories for a people who do not recognise themselves in the stories of the dominant. Following on from Chapters 2 and 3, we might say that this mythic function is the production of different narratives for different probe-heads, the invention of different life courses for different war machines. Mythopoesis names the locating, and constructing, of these lines of flight from consensual reality.

In fact, this future orientated practice might involve the utilisation of past myths, albeit in new and novel combinations (such myths will be precisely bastardised). Indeed, and as Raymond Williams once pointed out, residual cultures, residual myths, might hold a certain amount of potential resistance to those of the dominant culture, although it will be crucial to demarcate those that have been 'incorporated' (we might say those that have become major) from those that remain potentially resistant (or resolutely minor).[4] Deleuze says something similar in *Cinema 2* about this productive utilisation of yesterday's myths in relation to the films of Gabriel Rocha: 'it is not a matter of analysing myth in order to discover its archaic meaning or structure, but of connecting archaic myth to the state of the drives in an absolutely contemporary society, hunger, thirst, sexuality, power, death, worship' (*C2* 219).

This is a careful business for a people are often already colonised by myths of which they are not the origin (these are the myths imposed on them from outside). In *Cinema 2* Deleuze remarks that in the Third World: 'The cinema author finds himself before a people which, from the point of view of culture, is doubly colonised: colonised by stories that have come from elsewhere, but also from their own myths become impersonal entities at the service of the coloniser' (*C2* 222). In such a situation, the artist must not:

> make himself into the ethnologist of his people, nor himself invent a fiction which would be one more private story: for every personal fiction, like every impersonal myth, is on the side of the 'masters' ... There remains the possibility of the author providing himself with 'intercessors', that is, of taking real and not fictional characters, but putting these very characters in the condition of 'making up fiction', of 'making legends', of 'story-telling'. The author takes a step towards his characters, but the characters take a step towards the author: double becoming. Story-telling is not an impersonal myth, but neither is it a personal fiction: it is a word in act, a speech-act through which the character continually crosses the boundary which would separate his private business from politics, and which *itself produces collective utterances*. (*C2* 222)

Here myth-making is not impersonal and neutral, but is not purely personal either. In fact, it is explicitly collective: the production of collective enunciations, which itself involves a becoming-political, and indeed other stranger becomings. These are *minor* myths in which there is always a call to a people to whom the myth is addressed.

Traitor prophets

In a return to Chapter 1, we might call this mythopoesis the programmatic character of literature and of the literary moment in art. As Deleuze remarks in his collaborative essay 'On Anglo-American Literature': 'Programmes are not manifestos – still less are they phantasms, *but means of providing reference points for an experiment which exceeds our capacities to foresee ...*' (*DI* 48). Literary authors, and artists that tend towards the literary, are involved in this programmatic function; they offer up experimental adventures beyond the typical, beyond the foreseeable. They produce a different narrative to those offered to us on a daily basis. Indeed, this literary production is perhaps more important now than it has ever been, given the hegemonic power of the mass media which although increasingly operating on an affective register, also works precisely through narrative construction. In producing a new and different kind of narrative, a break with the norm, the author/artist must himself follow a line of flight. A flight from Oedipal configurations and from micro-fascisms, all the time avoiding the 'quick sands and the black holes' (*DI* 39). The author *and* his characters are caught up in these adventures beyond representation, becomings that the reader also enters into.[5]

Indeed, anything 'new' must involve a break with the dominant in this sense; a break or rupture that itself has to be protected: 'A true break may be extended in time, it is something different from an over-significant cut, it must constantly be protected not merely against its false imitations, but also against itself, and against the reterritorialisations that lie in wait for it' (*DI* 39). This, for Deleuze, is the tradition of Anglo-American writing, which always celebrates the rupture and as such calls us 'to take up the interrupted line, to join a segment to the broken line' (*DI* 39). For Deleuze then 'it is never the beginning or the end which are interesting; the beginning and end are points. What is interesting is the middle' (*DI* 39). Again, this is to return to the terrain of Chapter 1, to affirm the grass over the trees, to celebrate the rhizomatic nature of art and subjectivity.

In relation to this Deleuze gives us the example of Thomas Hardy:

> his characters are not people or subjects, they are collections of intensive sensations, each is such a collection, a packet, a bloc of variable sensations. There is a strange respect for the individual, an extraordinary respect ... because he saw himself and saw others as so many 'unique chances' – the unique chance from which one combination or another had been drawn. Individuation without a subject. (*DI* 39–40)

In such a landscape it is the traitor who occupies the 'central' position: 'A traitor to the world of dominant signification, and to the established order' (*DI* 41).[6] The traitor organises him or herself against the faciality machine of Chapter 2, turns away from 'what might be called the white wall/black hole system' (*DI* 45): 'We are always pinned against the white wall of dominant significations, we are always sunk in the hole of our subjectivity, the black hole of our Ego which is more dear to us than anything' (*DI* 45). The traitor involves him or herself in strange illegitimate becomings, which as Deleuze remarks, always involves the choice of a different kind of object (Captain Ahab's choice of the white whale for example).[7] We might say that it is the traitor who follows his or her own line of flight, makes his or her own myths, and produces his or her own reality.

The mythopoetic question is then 'how to unmake the face', how to break with dominant myth systems and also how to produce alternative myths and new becomings. This is the *raison d'etre* of much contemporary art practice: the production of idiosyncratic archives and inventories, the construction of alternative narratives and mythologies by traitor prophets.

Mythography: Matthew Barney's *Cremaster* cycle

A case study of this kind of counter-mythography can be found in the *Cremaster* films of Matthew Barney. These films, and especially the most recent, *Cremaster 3*, utilise past myth, and indeed non-mythic elements, in order to invent decidedly new myths. As Nancy Spector remarks in the catalogue that accompanied the *Cremaster* retrospective: 'Barney looked beyond biology as a way to explore the creation of form, employing narrative models from other realms, such as biography, mythology and geology' (2003, 5). Indeed, we might say that the films are addressed less to an already existing audience, who is familiar with an already existing narrative, but to a future audience, a people-yet-to-come, who as such require specifically new narratives, specifically contemporary myths.

Barney is very much the successor to Smithson in this sense: a producer of contemporary myths for a contemporary world. Indeed, the *Cremaster* films are involved in the production of hybrid narratives and the staging of specifically modern rituals. In the films we also see an emphasis on the sculptural element of film (we can compare this with Smithson's own view on film at the end of Chapter 2). As Barney himself remarks: 'The Cremaster cycle tries to take on a cinematic language ... I wanted to see how this sculptural project, which is what it is, could align itself with the cinematic form, and still come out as sculpture' (2002, 59). We might say then that the films are, as well as narratives, blocs of sensations. Indeed, this is precisely how myth operates: through blocs of signifying and asignifying matter.[8] The films are myth-machines in this sense, the linking together of disparate elements in a new and productive way, the construction of a novel assemblage through the utilisation of already existing fragments of other assemblages.

In *Cremaster 3* there is also the inclusion of Richard Serra, himself the most mythic of modern artists, who precisely operates as an intercessor for Barney (an intermediary between the fiction of the film and the 'reality' of the world). Serra is the master architect whom Barney himself, as apprentice (as traitor), and in his own mythology, must overcome in his own processual self-creation. As with Deleuze's take on Hardy, so with Barney's take on Serra, and indeed the other 'icons' that Barney uses in his films. For Barney such characters are as much 'physical states' as 'developed narrative characters' (Barney 2002, 59). The locations and landscapes of the *Cremaster* films also operate as kind of characters in this sense. As Barney remarks: 'it is important for that landscape to be drawable as a discrete object. That it should be possible to make a sculptural form from the Canadian Rockies or the Utah Salt Flats' (2002, 59). Of course, and as we have seen, Smithson produces just such a sculptural form from the Utah landscape. Indeed, Barney's films here mirror Smithson's earthworks, both operate on an epic scale, both are landscape-sculptures, and both involve the construction of new myths for a people yet-to-come.

Myth-science: Mike Kelley on Öyvind Fahlström

Another case study of mythopoesis within contemporary art is the bizarre and complex practice of Öyvind Fahlström, especially as the artist Mike Kelley writes about it in his remarkable essay, 'Myth-Science' (as we shall see, the latter term is taken from the musician Sun Ra). For Kelley, Fahlström's art, although involved in a critique of sorts (in what Kelley calls a deconstruction) is also creative and fundamentally constructive. As Kelley says: 'Fahlström saw his use of fracture and levelling as "a constructive Dadaism and thus not Dada at all" ' (1995, 19). Kelley goes on:

> it is easier to see Fahlström's practice as a kind of deconstruction, a deconstruction of the world using the popular signs which surround us everyday, rather than as an exercise in raising 'low' cultural material to the lofty realms of fine art. This deconstruction of the world is produced by the construction of an artistic world – a model of the world. Fahlström's preference is for multi-part works where the various elements are involved in complex interrelationships that imply system and narration. This pushes his work towards the theatrical, toward an art that has spatial and temporal aspects. (1995, 19)

Fahlström's assemblages then, like Barney's films, can be 'read as a kind of model universe' (Kelley 1995, 20). This involves 'not a play with low/high displacements ... but a play with temporality and narrative' (Kelley 1995, 20). For example, Fahlström's interest in comic books was that they 'offered a rich pictorial source reflecting contemporary mythologies, values, and belief systems' (Kelley 1995, 20). This is not the use of found images in pastiche and parody, but the use of the stuff of the world to produce something new. Fahlström then utilises the stuff of his life, producing his own inventory and archive, and ultimately his own worlds, in which nothing is excluded in advance.[9] This is the production of 'total art', and was why Fahlström was so attracted to Opera. As Kelley remarks, quoting Fahlström:

> Opera was his model, not only because it aspires to synthesis, but because, as he [Fahlström] wrote, 'it demonstrates the "amorality" of art, its readiness to profit from and transform into art anything at all to stimulate and broaden our self awareness ... which in turn can or need not be made to serve a political end'. (1995, 20–2)

For Kelley these two impulses, the deconstruction of dominant myth and the construction of alternative myth, go hand in hand. We might say that one cannot but help be produced by the other (as we saw in Chapter 3 dissent, the turning away from one world, produces affirmation, the turning towards another). As such, and as Kelley remarks:

> The only true political image must be the unnatural one, the one that challenges archetypal and unquestioned pictures of reality. This 'unnaturalism' need not be an escape from the pictorial; as in abstract art it can be a *dissection* of the pictorial. The secret language of pictorial conventions must be revealed as a construct, otherwise you remain the unwitting pawn of its shaping influence. (1995, 23)

For Kelley, the key is to understand that: 'Historical facts are as mythic as literary constructions; art, on the psychic level, is just as "real" as this worldly data. The artist, functioning in a symbolic world, nevertheless affects our perception of the everyday world' (Kelley 1995, 25). This then is the artist's production of myth. Kelley, in a nod to Sun Ra, gives this pursuit a name: Myth-science. For as Sun Ra announces, and Kelley quotes:

> Everything is of a particular science
> And myth is not exception

Witness: 'Science-fiction'
And the manifestation of its self
To a living what is called reality
Or so-called reality.

As a science Myth has many dimensions
And many degrees
Tomorrow is said to be a dimension of myth
Or even the very realm of myth itself. (1995, 26)[10]

Inevitably, technology plays a part in this myth-science.[11] Indeed new technologies allow the opening up of new incorporeal universes as Guattari might say (Virtual Reality being almost a literal example of world building, where the invocation of a people begins to coincide with their construction). We might say that new media will necessarily involve new myths, new narratives for a new (posthuman) subject. However, the sharp end of technology is more often than not at the service of dominant myth, thus art might well look to yesterday's technologies, or use technology in an unintended and unpredictable manner. We return here to the terrain of Chapters 1 and 3: art stammers the major, it uses all the means at its disposal but in a *different* way and so as to create a new world and with it the hope that comes from such an enterprise.

Ultimately, this hope is not just for a new story, a new myth, for if we are to follow Deleuze's Bergsonism closely here we must remember once more that this 'story-telling' function of art operates as a platform, a launch pad into something else: the cosmic, or what we might understand as simply the realm of potentiality (and thus the possibility of still more fictions). We might think this in the terms of Chapter 3: art operates as a specific production of subjectivity which in itself allows access to that which is beyond, or rather 'outside', that particular subjectivity. Art's power of fabulation then operates in two directions. It has a face turned to us and to the world, and a face turned to that which is precisely otherworldly.

Writing a book

This book has been about exploring the conjunction Deleuze *and* Art. Although attention has been given to Deleuze's own thoughts on the latter, I have been particularly keen to produce an encounter between Deleuze's conceptual resources and the expanded field of modern and contemporary art (and the methodological field of art history in general). Much of what I have had to say has been written against 'signifier enthusiasm', that desire to interpret art always on a signifying register, or from a deconstructive attitude. At other times I have positioned my arguments against the Frankfurt School, and particularly Theodor Adorno's 'melancholy science', attempting to rescue art from being positioned within a logic of negation. To a certain extent this has been a question of strategy, a way of making sense of my own position by relating it to pre-existent discursive fields. Later chapters have abandoned this somewhat contrary tone in order to embark on more experimental readings of Deleuze in relation to specific practices (the ending above being a case in point).

In retrospect, each of the chapters has always involved attending to the creative and affirmative aspects of Deleuze's thought, and in particular to the relevance both his and Guattari's writings have for the continuing production of our own subjectivities, our own processual self creation. As far as this goes, it is the power art has to break habit, and produce new and more spontaneous ways of being in the world that seems of particular importance. Here, creativity and recombination (difference and repetition) replace critique as art's *modus operandi*. This might involve only a small deviation from the typical, but this *clinamen* can operate as the germ of something new. It is in this sense that Deleuze and Guattari's work on the notion of a minor literature – the necessity of stammering, of stuttering, of foregrounding asignification – seems to me still to be one of their most important and productive texts for thinking the field of contemporary art. Such affective stammering operates as a kind of singularity that in itself counteracts already existing affective/signifying regimes, whilst at the same time opening up a gap into which creativity, understood as the pure past and future anticipations, can enter. Indeed, we might see this as a definition of freedom, at least freedom from habit. These glitches, or points of indeterminancy, open up the possibility of a multiplicity of pathways, and thus a multiplicity of possible worlds. Indeed, it is this functioning as an 'affective-event' that gives art its inspirational, we might even say hopeful tenor and also, I think, the potential to offer an escape from the manipulation performed by those other affective assemblages that increasingly operate in a parallel logic to art.[12] Other concepts that I have looked at and which I think could be productively put to more work are probe-heads and war machines, both of which point towards not merely the rupture with already existing modes of organisation but also the production of new and more experimental modes. Indeed, we might say that art, as well as being a name for a rupture, is also a name for these concomitant micro-technologies of reorganisation and resingularisation.

On a final note then I want to return once more to my own context and investments in this project, and particularly to what writing a book on the above conjunction means. On the one hand, and especially in today's academic climate, one writes to keep one's job. Antonio Negri's argument regarding the total subsumption of capital is nowhere more apparent than in academia where even one's dreams are utilised to meet research quotas. And yet, on the other hand, one writes as an accompaniment to thought, as a prop and platform for thinking the world differently. Writing in this sense is itself a technology of the production of subjectivity, at times an aesthetic project, at others a more stratified and neurotic pursuit. Indeed, in writing one is forced to come up against one's own subjectivity, one is reminded once again of one's own limitations and shortcomings. A book is always, at least in one sense, a record of these failings and aporias. This is not however to be lamented, for this understanding or awareness of one's self and one's habits is very much the ground clearing exercise for the production of something new. This book in particular is then a record of a process, containing its fair share of awkwardness and contradictions. It records an encounter with, and also the sampling and recombination of, other already existing assemblages, in the production of something that might, it is hoped, be mobilised elsewhere. Indeed, I hope very much that the book will have operated as a productive case study of one particular encounter with Deleuze and with art. If it moves any one reader to read Deleuze further and conduct their own transversal experiments, then it will have more than served its purpose.

Fiction: manifesto for future art practice

1. Activate immanence. Turn away from transcendent modes and points of organisation, especially religion and art, but also fashion, the mass media and other telematic standardisations. Refuse the priests and the police, affirm bottom-up formations and traitor prophets. Celebrate the 'isness' of all things. We call for a turn to matter, and a tracking of the latter's singularities and creative potentialities. Practice is the utilisation of that which already is (what else is there?) but in the production of new and specifically *different* combinations. Always affirm the eternal return.

2. Harness affect. Practice is the foregrounding of the world's intensive and affective properties. We are subject to the ambient affect of fear generated by others. We turn this fear-affect-assemblage back on itself, mimicking and bastardising their languages and their techniques. Affects as that which constitute the objects of our practice, (1), and affect as that which is 'communicated' through the work of the practice, (2). (1) The practice will involve the production of novel constellations of affects, away from opinion, away from habit, away from the clichés of so-called culture (the affective assemblages offered to us on a daily basis). (2) The practice will operate as a rupture in our overly anxious, paranoid and stratified habits of being (the practice will affirm new kinds of joy, and new kinds of becoming). This is an aesthetics. We affirm the necessity of style in this harnessing of affect.

3. Build probe-heads. The practice is an experimental device aimed at dismantling the strata that binds us and constitutes us as 'human' (our habitual states of being and responding). We will build probe-heads against faciality. In this practice both figuration and abstraction will be used (we will release the abstract from within the figurative). We offer access to the imperceptible from which the perceptible emerges and merges. We offer access to the unthought within thought, the nonsense within sense. And on the other side of the white wall? New territories, new polyvocalities.

4. Actualise the virtual. We locate the practice at that 'seeping edge' between the actual and the virtual. We turn away from the real and the possible as ontological co-ordinates for art (i.e. the clergy and their disciples). We attend to the 'matrix of emergence', the great screen that allows some things to pass, others to remain hidden (i.e. capitalism). And thus our practice is also one of *de*actualisation (the practice asks: how can we 'escape' the actual that surrounds us?) Our practice involves a switching of temporal registers, a speeding up, moving faster than any transcendent apparatus of capture, and also, at times, a slowing down, a remaining still. We open a gap between stimulus and reaction (i.e. creativity). We affirm speed, but also slowness and hesitancy. We are involved in mirror-travel and in the production of crystal objects.

5. Always stuttering, always stammering. Our practice is a collective enunciation, even when there is only one (we are always the group). Our practice is always linked to the larger political milieu (no oedipalisations and no nuclear families). Our practice as the general twisting, bending of a major language, a major tradition. The practice as centrifugal, reacting to, and attacking that which paradoxically produces the condition of possibility of the practice (*parasitical* function). The practice as centripetal, producing new forms and new modalities of being from within the same (*germinal* function). Always dissent *and* affirmation. Our practice is the precursor of that specifically immanent utopia to come, an exemplar of a new world that is already contained within this one. Our practice is a future fragment projected backwards in time. Stuttering and stammering we call forth the new clown-like people as the recipients of our practice.

6. *Always folding.* The inside as a fold of the outside (we refuse interiority and so-called 'essence'). We hold that our practice is the production of new folds, new worlds arising from these folds, and new myths appropriate to these future worlds (we will use past forms and yesterday's codes, but they will be made unrecognisable in their turn). The fold names our ontology, fractal and super-abundant (we believe in space and time travel conducted in the here and now). The fold names our processes of subjectivation, the relation we hold to ourselves, our capture of outside forces (everywhere we are subject *to*, but also subject producing). Our practice also affirms the 'new' folds of silicon with carbon, of the molecular, and of the secret fold at the heart of language – where language breaks free from meaning and cries like a wounded wolf.

Our practice is always one of ritual. We intend a performance that will allow those who dare participate to move from work time (utility) into sacred time (play). Our practice affirms transformation: we are concerned less with mundane consciousness than with cosmic consciousness. We believe in a Baroque practice as the only appropriate response to these troubled and terror-stricken times.

Notes

Introduction

1. In Deleuze's terms, an object of encounter's primary characteristic 'is that it can only be sensed' (*DR* 139). An object of recognition, on the other hand, is not only that which can be sensed, but that which may be attained by the other faculties (recalled, imagined, conceived): 'It therefore presupposes the exercise of the senses and of the other faculties in a common sense' (*DR* 139). It is common sense that predetermines, and we might say limits, typical experience. Common sense operates here as the cornerstone of representation.
2. In relation to this particular encounter I want to mention Keith Ansell Pearson's book, *Germinal Life: The Difference and Repetition of Deleuze* (1999) (London: Routledge), and Philip Goodchild's *Gilles Deleuze and the Question of Philosophy* (1996) (Madison: Fairleigh Dickinson University Press), both of which, although not referred to directly in my own work, played a crucial role in my understanding of Deleuze. A further volume that came later, but was equally inspiring, is John Rajchman's *The Deleuze Connections* (2000) (Cambridge, MA: MIT Press). I want also to mention the energy and inspiration offered by the *Virtual Futures* Conferences at the University of Warwick in the mid-1990s, which perhaps more than anything else determined that my encounter with Deleuze would be an exciting and productive one.
3. Henceforth, and unless I am specifically referring to joint works, I shall use the proper name 'Deleuze' to refer to all the writings Deleuze authored or co-authored.
4. We might productively note here the demarcation Jean-François Lyotard once made between philosophers and managers:

   If you look a little closer you will see that when the philosophers you have in mind decided to talk about the arts, it was not in order to explain works or interpret them. They wanted even less to make them fit into a system or build a system based on them. What then was their purpose? I'm not quite sure, and this is what we must try to grasp. But in any case these philosophers have had almost no part in the request for a system, except inadvertently. More often than not, they have purposely thwarted it as best they could. The request emanates instead from a new stratum: the managerial staff of the art institutions, the reading engineers, the maintenance crews for the big explanatory machines patented under the name of Ideology, Fantasy, Structure. (*LYO* 182)

   Indeed, for the philosopher it is precisely an art work's 'non-fitting' into any given system that constitutes its interest. This amounts to a certain evasive or what we might call bothersome quality of art that makes any given system 'malfunction' (*LYO* 182). For Lyotard, and I think for Deleuze also, this implies that art will always resist being 'transformed wholesale into signification'. (*LYO* 182)

5. There have been other books addressing a similar crossover. Most relevant to my own project is Ronald Bogue's *Deleuze on Music, Painting, and the Arts* (2003) (London: Routledge), the third volume of a three-volume introduction to Deleuze's writings. Although the former operates as an introduction to Deleuze's own writings on art, it is no less impressive for this (and indeed many of the themes of my own book inevitably parallel Bogue's). Bogue has also published a collection of essays, *Deleuze's Wake: Tributes and Tributaries* (2004) (Albany: State University of New York Press), which might be characterised as a series of deterritorialisations from the three-volume set. In this latter work Bogue brings Deleuze into encounter with fields not considered by Deleuze himself, perhaps most surprisingly death metal music. Gregg Lambert's *The Non-Philosophy of Gilles Deleuze* (2002) (London: Continuum) is another highly impressive thinking through of the encounter between art – or non-philosophy – and philosophy. Lambert offers up an astute reading of *The Fold: Leibniz and the Baroque* (1993a) (Trans. T. Conley) (Minneapolis: University of Minnesota Press), but also, like Bogue, takes Deleuze into other milieus, or develops Deleuze's own interests, for example in relation to the literature of Borges and the films of Resnai. A further work in this field is Dorothea Olkowski's *Gilles Deleuze and the Ruins of Representation* (1999) (Berkeley: University of California Press). This volume, like Lambert's, involves a reading of Deleuze's major philosophical works, and especially *Difference and Repetition* (1994) (Trans. P. Patton) (New York: Columbia University Press) and *The Logic of Sense* (1990) (Trans. M. Lester and C. Stivale) (Ed. C.V. Boundas) (New York: Columbia University Press). It also gives a compelling account of the phenomenology of Henri Bergson and Maurice Merleau-Ponty. Particularly interesting for myself as regards the latter volume is the utilisation of Mary Kelley's art practice as a case study, but also a kind of ally, in Olkowski's own project of rethinking feminism beyond representational paradigms. Although not strictly concerned with art – or for that matter Deleuze – Brian Massumi's book, *Parables for the Virtual: Movement, Affect, Sensation* (2002a) (Durham: Duke University Press), perhaps comes closest to what I attempt in my own volume, specifically in its emphasis on affirmation and invention and in the use of what Massumi calls 'examples'. In fact, for myself, Massumi's essay on 'The Autonomy of Affect', republished in the latter volume, was the first Deleuze inspired essay I read which effectively smeared Deleuze's own concepts into other areas. It is in this sense that Massumi's conference papers, specifically on a notion of affect, have also been highly instructive, and I occasionally reference them in what follows. Massumi's own commentary on Deleuze, *A User's Guide to Capitalism and Schizophrenia: Deviations from Deleuze and Guattari* (1993) (Cambridge, MA: MIT Press), had a similarly inspiring effect. If there is a difference between my own book and all of the above it is that it addresses itself specifically to the 'relevance' of Deleuze for the expanded field of modern and contemporary art, and for the field of art history in general.
6. The debates in *October* were constellated around the notion of an 'allegorical impulse' within postmodern art. See for example Craig Owen's article, 'The Allegorical Impulse: Towards a Theory of Postmodernism', republished in *The Art of Art History: A Critical Anthology* (1998) (Ed. D. Preziosi) (Oxford: Oxford University Press), pp. 315–28, and, most impressive, Stephen Melville's 'Notes on the Re-emergence of Allegory, the Forgetting of Modernism, the Necessity

of Rhetoric, and the Conditions of Publicity in Art and Art Criticism', *October* (1981), No. 19, 33–48.

7. See for example Manuel Delanda's *Intensive Science and Virtual Philosophy* (2002) (London: Continuum), which is specifically involved in 'wrenching his [Deleuze's] ideas from his collaboration with Felix Guattari' (Delanda 2002, 6). Delanda's rational is that he has a specific interest in that part of the collaboration that is Deleuze's, namely 'Deleuze's ontology and epistemology as exposed in his early works', thus, in his own work, Delanda uses 'only those parts of [Deleuze's] collaborative work which can be directly traced to those early works' (Delanda 2002, 6). For myself this is a misunderstanding of the nature of collaboration. Indeed, it seems to me that Deleuze's philosophy – as well as his philosophical attitude or style – was invariably affected by the encounter with Guattari, and in fact that the joint works were precisely experiments in thinking collectively (as the opening of *A Thousand Plateaus* (1988) (Trans. B. Massumi) (London: Athlone Press) makes clear: 'The two of us wrote *Anti-Oedipus* together. Since each of us was several, there was already quite a crowd' (*ATP* 3)).
8. It is in this sense that I am entirely in agreement with Alberto Toscano when he remarks, in his compelling Preface to Eric Alliez's own illuminating commentary on Deleuze and Guattari's *What is Philosophy?*:

   The commentary is not a contribution to the construction of an orthodoxy, with all its attendant disciplinary effects, but a necessarily partial, perhaps partisan, effort to revitalise a philosophy, by a judicious combination of detailed excavation, on the one hand, and the potentially catalytic adjunction of new components, on the other. (2004, xiv)

1 Rhizomes, Machines, Multiplicities and Maps

1. To quote Massumi:

   The best way of all to approach the book is to read it as a challenge: to pry open the vacant spaces that would enable you to build your life and those of the people around you into a plateau of intensity that would leave afterimages of its dynamism that could be reinjected into still other lives, creating a fabric of heightened states between which any number, the greatest number, of connecting routes would exist. (*ATP* xv)

2. Indeed, Deleuze and Guattari were themselves to be the subject of ideological critique. Frederic Jameson sums up this attitude in his afterword 'Afterword: Reflections in Conclusion', in *Aesthetics and Politics* (1977) (Ed. R. Taylor) (London: New Left Books), pp. 196–213. Here the so-called 'attack' on representation would only be finally 'understood' when it was itself situated *within* representation (which is to say, ideology):

   Meanwhile, poststructuralism has added yet a different kind of parameter to the Realism/Modernism controversy ... The assimilation of realism as a value to the old philosophical concept of mimesis by such writers as Foucault, Derrida, Lyotard or Deleuze, has reformulated the Realism/Modernism debate in terms of a Platonic attack on the ideological effects of representation ... yet my own feeling is that we will not fully be able to assess the consequences of the attack on representation, and of poststructuralism generally, until we are able to situate it *within the field of the theory of ideology itself* [my italics]. (Jameson 1977, 199)

3. See for example Peter Hallward's *Absolutely Postcolonial: Writing Between the Singular and the Specific* (2001) (Manchester: Manchester University Press) in which Deleuze's project is characterised as one of 'counter-actualisation':

   The great purpose of Deleuze's work is thus the invention of various mechanisms whereby the given can be counter-actualised, 'real'-ised, deterritorialised, or otherwise transfigured. One becomes real, naturally, by escaping the equivocal, the territorial, the relative, the mediate, the figural, the significant, the perceptible, and so on. (2001, 13)

   Hallward finds confirmation of this take on Deleuze from Deleuze himself, quoting from *Cinema 1*: 'how can we rid ourselves of ourselves and demolish ourselves?' (*C1* 66). My particular take on this matter is that this apparent negation of ourselves also, and more importantly, involves the production of 'new' selves – a fundamentally constructive project.
4. At stake in such a resonance is a paradigmatically different relationship to another's intellectual or artistic practice; an affective relationship often resulting in an affective homage. In a similar vein the contemporary artist Thomas Hirschorn has referred to his relation to Deleuze – and also Bataille, Spinoza and Gramsci – as being one of a 'fan' (Hirschorn, paper presented at *Field Work: Reports from the Fields of Visual Culture* Conference (2003), London, Victoria Milo Gallery). Hence Hirschorn's monuments that he builds to these philosophers (for example the *Bataille Monument* built for Documenta XI (see Fietzek, G. (Ed.) *Documenta XI: The Catalogue* (2002) (London: Art Books International)).
5. There have been recent volumes that map the connections between Deleuze and Derrida. See for example Paul Patton and John Protevi's edited collection *Between Deleuze and Derrida* (2003) (London: Continuum). See also Protevi's own impressive volume *Political Physics* (2001) (London: Athlone Press), in which the Derridean deconstruction of logocentrism is allied with Deleuze's own project of mapping out a non-hylomorphic philosophy of matter (see also my review of Protevi's volume in *Parallax* (2003), vol. 9, no. 1, 126–7.
6. In relation to this Deleuze has remarked in an interview: 'It's easy to set up a correspondence between any society and some kind of machine, which isn't to say that their machines determine different kinds of society but that they express the social forms capable of producing them and making use of them' (*N* 180).
7. We might also note recent developments in neuroscience and in embodied Artificial Intelligence, both of which appear increasingly 'Deleuzian'.
8. A crucial question here, which I address at this stage in just a footnote, is the relationship of rhizomatics to capitalism. Put bluntly the question might be formulated thus: if capitalism operates in a specifically rhizomatic manner – which it increasingly seems to – how might rhizomatic art practices resist and/or critique this? Put even more bluntly, what are we to think when the

management strategies of multinationals such as *Microsoft* seem to parallel the artistic strategies of expanded contemporary practices? Chapter 4 goes some way to address this via the introduction of the notion of the minor, and the necessity of stuttering and stammering these new models. It is important also to point out that the relationships between different rhizomatic formations must always be scrutinised and attention given to the power relations in what might appear bottom up systems of organisation. Equally important is to note Deleuze's notion that 'resistance is primary', which is to say, the question is really why an ontologically prior rhizomatics becomes blocked and captured. In fact Deleuze, when asked 'whether control or communication societies will lead to forms of resistance that might reopen the way for a communism understood as the "transversal organization of free individuals" ', confesses that he is not sure, or indeed whether 'resistance' as it were can proceed through speech and communication at all (for Deleuze the latter have all but been corrupted by money and the profit motive) (*N* 175). Thus Deleuze posits the intriguing idea that resistance might well involve creating 'vacuoles of non communication, circuit breakers, so we can elude control' (*N* 175). As Deleuze remarks: 'It's not a question of worrying or hoping for the best, but of finding new weapons' (*N* 178). See also Hardt and Negri's chapter on 'Postmodernization, or the Informatization of Production', in *Empire* (2000) (Cambridge: Harvard University Press), pp. 280–303.

9. See for example Association Metaworx (Ed.), *Metaworx: Approaches to Interactivity* (2004) (Zurich: Birkhauser), which provides an interesting survey of predominantly Swiss practices that might be said to be located at the sharp end of technological developments especially as regards the conjunction of interactive media and complexity theory. See also Vera Buhlman's informative introduction to this volume, 'Volatile Milieu: The Poetics of Interactivity', which utilises the writings of Deleuze and Guattari and Brian Massumi in mapping out a framework for interactive multidisciplinary research.
10. Deleuze and Guattari return to this theme of a rhizomatic, or 'counterpunctual' universe in their last work together. See *WP* 185–6.
11. It is Nicolas Bourriaud who first coined the phrase 'relational aesthetics' in relation to contemporary art. See his *Relational Aesthetics* (1998) (Trans. S. Pleasance, F. Woods and M. Copeland) (Paris: Les Presses du Reel) in which relational art is defined as 'the possibility' of 'an art taking as its theoretical horizon the realm of human interactions and its social context rather then the assertion of an independent and *private symbolic* space' (Bourriaud 1998, 14). One might argue that all art is relational in this sense (and always has been), and indeed that these relations involve more than just the social. One might also want to ask what *kinds* of social relations art produces? Are they all to be applauded (are there practices that merely restage dominant power relations)? Much of what Bourriaud goes on to say in *Relational Aesthetics* relates to the subject matter of this chapter, although later chapters might be seen to take issue with the opposition he sets out above.
12. This turn away from traditional disciplinary boundaries has its correlate in the emergent field/academic discipline of Visual Culture. This is not necessarily to focus purely on the visual, rather it is to recognise that the expanded field of artistic practice has gone beyond those objects, practices and discourses typically contained within the remit of art history.

13. See Derrida, *The Truth in Painting* (1987) (Trans G. Bennington and I. McLeod) (Chicago: University of Chicago Press), pp. 21–2.
14. Donald Preziosi conducts a similar analysis of art history, which is to say a critique of representation, in his *Rethinking Art History: Meditations on a Coy Science* (1991) (New Haven: Yale University Press). For Preziosi

    the art of art history is inextricably grounded in a logocentric paradigm of signification, and the business of the discipline is addressed above all to the task of reading objects so as to discern meaning, to hear the Voice behind what is palpable and mute. (1991, 16)

    Preziosi continues:

    Disciplinary practice has rested upon a series of metaphors and tropes that remain grounded in classical theories of signification and representation. Such rhetorical protocols ... have tended to be held in common by seemingly distinct schools of theory and methodology in art history. However much they might contrast with each other in programmatic ways, iconographic analysis, Marxist social history, and (structuralist) visual semiotics, among others, have shared basic assumptions on how artworks mean and how they reflect social and historical processes. (1991, 16)

15. Andrew Benjamin gives this problem an interesting temporal slant in his 'Introduction' to a special issue of *Art and Design* on *Complexity: Architecture/Art/Philosophy* (1995) (Ed. A. Benjamin) (London: Academy Editions):

    With representation there is the already implicated presence of the ontology of stasis. Consequently, opening up the possibility of a founding complexity will give rise to two immediate demands. The first is a repositioning of the ontological, while the second will involve a recasting of how the process of production – that is, the work's effectation – is to be understood. (Benjamin 1995, 7)

    This first chapter is precisely an attempt to think through these two demands. Importantly, and like myself, Benjamin sees this rethinking and reworking as not nihilistic – not stemming from a destruction of metaphysics – but rather as the 'affirmation of other practices, activities and works' (Benjamin 1995, 7).
16. See for example de Man's essay 'The Rhetoric of Temporality', *Blindness and Insight: Essays in the Rhetoric of Contemporary Criticism* (1983a) (London: Methuen), pp. 187–228.
17. It is worth noting Lyotard's take on the 'origin' of representation here – that it is premised on a crisis, or a *lack*. Here is Lyotard from his essay on Anton Ehrenzweig, 'Beyond Representation' (Trans. J. Culler), *The Lyotard Reader* (1989b) (Ed. A. Benjamin) (Oxford: Basil Blackwell):

    In this methodological nihilism, which transforms entities of language, painting or music into signs or groups that *stand for* something else, and therefore treats the material and its organisation as a surface to be penetrated, one finds the same prejudice: the notion that works have a substitutive or vicarious function. They are only there in place of a missing object, as the accepted formula has it; and they are there only *because* the object is missing. (1989b, 158)

    Lyotard goes on to remark:

    An account of the economy of works of art that was cast in libidinal terms (but should we still, in this case, continue to speak of *works*?) would have as its central presupposition the affirmative character of works: they are not in place of anything; they do not *stand for* but stand; that is to say, they function through their material and its organization. (1989b, 158)

18. This is not to say that deconstruction cannot be utilised in a more affirmative manner. Derrida's notion of *différance* for example might be productive in thinking through how art generates certain signifying effects, that is, through a variety of differential relations within a specific art work, between art works, and between art and non-art – as well as through a deferral of what the art work appears to 'represent'.
19. There is certainly a role for this type of critique that inhabits its object of criticism like a virus or parasite. The danger is that this critique can become the very horizon of thought in general.
20. Robert Smithson characterises the art of Donald Judd, and the work of Alain Robbe-Grillet, in precisely this way – as breaking with a certain 'empathy' between self and object. Here he is from his essay on 'The Pathetic Fallacy in Esthetics':

    The empathic projection of the 'self' into an art-object has determined all esthetics of the last fifty years or so. Recently, both Alain Robbe-Grillet and Don Judd have attacked this empathic esthetic. In Judd's *Specific Objects*, one detects a dissatisfaction with the problems of space. In Robbe-Grillet's essay *Nature Humanism Tragedy*, one finds an explicit rejection of anthropomorphic 'complicity'. Things are not filled with any *humanist* justifications. 'Things are things, and man is only man'. Abstract art is not a self-projection, it is indifferent to the self. (*CW* 338)

    We might productively compare this with Nietzsche who also abhorred, and wrote against, this endemic anthropomorphism:

    Nothing is more difficult for man than to apprehend a thing impersonally: I mean to see it as a thing, *not as a person*: one might question, indeed, whether it is at all possible for him to suspend the clockwork of his person-constructing, person-inventing drive even for a moment. (Nietzsche 1977, 30–1)

    Deleuze and Guattari also attend to this 'person-constructing' mechanism in *A Thousand Plateaus* (1988) (Trans. B. Massumi) (London: Athlone Press). In the plateau '1440:The Smooth and the Striated' they write about two kinds of line: the organic, which delineates form, encloses with verticals and horizontals, sticks to a centre, that is *representational* (represents something other than what it is); and the abstract or nomadic line that disrupts this function (*ATP* 492–9). The former line, and the form that it delineates, works to unite representation with the subject. An empathy is produced between the form of the art object and the (form of the) human subject (to pre-empt the argument of Chapter 2, we might call this the workings of the faciality-machine). Deleuze explores this further in his book *Francis Bacon: The Logic of Sensation* (2003) (Trans. D.W. Smith) (London: Continuum). See p. 46 of the latter for a description of the 'northern gothic line' as that which maps out a 'powerful non-organic life'. See also p. 105, and pp. 129–30.
21. Edgar Schmitz has developed an interesting concept of the 'ambient' in relation to contemporary art to describe a kind of super-connectivity and super-relationality, which in itself involves a critique of the more restricted

economies of institutional critique, site specificity and 'relational aesthetics' (all of which, as Schmitz demonstrates, maintain a binary logic) (Schmitz, *Ambient Mode: Poetics and Politics of Dispersed Engagements* (forthcoming) (New York: Lukas and Steinberg)).

22. See for example the 'counter cartographies' project by the art collective C.CRED (www.ccred.org). See also my essay on C.CRED's practice, 'Four Moments/Movements for an Expanded Art Practice (Following Deleuze, Following Spinoza)', *The Issues (In Contemporary Culture and Aesthetics)* (2005a), vol. 1, 67–8.
23. See the plateau '1933: Micropolitics and Segmentarity', *ATP* 208–31.
24. The smearing of complexity theory into the humanities has been particularly productive. See for example Paul Cilliers' bringing together of Derrida and Lyotard with the former in 'Post-structuralism, Connectionism and Complexity', in *Complexity and Postmodernism: Understanding Complex Systems* (1988) (London: Routledge) pp. 37–47, and in relation to contemporary art and art theory see the edited collection *Complexity: Architecture/Art/Philosophy* (1995) (Ed. A. Benjamin) (London: Academy Editions).
25. See for example Mike Nelson's *Forgotten Kingdom* (2001) (Ed. W. Bradley) (London: ICA), an exhibition catalogue that takes the form of a collection of extracts from Science Fiction, horror and other novels – including Stanislaw Lem's *Solaris* and Philip K. Dick's *Do Androids Dream of Electric Sheep*?
26. The rhizome then follows closely Barthes' definition of 'text', especially as it is laid out in the essay 'From Work to Text', in *Image/Music/Text* (1977a) (Trans. and Ed. S. Heath) (London: Fontana), pp. 155–64. However it also announces a more general principle of connectivity – beyond textuality – with organic and inorganic matter. A case study of this principle of connectivity is *arte povera*, at least as it is characterised by Germano Celant:

    Animals, vegetables and minerals take part in the world of art. The artist feels attracted by their physical, chemical and biological possibilities, and he begins again to feel the need to make things of the world, not only as animated beings, but as producer of magic and marvellous deeds. The artist–alchemist organizes living and vegetable matter into magic things, working to discover the root of things, in order to re-find them and extol them. His work, however, does include in its scope the use of the simplest material and natural elements (copper, zinc, earth, water, rivers, land, snow, fire, grass, air, stone, electricity, uranium, sky, weight, gravity, height, growth etc.). (1992, 886–7)

27. We are always forming rhizomes with art in this sense, perhaps most obviously becoming music when we dance. A further study would be needed to think through different artist's various becomings involved in *making* their art. We might point briefly to one such case study of Jackson Pollock 'becoming painting':

    When I am *in* my painting, I'm not aware of what I'm doing. It is only after a sort of 'get acquainted' period that I see what I have been about. I have no fears about making changes, destroying the image etc., because the painting has a life of its own. I try to let it come through. It is only when I lose contact with the painting that the result is a mess. Otherwise there is pure harmony, an easy give and take, and the painting comes out well. (Pollock quoted in Read 1974, 266–7)

There are also of course the various becomings that *allow* for creativity (a veritable becoming plant in the case of Pollock's alcoholism).

28. See Jean-François Lyotard, 'The Tensor', *Libidinal Economy* (1993) (Trans. I. H. Grant) (London: Athlone Press), pp. 43–94.
29. An interesting case study of how this principle of 'interpretation' might be thought in relation to art practice is the work of the contemporary artist Simon Starling, which involves precisely the 'actualisation' of the different processes – or durations – encapsulated in the object. See for example Katrina M. Brown's introductory essay 'Djungel Dwelling', in *Simon Starling: Djungel* (2002) (Dundee: Dundee Contemporary Arts), pp. 23–36. As Brown remarks:

[Starling's] ... projects bring diverse sources and elements together in configurations which undermine the latent hierarchy – of object over process, end-product over source material, design over craft. They are synthetic rather than analytic, with each present, tangible and concrete element insisting on an awareness of the disparate histories and journeys necessary to the creation of the whole. (2002, 23)

30. Action painting would be a paradigmatic case study of this encounter between artist and material. Here for example is Harold Rosenberg writing about this particular encounter/confrontation:

At a certain moment the canvas began to appear to one American painter after another as an arena in which to act – rather than as a space in which to reproduce, redesign, analyse or 'express' an object, actual or imagined. What was to go on the canvas was not a picture but an event. The painter no longer approached his easel with an image in his mind; he went up to it with material in his hand to do something to that other piece of material in front of him. The image would be the result of this encounter. (1970, 36–7)

31. In much the same way as Barthes' reader operates as the limit point and unity of a written text. See 'The Death of the Author', in *Image/Music/Text* (1977b) (Trans. and Ed. S. Heath) (London: Fontana), pp. 142–8.
32. And it is not just 'radical' and dissenting machines that are constructed. We might think, for example, of the films and other propaganda of the Third Reich; 'art' here was precisely a 'fascist machine'. But a fascist machine can itself be redirected and used against its original masters (hence the Situationist strategy of *détournement*). More worrying perhaps is that a radical, dissenting machine can likewise be redirected against its original mechanics (staying with Hitler's Germany, the exhibition of 'Degenerate art' would be a case in point). Ultimately any machine can produce any number of different effects depending on its conjunction with other machines.
33. George Bataille has written a whole 'history' of the world in terms of this 'production'. See *The Accursed Share: An Essay on General Economy Volume 1: Consumption* (1991) (Trans. R. Hurley) (New York: Zone Books) where Bataille 'fleshes' out his theory on consumption and surplus as a general theory of production. Like Deleuze and Guattari, Bataille's notion of production is global; all production is to be thought of in terms of 'the movement of

energy on the globe' (Bataille 1991, 20). As Bataille remarks: 'Shouldn't productive activity as a whole be considered in terms of the modifications it receives from its surroundings? In other words, isn't there a need to study the system of human production and consumption within a much larger framework?' (1991, 20). We might see this as a critique of Marx and Engel's own theory of production inasmuch as the latter, although it recognises the importance of natural resources, restricts production to the human realm. See 'History: Fundamental Conditions', in *The German Ideology: Part One* (1970) (Ed. C. J. Arthur) (London: Lawrence and Wishart), and especially pp. 48–50.

34. Here is Ronald Bogue writing about these 'flows' as they are written about in *Anti-Oedipus*:

    A flow of electricity, for example, can be conjoined with a flow of words, a flow of images, a flow of music, or a flow of digital commands controlling any number of technical machines; but the conjoined flows never mean anything, they simply channel flows in different directions, each sign resembling a cloverleaf junction into which and out of which stream various entities. (1989, 102)

35. As Deleuze and Guattari remark: 'Desiring-machines work only when they break down, and by continually breaking down' (*AO* 8).
36. See the plateau '10,000 B.C.: The Geology of Morals (Who Does the Earth Think It Is?)' (*ATP* 39–74).
37. I am following Deleuze and Guattari's notion of 'schizophrenia' here, which is to say *not* the clinical diagnosis as such, but a certain logic of desire and 'unfixing' that is produced *by* capitalism. Eugene Holland puts this well in his 'Introduction' to *Deleuze and Guattari's* Anti-Oedipus: *Introduction to Schizoanalysis* (1999) (London: Routledge):

    It is important ... to dispel the most common misconception about schizoanalysis, by explaining what Deleuze and Guattari do not mean by 'schizophrenia', and why they claim never to have seen a schizophrenic. For schizoanalysis, schizophrenia is not the disease or mental disturbance characterising or defining schizophrenis. Schizophrenics as clinical patients (and 'schizophrenia' as a reductive and ill-conceived psychiatric diagnosis) result, on the contrary, from the incompatibility between the dynamics of schizophrenia unleashed by capitalism and the reigning institutions of capitalist society. (1999, 2)

38. There has been much said about the apparent emphases on absolute deterritorialisation in *Anti-Oedipus*, as opposed to the more sober emphasis on caution in *A Thousand Plateaus*. See for example Charles Stivale's 'Rhizomatics in Cyberspace' (from his book, *The Two-Fold Thought of Deleuze and Guattari: Intersections and Animations* (1988) (New York: Guildford Press), pp. 71–99) for a 'blow-by-blow' account of this debate as it was constellated around the Warwick *Virtual Futures* conference in 1994 – initiated by Nick Land's paper there, and subsequent publication ('Making it with Death: Remarks on Thanatos and Desiring-Production', *Journal of the British Society for Phenomenology* (1993), vol. 24, no. 1, 66–76). Stivale, in reporting this

exchange, also gives an interesting example of a rhizomatic, virtual community. My particular take on this is pragmatic, and as such, closer to the strategies for self-creation in *A Thousand Plateaus*, than the absolute deterritorialisations of *Anti-Oedipus*, although the former does in fact demarcate the possibility of a positive absolute deterritorialisation:

> It seems necessary to distinguish between three types of deterritorialization: the first type is relative, proper to the strata, and culminates in signifiance; the second is absolute, but still negative and stratic, and appears in subjectification ... finally, there is the possibility of a positive absolute deterritorialization on the plane of consistency or the body without organs. (*ATP* 134)

39. I attend to this notion of the war machine in Chapter 3.
40. 'In control societies ... the key thing is no longer signature or number but a code: codes are *passwords* ... The digital language of control is made up of codes indicating whether access to some information should be allowed or denied' (*N* 180).
41. Of course people resingularise themselves everyday outside of any clinic. White collar workers plant allotments, blue collar workers visit the theatre. Different activities take on what we might call, following Guattari, an *ethicoaesthetic* function.
42. As Deleuze and Guattari remark: 'Smooth space is filled by events or haecceities, far more than by formed and perceived things. It is a space of affects, more than one of properties' (*ATP* 479).
43. As Germano Celant suggests, quoting John Cage: ' "Art comes", states Cage, "from a kind of experimental condition in which one experiments with living". To create art, then, one identifies with life and to exist takes on the meaning of re-inventing at every moment a new fantasy, pattern of behaviour aestheticism, etc. of one's own life' (1992, 887). See also Deleuze's interview 'Life as a Work of Art' in relation to Foucault, and to an aesthetics of living that is also an ethics (*N* 94–101).
44. Or as Deleuze and Guattari put it in relation to psychoanalysis, we need to find the rhizome 'beneath' the 'family photo' (*ATP* 14).
45. We have examples of Deleuze's child mapmaker in the psychoanalytical case studies of Little Hans and Little Richard. An even more intriguing example is the young Walter Benjamin, at least as the older Benjamin writes about him and his childhood wanderings around the city of Berlin:

> I have long, indeed for years, played with setting out the sphere of life – bios – graphically on a map. First I envisaged an ordinary map, but now I would incline to a general staff's map of a city centre, if such a thing existed ... I have evolved a system of signs, and on the grey backgrounds of such maps they would make a colourful show if I clearly marked in the houses of my friends and girl friends, the assembly halls of various collectives. And even without this map, I still have the encouragement provided by an illustrious precursor, the Frenchman Leon Daudet, exemplary at least in the title of his work, which exactly encompasses the best that I might achieve here: *Paris vecu*. 'Lived Berlin' does not sound so good but is as real. (W. Benjamin 1997a, 295)

2 The Ethicoaesthetics of Affect and the Bloc of Sensations

1. In this sense I am very much in agreement with Ian Buchanan's notion in his book, *Deleuzism: A Metacommentary* (2000) (Edinburgh: Edinburgh University Press), that *What is Philosophy*? is a kind of *revisionary* text. It is important also to point out that the different speed and tone of this volume is the result of it having a different kind of function to earlier works, namely to counteract the increasing hegemony of opinion, as Deleuze and Guattari saw it, within contemporary culture. For myself, Buchanan's reading of Deleuze is interesting precisely because it is made through the optic of Frederic Jameson's writings – we might even say is read *through* this broadly representational paradigm (see also Chapter 1, note 2). Another example of more extreme capture is Slavoj Zizek's book on Deleuze, *Organs without Bodies: Deleuze and Consequences* (2004) (London: Routledge), which perhaps inevitably involves the reading of Deleuze via a Lacanian optic.
2. This is then a specifically Spinozist project. As Deleuze remarks:

   What does Spinoza mean when he invites us to take the body as model? It is a matter of showing that the body surpasses the knowledge that we have of it, *and that thought likewise surpasses the consciousness that we have of it*. There are no fewer things in the mind that exceed our consciousness than there are things in the body that exceed our knowledge. So it is by one and the same movement that we shall manage, if possible, to capture the power of the body beyond the given conditions of our knowledge, and to capture the power of the mind beyond the conditions of our consciousness. (*PP* 18)

3. Lyotard 'defines' these fantasies as operating:

   whenever the objective is to stabilise the referent, to arrange it according to a point of view which endows it with a recognisable meaning, to reproduce the syntax and vocabulary which enable the addressee to decipher images and sequences quickly, and so to arrive easily at the consciousness of his own identity as well as the approval which he thereby receives from others – since such structures of images and sequences constitute a communication code among all of them. This is the way the effects of reality, or if one prefers, the fantasies of realism, multiply. (1984, 74)

   Hence, for Lyotard the importance of the artist who counteracts this 'reality effect', who is precisely 'working without rules in order to formulate the rules of what *will have been done*' (Lyotard 1984, 81).
4. Indeed, there is a 'tradition' of positioning critical art history as a form of ideological critique, and specifically as a critique of aesthetics. See for example Kurt Foster's polemical essay, 'Critical History of Art or a Transfiguration of Values', *New Literary History* (1972), vol. 3, No. 1, 459–70.
5. See Derrida's *The Truth in Painting* (1987) (Trans. G. Bennington and I. McLeod) (Chicago: University of Chicago Press) and specifically the section 'Parergon', pp. 37–82.
6. Affects are events that are irreducible to discourse, understood as structure. Affects might however be understood as textual in a kind of expanded Derridean sense, in that they are felt as *differences in intensity*.

7. For Brian Massumi, in his essay 'The Autonomy of Affect', *Deleuze: A Critical Reader* (1996) (Ed. P. Patton) (Oxford: Basil Blackwell), pp. 217–39, affects are likewise understood as passages of intensity, which might resonate with linguistic expression but which strictly speaking are of a different, and prior, order. For Massumi, as for myself: 'Approaches to the image in its relation to language are incomplete if they operate only on the semantic or semiotic level, however that level is defined (linguistically, logically, narratologically, ideologically, or all of these combinations, as a Symbolic). What they lose, precisely, is the *event* – in favour of structure' (1996, 220). Massumi identifies the realm of affect as being of increasing importance within 'media, literary and art theory' but specifies the problem that there is 'no cultural-theoretical vocabulary specific to affect', and that indeed 'our entire vocabularies has derived from theories of signification that are still wedded to structure' (1996, 221). From one perspective Massumi is right; there is no vocabulary of affect. However, it might not be so simple as to invent one, for from one perspective at least (that is to say, the deconstructive perspective) to come up with a language for, or of, affect is to bring the latter into representation and hence to invite deconstruction. In a sense there is no way out of this predicament except to acknowledge it as a problem within a certain intellectual field and move beyond it.
8. See 'Beatitude', the final section of Deleuze's *Expressionism in Philosophy: Spinoza* (1992) (Trans. M. Joughin) (New York: Zone Books), for a further exploration of this third kind of knowledge and what can only be called the super-human state it produces (*EX* 303–20).
9. In Guattari's own writing affects are understood as precisely that which 'make up' life. Affects establish a kind of centre – or 'self-affirmation' – that occurs parallel to the discursive (what Guattari terms *linear*) elements of subjectivity. For Guattari, this affective element is present in Freud's theory of the drives, but has been overlooked by 'the structuralists' (and here Guattari has in mind Lacan). I quote Guattari at some length from his essay 'On Machines':

   I consider that limiting ourselves to this coordinate [i.e. linearity] is precisely to lose the element of the machinic centre, of subjective autopoiesis and self affirmation. Whether located at the level of the complete individual or partial subjectivity, or even at the level of social subjectivity, this element undergoes a *pathic* relationship by means of the affect. What is it, then, that makes us state phenomenologically that something is living? It is precisely this relation of affect. This is not a description, nor a kind of propositional analysis resulting from a sense of hypotheses and deductions – i.e., it is a living being, therefore it is a machine; rather an immediate, pathic and non-discursive apprehension occurs of the machine's ontological autocomposition relationship. (*OM* 10)

   Interestingly, Guattari's notion of this non discursive affective *foyer* has much in common with Bergson, and with the latter's notion of living beings as affective 'centres of indetermination'. See later in this chapter and also *Matter and Memory* (1991) (Trans. N.M. Paul and W.S. Palmer) (New York: Zone Books), especially pp. 28–34.
10. As we saw in the previous chapter, it is Lyotard who addresses this double functioning of the sign in *Libidinal Economy* (1993) (Trans. I. H. Grant)

(London: Athlone Press). Like Guattari (see note 9 above), Lyotard's point of departure is Freud's theory of the drives. Lyotard merely points out that the sign can operate within two (or presumably even more) economies: metonymic and metaphoric systems but also affective ones: 'At the same time a sign which produces meaning through difference and opposition, and a sign producing intensity through force [*puissance*] and singularity' (Lyotard 1993, 54). Again, Brian Massumi is instructive on the relation of affect to the human brain-body configuration, suggesting that affects – understood as asignifying 'events' that pass across the body – everywhere and always accompany (and in some senses determine) the more obvious (i.e. signifying and structuring) elements of subjectivity (Massumi 1996). In fact, we might say, with Massumi, that the universe of affect (or, for Massumi, the universe of the *virtual*) often works to *interfere* with linguistic expression and indeed the other 'subject constructing' mechanisms of late capitalism (Massumi 1996, 219).

11. It is, at least in one sense, against de Man's melancholy writings on the aesthetic that this polemical first section of Chapter 2 was written. See for example his 'Rhetoric of Temporality', *Blindness and Insight: Essays in the Rhetoric of Contemporary Criticism* (1983a) (London: Methuen), pp. 142–65, where the symbol (the aesthetic moment) is portrayed as a mechanism, or 'defence strategy' as de Man calls it, that tries to hide from the 'negative self knowledge' of man's temporal predicament (his mortality) (de Man 1983a, 208). It is, of course, de Man's point that this strategy is always already frustrated (the symbol is but a special case of its supposed opposite, allegory). The promise of the aesthetic is, for de Man, always being broken.
12. Once more Massumi is useful here, on rethinking the relationship between the event – as intensity – and experience:

    Although the realm of intensity that Deleuze's philosophy strives to conceptualise is transcendental in the sense that it is not directly accessible to experience, it is not transcendent, it is not exactly outside experience either. It is immanent to it – always in it but not of it. Intensity and experience accompany one another, like two mutually presupposing dimensions, or like two sides of a coin. Intensity is immanent to matter and to events, to mind and to body and to every level of bifurcation composing them and which they compose. (Massumi 1996, 26)

    Hence intensity, for Massumi is indeed experienced 'in the proliferations of levels of organisation it ceaselessly gives rise to, generates and regenerates, at every suspended moment' (Massumi 1996, 226).
13. See for example the debates of *October* journal (see note 6 to my 'Introduction').
14. For an interesting take on this problematic (how to think the event) – especially in relation to Deleuze's project of thinking multiplicity – see Alain Badiou, *Deleuze: the Clamour of Being* (1999) (Trans. L. Burchill) (Minneapolis: University of Minnesota Press).
15. See *Derrida: The Movie* (2002) directed by A. Z. Kofman and K. Dick, distributed by Jane Doe Film.
16. As Deleuze suggests in *The Logic of Sense* (1990) (Trans. M. Lester and C. Stivale) (Ed. C. V. Boundas) (New York: Columbia University Press), there is an order of bodies, or states of affairs, but these should not be confused

with the events – incorporeal 'surface-effects' – that in some senses pass over and infuses them. The world of these events is a virtual world of becoming:

> These *effects* are not bodies, but properly speaking, 'incorporeal' entities. They are not physical qualities and properties, but rather logical or dialectical, attributes. They are not things or facts, but events. We cannot say they exist, but rather that they subsist or inhere (having this minimum of being which is appropriate to that which is not a thing, a nonexisting entity). They are not substantives or adjectives but verbs. They are neither agents nor patients, but results of actions and passions. They are 'impassive' entities – impassive results. (*LS* 5)

17. As Deleuze and Guattari remark, art is:

> (a) zone of indetermination, of indiscernability, as if things, beasts, and persons ... endlessly reach that point that immediately precedes their natural differentiation. This is what is called an *affect* ... Life alone creates such zones where living beings whirl around, and only art can reach and penetrate them in its enterprise of co-creation. (*WP* 173)

18. In Bergson's writing affection names something else: the action of the body on itself, which is to say the complete closure of the gap between bodies – or between excitation and reaction. See p. 57 of *Matter and Memory* (1991) for a discussion of affection in this sense.
19. For Bergson it is the increasing complexity of the organism – the increase in perceptual mechanisms and the possibilities of response – that ultimately results in a kind of 'free will'. For Spinoza too it is this increase in the body's perceptive and reactive capabilities that results in an increase in power:

> I say in general, that in proportion as a body is more capable than others of doing many things at once, or being acted on in many ways at once, so its mind is more capable than others of perceiving many things at once. And in proportion as the actions of a body depend more on its self alone, and as other bodies concur with it less in acting, so its mind is more capable of understanding distinctly. (Deleuze quotes Spinoza, *EX* 256–7)

20. Walter Benjamin also attends to this aspect of fabulation. For Benjamin, story telling is a kind of precondition that allows new forms of experience to emerge. See the essay 'The Storyteller: Reflections on the Work of Nikolai Leskov', *Illuminations* (1999a) (Trans. H. Zorn) (London: Pimloco), pp. 83–107, where Benjamin writes of the boredom of story telling being the 'dream bird that hatches the egg of experience' (1999a, 90) (Thanks to Ditte Villstrup for this connection).
21. Indeed, new technologies do not in themselves necessarily produce creative deterritorialisations, which is to say neither a switching of temporal or spatial registers, or both (which might be a definition *of* technology) necessarily produces 'art' (it can in fact merely reinforce already existing perceptual and psychic habits).
22. See 'November 28, 1947: How to Make Yourself a Body without Organs?' (*ATP* 149–66).
23. Deleuze gives us a case study of the masochistic BwO in his own work on *Masochism: Coldness and Cruelty* (1991b) (Trans. J. McNeil) (New York: Zone Books). See in particular the chapter 'The Art of Masoch' (*M* 69–80).

24. We might in this sense wish to contest Adorno and Horkheimer's notion that magic is necessarily a regression of sorts, a 'pre-Enlightenment' modality of understanding (see Adorno and Horkheimer, *Dialectic of Enlightenment* (1979) (Trans. J. Cumming) (London: Verso), especially pp. 8–14). I go into this further, in relation to myth, in the conclusion to this book, suffice to say here that apparently 'primitive' technologies might have a residual power of 'resistance' to late capitalist practices and procedures.
25. To quote Warburg: 'Telegram and telephone destroy the cosmos. Mythical and symbolic thinking strive to form spiritual bonds between humanity and the surrounding world, shaping distance into the space required for devotion and reflection: the distance undone by instantaneous electric connection' (1998, 206).
26. As Benjamin remarks:

    We know that the earliest art works originated in the service of ritual – first the magical, then the religious kind. It is significant that the existence of the work of art with reference to its aura is never entirely separated from its basis in ritual. (1999b, 217)

    For Benjamin modernity – and especially new reproductive technologies – emancipates the work of art 'from its parasitical dependence on ritual' (Benjamin 1999b, 218). This means that the function of art changes; instead of being based in ritual it becomes involved in politics. Here art's authenticity – its auratic power – is divorced from its political function. For Benjamin this is however not a simple progression; the loss of aura is not without its problems, specifically in terms of an increasing alienation from the world.
27. I will be returning to Raymond Williams in my conclusion.
28. In general Lyotard tends to configure this unknown event in Kantian terms, specifically in relation to the sublime. Following Lyotard we might describe the affective-event as a form of *micro* sublime.
29. John Rajchman, in his essay 'Abstraction', *Constructions* (1998) (Cambridge, MA: MIT Press), pp. 55–76, writes well on this notion of the abstract and about its difference to the more typical, one might say Greenbergian, notion of abstraction as reduction and purity. For Rajchman abstraction must be understood in terms of the realm of possibilities – or realm of *potentialities* – prior to figuration. As such, and in order to paint 'one must come to see the surface not so much as empty or blank but rather as intense, where "intensity" means filled with the unseen virtuality of other strange possibilities' (Rajchman 1998, 61). This question of how to 'paint outside forces', is according to Rajchman's reading of Deleuze, 'the basic question of modernity' (Rajchman 1998, 60).
30. As Deleuze and Guattari remark in '587 B.C.–A.D. 70: On Several Regimes of Signs': 'The principal strata binding human beings are the organism, significance and interpretation, and subjectification and subjection' (*ATP* 134). It is the function of the next plateau, 'November 28, 1947: How Do You Make Yourself a Body without Organs?', to offer strategies precisely for destratification (*ATP* 149–66). See also my 'In Violence: Three Case Studies Against the Stratum', *Parallax* (2000), vol. 6, no. 2, 104–9.
31. See my article 'Writing on Art (Case Study: The Buddhist Puja)', *Parallax* (2001), vol. 7, no. 4, 155–21, for a case study of just such a ritual practice.

32. We might say in this sense that there is a difference between what art *says* its doing (what is represented) and what it *actually* does (the affects it produces).
33. For Deleuze and Guattari philosophy is not a utopian pursuit in the sense of positing transcendent (and thus authoritarian) utopias. However, philosophy might be figured as utopian if we understand by this term *immanent, revolutionary* utopias. I go into more detail about this in Chapter 4.
34. A good example of this rethinking of art away from the horizon of instrumental reason (and of the latter's critique) is Ronald Bogue's essay, 'Art and Territory', in *A Deleuzian Century*? (1999) (Ed. I. Buchanan) (Durham: Duke University Press), pp. 85–102. Here Bogue, taking his lead from Deleuze's notion of the refrain, argues that bird song, as a kind of art practice, has a specific function; it is involved in the production of a territory, that itself operates as a platform for further deterritorialisations.
35. For a somewhat different thinking through of the notion of a 'post-medium practice' – in relation to Broodthaers and the development of ubiquitous installation art – see Rosalind Krauss' *A Voyage on the North Sea: Art in the Age of the Post-Medium Condition* (1999) (London: Thames and Hudson).
36. Again, Ronald Bogue has outlined this 'aesthetics of force' in relation to painting and music in his essay 'Gilles Deleuze: The Aesthetics of Force', in *Deleuze: A Critical Reader* (1996) (Ed. P. Patton) (Oxford: Basil Blackwell), pp. 257–69. Bogue reads Deleuze as offering an 'open system' of the arts where at stake is less a definition of art, or indeed any demarcation between the aesthetic and non-aesthetic, but rather a general function of art as that which 'harnesses forces'.
37. And these three types of 'compound sensations', or 'vibrations', are, I would argue, not just characteristic of art. In art they take the form of an apparently static 'compound of materials', but elsewhere these vibrations are faster or occur in less dense materials. All life, organic and inorganic, is 'vibrational' in this sense (as the new sciences tell us 'matter' is merely the most dense frequency).
38. To pre-empt slightly my argument of Chapter 5, we might quote the Situationists here (in this case the English section) who called for a similar approach to art. Here they are from 1958, quoted in the pamphlet *The Revolution of Modern Art and the Modern Art of Revolution* (1994) (London: Chronos Publications):

    The goal of the Situationists is immediate participation in a varied and passionate life, through moments that are both transient and consciously controlled. The value of these moments can only lie in their real effect. The Situationists see cultural activity, from the point of view of the totality, as method of experimental construction of everyday life ... *Art can stop being an interpretation of sensations and become an immediate creation of more highly evolved sensations*. [my italics] (Clarke *et al.* 1994, 10)

39. In relation to this we might note the aporia which a 'materialist' art history can come up against, and which, very briefly, goes something like this: How to attend to the material object behind the ideological veils (the cultural readings/meanings) whilst still attending to the object's history? The problem arises because ideology and history are here synonymous, both positioning art in, and as, representation. With 'The Social History of Art' for example,

the always already ideological character of art is assumed (indeed art *is* ideology). From such a perspective, a language of material and matter would be a kind of fetishisation, a haemorrhaging out of meaning, or of that trope of meaning: history. Such a 'language' of art (if it could still be called as such) would be guilty of the very ideological mystification that 'The Social History of Art' orientates itself against. It is only within a different model – a different paradigm if you like – that such a language of materials and matter makes 'sense' (and this latter paradigm will always be judged as naïve, if not reactionary, from the other).

40. Deleuze and Guattari talk about 'revolution' in the same way as they do art:

> revolutions do not survive their victory. But the success of revolutions resides only in itself, precisely in the vibrations, clinches and openings it gave to men and women at the moment of its making and that composes in itself a monument that is always in the process of becoming, like those tumuli to which each new traveller adds a stone. The victory of a revolution is immanent and consists in the new bonds it installs between people, even if these bonds last no longer than the revolution's fused materials and quickly give way to division and betrayal. (*WP* 177)

Here, in Deleuze and Guattari's discussion of revolution, we have a case study of how they differ from other 'representational' thinkers. Revolution, for Deleuze and Guattari, is to be understood as the affirmation of connectivity and becoming, of life as it is *now* and not as the desire for a 'new beginning/lost origin' with all the attendant problems and limitations.

41. See Deleuze's book on Nietzsche, and especially the final section, 'Dionysius and Zarathustra', for a discussion of the 'laughter, play and dance' that 'affirms becoming' and 'always accompanies the eternal return' (*NI* 189–94). See also Keith Ansell Pearson's compelling account, 'Towards the Overhuman: On the Art and Artifice of Nietzsche's Selection', in *Viroid Life: Perspectives on Nietzsche, and the Transhuman Condition* (1997) (London: Routledge), pp. 37–56.
42. For Michaux this 'becoming molecular' was enabled through his utilisation (amongst other practices) of mescaline:

> Mescaline multiplies, sharpens, accelerates, intensifies the inner moments of becoming conscious. You watch their extraordinary flood, mesmerized, uncomprehending. With your eyes shut, you are in the presence of an immense world. Nothing has prepared you for this. You don't recognise it. Tremendously present, active, coloured, swarming in tiny islands very close together with no empty space, teeming, vibrating but stationary, festering with ornaments, saturating the space which still remains immeasurable, which keeps coming to life in seethings, intertwinings, in unpreventable accumulations. (Michaux 1999)

43. As Deleuze suggests: 'If representation is related to an object, this relation is derived from the form of representation; if this object is the organism and organisation, it is because the form of representation is first of all organic in itself, it is because the form of representation first of all expresses the organic life of the man as subject' (*FB* 126).
44. We might note here the different kinds of 'houses' or territories built by modern art, from Tatlin's Tower to Alan Kaprow's Happenings. I return to

this notion of urbanism in Chapter 5 in relation to the foldings produced by art (and specifically the expanded architectural practices of the Situationists).

45. I shall be looking at another example of the diagram in painting – in relation to Gerhard Richter's Abstracts – in Chapter 5.
46. In contemporary electronic music we might also note the 'glitch' genre that utilises noise in this way; random 'mistakes' producing the possibility of new refrains. Jacques Attali has a similar take on noise, as that which breaks, but also creates:

    A network can be destroyed by noises that attack and transform it, if the codes in place are unable to normalise and repress them. Although the new order is not contained in the structure of the old, it is nonetheless not a product of chance. It is created by the substitution of new differences for the old differences. Noise is the source of these mutations in the structuring codes. For despite the death it contains, noise carries order within itself; it carries new information. (Attali 1985, 33)

47. Bacon's paintings are involved in the production of 'rhythmic characters' in this sense. See *FB* 65–73.
48. Deleuze explores the logic of another painter – Gerard Fromanger – in his essay 'Cold and Heat', in *Photogenic Painting* (1999) (Trans. D. Roberts) (Ed. S. Wilson) (London: Black Dog Publishing), pp. 61–77, although here it is the artist's use of a kind of *hyper* cliché that disrupts everyday reality: 'To push the copy, the copy of the copy, to the point at which it reverses itself and produces the model: Pop Art, or painting that produces a "heightened reality" ' (*CH* 65).
49. Octavio Paz has a remarkably similar take on Pollock's paintings, and is worth quoting at length:

    Painting is *like* the action of sun, water, salt, fire, or time on things. To a certain degree abstract painting and natural phenomena are an *accident*: the sudden, unforeseen intersection of two or more series of events. Many times the result is striking: these paintings are fragments of living matter, chunks sliced out of the cosmos or heated to a seething boil. Nonetheless, it is an incomplete art, as can be seen in Pollock. His great canvases have no beginning or end; despite their huge dimensions and the energy with which they are painted, they seem to be great chunks of matter rather than complete worlds. (1983, 29)

50. See Clarke, *Farewell to an Idea: Episodes from a History of Modernism* (1999) (New Haven: Yale University Press), pp. 324–6.
51. To quote Kristeva:

    Le Flacon Scent, 1955, is, together with *Search*, 1955, Pollock's last great painting. The almost joyous sensuality of the brush (this is not a 'drip' and so synthetic pigments were used) that traces the daring but controlled arabesques from which no figure emerges, leads me to see – or to feel? or to penetrate? – not a *surface*, but the intense fibrousness of an unknown and opaque substance which resists me. We might call it *matter*, and the artist's gesture, even the artist himself, is now inseparable from it. (1989, 35)

52. See Clarke, *Farewell to an Idea*, pp. 310–13.

53. For myself a case study of just such a practice is the complex and compelling assemblages made by Cathy Wilkes. See *Cathy Wilkes* (2001) (Glasgow: The Modern Institute), and also my essay on Wilkes' practice, 'Ten Concepts Following Cathy Wilkes' Practice,' *Afterall* (2005), vol. 12, 65–70.
54. See Craig Owen's seminal essay, 'The Allegorical Impulse: Towards a Theory of Postmodernism', reprinted in *The Art of Art History: A Critical Anthology*, (1989) (Ed. D. Preziosi) (Oxford: Oxford University Press), pp. 315–28. Owen's identifies an allegorical impulse in 'postmodern' art that we might characterise as involving the disruption of the aesthetic (or the *symbolic* moment). Owen's essay utilises the writings of Walter Benjamin in mapping out this allegorical impulse – understood as an attitude, or precisely mode, of *reading* ('one text is *read through* another' (316)). It is here that we encounter the specifically deconstructive attitude in which such practices 'both solicit and defer a promise of meaning' (Owens 1998, 318). For Owens allegory also names the actual internal structure as it were to much contemporary art, hence the 'allegorical impulse':

    Appropriation, site specificity, impermanence, accumulation, discursivity, hybridisation – these diverse strategies characterise much of the art of the present and distinguish it from its modernist predecessors. They also form a whole when seen in relation to allegory, suggesting that postmodernist art may in fact be identified by a single, coherent impulse. (Owens 1998, 321)

    In a passage in *The Fold* Deleuze also attends to Benjamin's notion of allegory, although it is understood less as a mechanism of deferral and more as the multiplicity of different 'points of view' (*F* 125–7).
55. See my essay, 'The New Moderns?', *The Showroom Annual* (2005b) (London: The Showroom Gallery), pp. 45–61, in which I explore this utilisation of previous art, specifically modern forms, within contemporary art practice. Nicolas Bourriaud in *Postproduction* (2002) (Trans. J. Herman) (Ed. C. Schneider) (New York: Lukas and Steinberg), also attends to contemporary art's utilisation of previous art – and indeed other cultural forms (often more popular cultures). Hence the 'twin figures of the DJ and the programmer' are characteristic of our age, 'both of whom have the task of selecting cultural objects and inserting them into new contexts' (Bourriaud 2002, 6). We move here to a paradigm of *montage* and *détournement*: artists become archivists, and the exhibition, as much as the studio (or indeed any other site) becomes a site of production. At stake here, as Bourriaud points out, is also the blurring of the distinction between artist and spectator ('These artists who insert their work into that of others contribute to the eradication of the traditional distinction between production and consumption, creation and copy, readymade and original work' (2002, 6)). To a certain extent Bourriaud's argument returns us to the terrain of the previous chapter, in its outlining of an expanded notion of production, and inasmuch as he diagnoses on the part of contemporary artists a 'willingness to inscribe the work of art within a network of signs and significations, instead of considering it an autonomous or original form' (Bourriaud 2002, 10), hence his new name for such cultural practitioners: 'semionauts' (Bourriaud 2002, 12). We might however want to ask what has happened to the aesthetic, or the affective aspect of art, in Bourriaud's

account (where are the becomings?). We might also want to ask how these sampling and mixing practices championed by Bourriaud differ from the sampling and mixing practices offered by consumer culture (here Deleuze and Guattari's notion of style is crucial).

3 Art and the Political

1. As Hardt and Negri themselves remark in a footnote to the Preface of *Empire*: 'Two interdisciplinary texts served as models for us throughout the writing of this book: Marx's *Capital* and Deleuze and Guattari's *A Thousand Plateaus*' (*E* 415, n4).
2. We might also think about 'mythic language' as involving the production of 'possible worlds'. Depending on their trajectory these mythic reterritorialisations might be transcendent or specifically immanent in character. I will be returning to this in my conclusion.
3. This 'community-effect' can also be understood as a becoming autonomous. As Deleuze and Guattari remark elsewhere:

   Becoming Minoritarian as the universal figure of consciousness is called autonomy. It is certainly not by using a minor language as dialect, by regionalising or ghettoising, that one becomes revolutionary: rather by using a number of minority elements, by connecting, conjugating them, one invents a specific, unforeseen, autonomous becoming. (*LMM* 151)

4. In the plateau 'November 20, 1923: Postulates of Linguistics' Deleuze and Guattari refer to minorities as 'crystals of becoming' that precisely trigger 'uncontrollable movements' (*ATP* 106).
5. To take just two examples in relation to art history, we have Griselda Pollock's feminist critique of T. J. Clarke's own critical attitude towards modernist critics such as Michael Fried (see Pollock, 'The "View from Elsewhere": Extracts from a Semi-public Correspondence about the Visibility of Desire', in *Twelve Views of Manet's Bar* (1993) (Ed. B.R. Collins) (New Jersey: Princeton University Press), pp. 278–315) and we have Irit Rogoff's 'deterritorialisation' of typical feminist art histories in her turn to post colonial subjectivities and practices (see Rogoff, *Terra Infirma: Geography's Visual Cultures* (2000) (London: Routledge).
6. For example, Paul Wood's essay 'Truth and Beauty: The Ruined Abstraction of Gerhard Richter', in *Art has No History: The Making and Unmaking of Modern Art* (1994) (Ed. J. Roberts) (London: Verso), pp. 180–99, calling for a return to the aesthetic as a strategy for moving beyond the impasses of postmodern theory. As Wood remarks: 'When management comes to conceive of itself as radical, extreme and paradoxical counter-strategies may be required' (1994, 91).
7. And in which case we might make the argument that *The Communist Manifesto* is an exemplar of minor literature.
8. Francis Bacon, at least as Deleuze portrays him, would be a specifically minor painter in this sense. See especially the chapter on 'The Diagram' in *Francis Bacon: The Logic of Sensation* (2003) (Trans. D. W. Smith) (London: Continuum), and especially pp. 99–110. See also the second section of my Chapter 2.
9. Hirschorn's Bataille monument was a kind of 'self-producing community site' involving the use of a whole variety of non-artistic materials and the

involvement of the inhabitants of the housing scheme in whose public area the monument was built. See Fietzek (Ed.) *Documenta XI: The Catalogue* (2002) (London: Art Books International), pp. 334–7.

10. A case study of such an affirmative violence is the practice of the London based art collective *Bank*. *Bank*, as part of their practice, curated a series of open and anarchic group shows occupying disused and derelict spaces. They also produced papers and proclamations intended specifically to poke fun at, and provoke, the art establishment, to show up its pretensions and affectations (a certain indifference to the art world was crucial here). It is also worth remarking that *Bank* were as much a scene as a collaboration, a scene involving a certain dynamic, a kind of energetics, as opposed to anything specifically concrete (and thus inevitably in opposition and irreducible to any institutional framing). Thanks to Robert Garnett for his conversations on *Bank*. For more on *Bank* see their catalogue, *Bank* (2000) (London: Black Dog Publications).
11. For details of *Superflex*'s practice see their website at www.superflex.net. *Superflex* talk about their socially and economically engaged practice in an interview with Åsa Nacking. See Nacking, 'Interview with Superflex', *Afterall* (1999), O, 52–61. *n55*'s website is at www.n55.dk.
12. A case study of the latter is the art collective *COUM Transmissions*. *COUM* involved themselves in the production of new types of subjectivity through performances, through exploring the limits and possibilities of 'acceptable' sexuality, through experimenting with collective living, and through generally being involved in processes and practices outside the mainstream. Indeed, *COUM* were involved in what we might call the exploration of *ludic* practice and in the possibilities of improvisation that this implies. We might add that a group such as *COUM* found themselves inevitably and constantly at odds with the state machine, whether it be in a soft form (the difficulty of securing funding grants, exhibition spaces and so on), or in a harder one (arrests and general harassment by the police). *Throbbing Gristle*, the band that emerged from *COUM*, expanded the accessibility of the group's activities, their 'music' reaching a far wider audience than performance art ever could. It also extended their critique of 'art' to the music industry. In relation to this, we might note *Throbbing Gristle*'s interest in noise as a form of 'warfare', as precisely counteracting the functioning of 'order-words'. See Simon Ford's book, *Wreckers of Civilisation: The Story of COUM Transmissions and Throbbing Gristle* (2000) (London: Black Dog Publications).
13. It is interesting to note in this context that artistic collaborations, in the 1970s and 1980s, often involved bands: Art and Language collaborating with *Red Crayola* for example, or as was mentioned above, *COUM Transmissions* morphing into *Throbbing Gristle*.
14. Dance music would be a particularly good example of 'becoming minor', involving as it does the neutralisation of sense, the foregrounding of the intensive and affective (a becoming music) and also the production of new communities (club culture). Indeed, the real indicator of dance music's status as minor comes from the state's attitude towards it when the former is in its most deterritorialised form: the illegal raves of the 1980s, the free party sound systems of the 1990s. Both of these might be understood as Deleuzian 'war machines'. See later in the chapter and also Hemment, 'E is for Ekstasis', *New Formations* (1997), 31, 23–38.

15. We might note that such collectivities often involve a particular idiosyncratic language and style of communication. We might also note here the way in which jokes and humour can often be involved in the formation of a community in this sense.
16. The collective and expanded practice of *Atelier Van Lieshout* for example, which in 1991 involved the production of a whole alternative settlement, or 'free state', in Rotterdam ('AVL-ville'). For details of *Atelier van Lieshout*'s expanded practice see the website: www.ateliervanlieshout.com. The group *Transnational Republic* (www.transnationalrepublic.org) have a similar, if less 'realised' utopian aspect. For a whole selection of practices involved in this area see the 'Utopia Station' exhibition at the 50th Venice Biennale (Bonami and Frisa, 'Utopia Station', *Dreams and Conflicts: The Dictatorship of the Viewer* (*50th Venice Biennale*) (2003) (Venice: Marsillo), pp. 319–415). We might extend this notion of artistic community further to include the production of artistic *scenes*. In the UK for example there was the *yba* 'phenomena' in London, or the various scenes that emerged in Glasgow in the 1990s. In all these cases a kind of 'ambient creativity' and an all-important 'self-referentiality' is produced through a complexity of factors, which include a relative isolation (on the *yba*'s – and the 'Glasgow scene' – see Michael Bracewell's 'New Image Glasgow to Young British Art: Introducing the 1990s', *New Formations* (2003), no. 50, 22–7. For the generation of Scottish artists – and their 'scene' – after this moment see Neil Mulholland's 'Learning from Glasvegas: Scottish Art after "the 90" ', *Journal of the Scottish Society for Aesthetics* (2002), vol. 7, 61–9. For a social history of both these moments (in Glasgow) see Sarah Lowndes' *Social Sculpture: Art, Performance and Music in Glasgow: A Social History of Independent Practice, Exhibitions and Events since 1971* (2003) (Glasgow: Stopstop).
17. A case study of this might be the utilisation of the 'collective name' within art practice – and wider culture in general. For example the use of the name 'Monty Cantor' or 'Luther Blissett'. This also has political implications: any individual can operate as Luther Blissett, thus plugging into any operational benefits that the name has assumed. Thanks to Jim Backhouse, and his unpublished manuscript, 'The Invisible Insurrection of a Million Minds: Networking and Cultural Resistance from *The Sigma Project* to *Luther Blissett*' (2004), Goldsmiths College, University of London, for this point. Backhouse also alerts us to the political implications of the Luther Blissett project understood as a kind of counter mythology:

    Mythopoesis is a literary term for the exploration of myth as a social process, and the constitution of myth into social reality is 'central' to the Luther Blissett project. Luther Blissett enacts information warfare against the dominant myths that underwrite the concrete power of capital. By disseminating transformative counter-mythologies, articulated in the appropriate rhetoric, capitalist institutions can be seduced into acting as replication-machines distributing semiotic viruses into the collective imagination. (Backhouse 2004)

    I will be returning to a notion of mythopoeisis in my conclusion.
18. We might note here the similarities with Hardt and Negri's reading of Spinoza in *Empire*: 'Perhaps we need to reinvent the notion of the materialist teleology that Spinoza proclaimed at the dawn of modernity when he

claimed that *the prophet produces its own people'* [my italics] (*E* 65). Hardt and Negri also make an interesting distinction between the people and the multitude, the former in fact being a 'representation' of the latter, who are then represented in the nation, itself represented in the state (*E* 34). 'Representation in each case means a further step of abstraction and control' (*E* 34).

19. To take just two examples of this 'future orientation' from the field of contemporary art: Mike Nelson, whose work we might say stages, and indeed relies on, a missing people (see especially *The Amnesiacs* art work in Nelson, *Extinction Beckons* (2000) (London: Matt's Gallery)); and Cathy Wilkes, whose work seems precisely to call an audience into being inasmuch as it seems to contain a 'language' albeit one that it is difficult to 'read' (see Chapter 2, note 53). See also my 'Conclusion' that makes an argument for Matthew Barney's myth-making films as future orientated.
20. This is to reinstate the imagination as crucial to the working of art. It is in this sense that I ultimately part company with Nicolas Bourriaud's 'relational aesthetics', inasmuch as he differentiates and champions the latter, to do with 'the realm of human interactions and its social context' over the 'assertion of an independent and *private* symbolic space' (Bourriaud 1998,14). I do not see the two as mutually exclusive, and indeed one might argue that the latter is intrinsic to any effective art practice. In fact for Deleuze, as we shall see in Chapter 6, art might be characterised as precisely the assertion, or rather *expression*, of an independent and private symbolic space, that is to say, the production of a 'possible world'.
21. It is this that gives minor practices a certain lightness. An example of this kind of oblique practice is Francis Alÿs' walking projects, for example *Narcotourism*, in which the artist spent a number of days wandering city streets under the influence of different drugs. See Alÿs' *Walking Distance from the Studio* (2005) (Ostfildern: Hatje Cantz Publishers) for an account of this and Alÿs' other 'walking' practices.
22. See the section 'Two Europes, Two Modernities' (*E* 69–90).
23. For an interesting counter-argument to this, and from the same historical moment as Negri, see Paolo Virno's *A Grammar of the Multitude* (2004) (Trans. I. Bertoletti, J. Cascaito and A. Casson) (New York: Semiotext(e)). As Sylveire Lotringer remarks in his foreword to the above (pp. 7–19), Virno's notion is that capitalism is revolutionary in and of itself, hence producing a kind of communism (the 'Communism of Capital') (2004, 11). In fact, Virno's position is, as Lotringer also remarks, close to Deleuze and Guattari's own position on capitalism as 'fluid, inventive and adaptive' (2004, 11). Indeed, the question here becomes one of 'beating capital at its own game', 'decoding its flows even further, or constantly displacing oneself in relation to them' (Lotringer 2004, 11–12). We might say that creative practices are involved in exactly this latter strategy.
24. I am thinking here of Bergson's gap, or hesitation, between stimulus and reaction which in itself allows creativity to arise. See Bergson's *Matter and Memory*, and especially chapter 3 'On the Survival of Images' (*MM* 133–77). See also my Chapter 4.
25. It is in this sense, paradoxically, that the minor does not necessarily denote the *weaker*, or rather it is the minor's apparent weakness – its flexibility,

fluidity, openness – as well as its ontological prior status (to that of the major) that makes it always a *force* that must be controlled by the major.

26. Alain Badiou, in his paper presented at the *Return(s) to Marx* Conference (2002), London, Tate Modern Gallery. In fact Hardt and Negri have a slightly different take on this point. They 'understand the concept "proletariat" ' as referring 'not just to the industrial working class but to all those who are subordinated to, exploited by, and produce under the rule of capital' (*E* 256). That is to say the proletariat is less a people-to-come than the state of those already here.
27. As Spinoza remarks in 'A Political Treatise', *Works of Spinoza: Volume One* (1951) (Trans. R.H.M. Elwes) (New York: Dover Publications): 'If two come together and unite their strength, they have jointly more power, and consequently more right over nature than both of them separately, and the more there are that have so joined in alliance, the more right they all collectively will possess' (1951, 296). For Negri's own take on Spinoza, that at least in part theoretically underpins his collaboration with Hardt, see *The Savage Anomaly: Power of Spinoza's Metaphysics and Politics* (1991) (Trans. M. Hardt) (Minneapolis: University of Minnesota Press), and the more recent collection of essays *Subversive Spinoza: (Un)contemporary Variations* (2004a) (Ed. T. S. Murphy) (Manchester: Manchester University Press).
28. Interestingly, and perhaps surprisingly, right at the end of *Empire* we get another manifesto of affirmation and friendship in the figure of St Francis of Assisi. This was an individual who discovered 'the ontological power of a new society' by 'adopting the common condition', who refused the 'instrumental discipline' of a 'nascent capitalism', instead celebrating a joyous life based on friendship and on a '*community* of friendships which includes all beings' (*E* 412). We might say then that this friendship is to be understood as operating between men, but also with the world in general. It is here, as perhaps Guattari would say, that politics joins hands with ecology.
29. Another way of thinking this immanent formation is as a community of Giorgio Agamben's 'whatever singularities', the latter understood as those beings 'devoid of any representable identity', irrelevant to, and disposable by, the state – and yet also a threat to that very same mechanism of capture (Agamben, *The Coming Community* (1993) (Trans. M. Hardt) (Minneapolis: University of Minnesota Press), p. 86.7). Such 'whatever singularities' pose a threat because they do not obey the rules of the state – even as a negative formation; they do not have transcendent coordination points (such a community is in this sense self-organising in nature). For Agamben the coming politics will be precisely a struggle between this non-State or common humanity and the State (Agamben 1993, 86.7). We might say between a state constituted by sad passions (by hatred and by guilt) and a community constituted by joy (by friendship and by self-affirmation).
30. This is as true for modern art as it is for contemporary art. Mondrian's paintings for example were intended for future subjects – or at least to call this future subject forth (see Read, *A Concise History of Modern Painting* (1974) (London: Thames and Hudson), pp. 196–203).
31. To quote Deleuze and Guattari:

    We are trying, then, to make a distinction between a paranoid, signifying, despotic regime of signs and a passional or subjective, postsignifying authoritarian regime. Authoritarian is assuredly not the same as despotic, passional is not the same as paranoid, and subjective is not the same as signifying. What happens in the second regime, with comparison with the signifying regime as we have already defined it? In the first place, *a sign or packet of signs detaches from the irradiating circular network* and sets to work on its own account, starts running a straight line, as though swept into a narrow, open passage. (*ATP* 121)

It is a people who follow this line, 'a people effectuates the assemblage that assures the relative dominance of that regime under certain historical conditions' (*ATP* 121). Deleuze and Guattari give the example of the Jews, detaching themselves from the imperial network of Egypt (the flight into the desert). Here the most 'authoritarian' of subjectivities is pitted against 'despotic signifiance' (*ATP* 122).

32. In relation to this confusion between war and the war machine, *and* between the war machine as it is popularly understood (i.e. the military-industrial complex) and war machine in the Deleuzian sense, Paul Patton has suggested another name for the latter: 'metamorphosis machine'. To quote Patton: 'The real object of Deleuze and Guattari's War machine concept is not war but the conditions of creative mutation and change' (2000, 110).
33. Nick Land addresses precisely this issue – the repression of desire – in his compelling article, 'Making it with Death: Remarks on Thanatos and Desiring-Production', *Journal of the British Society for Phenomenology* (1993), vol. 24, no. 1, 66–76. As Land says (referring to *Anti-Oedipus*):

    The revolutionary/fascist disjunction is used to discriminate between the broad tendencies of deterritorialisation and reterritorialisation: between the dissolution and reinstitution of social order. Revolutionary desire allies itself with molecular death that repels the organism, facilitating uninhibited productive flows, whilst fascist desire invests the molar death that is distributed by the signifier; rigidly segmenting the production process according to the borders of transcendent identities. (1993, 72)

34. In what follows I am attending to the first generation RAF, specifically the grouping of Andreas Baader, Ulrike Meinhof, Gudrun Ensslin, Horst Mahler and Jan Karl Raspe. For an exhaustive account of this moment see Stefan Aust's *The Baader-Meinhof Group: The Inside Story of a Phenomenon* (1987) (Trans. A. Bell) (London: The Bodley Head). Two alternative histories, each at either end of the political spectrum (and ten years apart), are Jillian Becker's *Hitler's Children: The Story of the Baader-Meinhof Gang* (1978) (London: Panther Books), and Tom Vague's *Televisionaries: The Red Army Faction Story 1963–1993* (1994) (Edinburgh: AK Press).
35. Capitalism–imperialism also 'produced' the RAF in the sense that it produced the conditions for the latter's emergence in the form of a subjectivity 'brain washed through the media, consumerism, physical punishment and the ideology of non-violence', suffering from 'depression, sickness, declassification, insult and humiliation' (Meinhof 2001b, 276). Capitalism had produced an exploited third world but also an alienated 'metropole individual': 'He or she comes from the process of decay, the false, alienated surroundings of living in the system – factory, office, school, university, revisionist group, apprenticeship and temporary jobs' (Meinhof 2001b, 275). In such a situation the Westerner is doomed, as Debord might say, to be a spectator on his or her

own life. Hence, according to Meinhof, the 'shock' of the RAF's first action, which was nothing other than the shock of people acting 'without being determined by the pressure of the system, without seeing themselves with the eyes of the media, without fear' (Meinhof 2001b, 278).

36. Irit Rogoff has written an essay, 'Engendering Terror', in *Geography and the Politics of Mobility* (2003) (Ed. U. Bieman) (Wien: Generali Foundation), pp. 48–63, that attempts a similar recuperation, or rereading, of the RAF, albeit from a different direction. Rogoff's argument is that so-called terror groups (the RAF included) might constitute an alternative, or counter cartography to that of nation states. Rogoff terms this new kind of mapping, that occurs throughout time and space (the linking of European groups with African liberation movements), 'relational geography': 'we have a map that is composed of aggregates of intensities, of insurgences that link and empathise and spark off each other' (Rogoff 2003, 56).
37. For a vivid display of this 'use' of language by the RAF see the film *Stammheim: the Trial of the RAF* (1985) directed by R. Hauff, distributed by Bioskop.
38. Guattari in fact wrote on the actions of the RAF as a mirror-image of the very thing they fought against, albeit for Guattari this was their failing: 'the altogether absurd confrontation between a monstrous state-power and pitiful politico-military machines' (Guattari, *Soft Subversions* (1996) (Trans. D.L. Sweet and C. Wiener) (New York: Semiotext (e)), p. 187). Indeed, Guattari felt the actions, especially of the later RAF, were misguided – mimicking and reproducing the very structures of domination they sort to attack:

    the real drama is not that a man was killed [the assassination of Schleyer], but that these actions were conducted in a way that simply does not break free of the repressive bourgeois system, fascist assassinations, or kidnappings carried out by unofficial police gangs, and that in the final account, their only result will have been to echo the collective melancholy that has present-day Germany in its grip. (*SS* 185)

    For Guattari this was especially the case with the RAF's attempted 'use' of the media, specifically the dissemination of images of Schleyer with placards across his chest announcing his capture ('To Claim to lead a revolutionary movement without attacking these phenomena of mass manipulation is an absurdity' (*SS* 185)). Guattari's critique is then that the particular axis of violence and the media which was one of the key tropes of the RAF was also a key trope of that which they attacked:

    Like it or not, in today's world, violence and the media work hand in glove. And when a revolutionary group plays the game of the most reactive media, the game of collective guilt, then it has been mistaken: mistaken in its targets, mistaken in its method, mistaken in its strategy, mistaken in its theory, mistaken in its dreams. (*SS* 186)

    We might note that for Guattari revolution must involve a break with any and all of these systems of repression, hence Guattari's thesis on the production of subjectivity. At stake here is the theorisation of the war machine and whether a guerrilla cell such as the RAF was a war machine, whether it contained, or connected with a war machine, or merely operated, as Guattari argues, as a mini state machine (was, if you like, the formation of a state machine from within a war machine).

39. To quote from an RAF communiqué in 1972 (quoted in *In Love With Terror* (2000) directed by B. Lewis, produced by A–C Schröder, distributed by BBC/Mentorn): 'The American Air Force has dropped more bombs on Vietnam in the last seven weeks than they have dropped on Germany and Japan combined during the whole of world war two. That is the final solution. That is Auschwitz'.
40. As Gudrun Ensslin remarked in 1967 following the police shooting of Benno Ohnesorg during a Berlin demonstration:

    They will kill us all. You know what kinds of Pigs we're up against. This is the generation of Auschwitz we've got against us. You can't argue with people who made Auschwitz. They have weapons and we haven't. We must arm ourselves. (quoted in *In Love With Terror* (2000))

41. This is Walter Benjamin's divine violence (law destroying) that opposes itself to the mythical violence (law making) of the state. Benjamin's example is the proletarian general strike over and above the political strike, which is to say revolution as not a mean to ends but as an end in itself. See Walter Benjamin's 'Critique of Violence', in *One Way Street* (1997b) (Trans. E. Jephcott and K. Shorter) (London: Verso), pp. 132–54.
42. Alain Badiou makes a similar point about fraternity and violence in a recent article, 'Seven Variations of the Century', *Parallax* (2003), vol. 9, no. 27, 72–80:

    fraternity is the real manifestation of the new world, and thus of the new man. What is experimented – in the Party, in action, in the subversive artistic group, in the egalitarian couple – is the real violence of fraternity. And what is the content of this fraternity, if not the acceptance that the infinite 'we' prevails over the finitude of the individual? This is what is named by the word 'comrade', which today, for all intents and purposes, has fallen into disuse. My comrade is one who, like myself, is only subject by belonging to a process of truth that authorises him or her to say 'we'. (2003, 74)

43. Antonio Negri, in *Negri on Negri: Antonio Negri in Conversation with Anne Dufourmantelle* (2004b) (Trans. M.B. DeBevoise) (London: Routledge), has something similar to say when asked in interview about the Red Brigades in Italy:

    One must be careful not to think of the Red Brigades as making up the whole of the movement of the 1970s, and of this movement as a historical parenthesis, an absolutely isolated, singular, separate term; in reality, the movement was a path in life, one taken by a great many of my generation. (2004b, 31)

44. Thanks to Ola Stahl, and his '*Die Meinhof hat Alles Verraten*: Ulrike Meinhof: Memories, Forgettings, Remembrances' (2001), dissertation, University of Leeds (unpublished), for this point. Irit Rogoff also attends to the figure of Ulrike Meinhof in her essay 'Engendering Terror', where the 'enduring artistic circulation', as image, of Meinhof (as terrorist *and* woman) is explored and seen as 'an attempt at recovering an ethical and political complexity in which it is possible to entertain sympathy, rather than echo the binary opposites of terrorism versus the state' (Rogoff 2003, 52).

45. Meinhof's prison letters are especially revealing about how this isolation produced self-criticism. Meinhof ended up questioning her own relationship to Baader and Ensslin: she saw herself as 'toadying' – or 'treating them like cops' – and thus, in her words, becoming a kind of cop herself (See the film *Stammheim*, Aust 1985).
46. Hardt and Negri also attend to this joyous aspect of the militant. Indeed, for Hardt and Negri the template for the modern day 'communist' is not the 'sad, ascetic agent of the Third International whose soul was deeply permeated by Soviet state reason, the same way the will of the pope was embedded in the hearts of the knights of the Society of Jesus' (*E* 411–2), which is to say, not a *sad* communist, but rather the libratory and anti-fascist fighters of the twentieth century.
47. We might note here the mass media's general fascination with 'rebels' and 'revolutionaries'. The glamorisation of such figures, from Che Guevera through to the fictional heroes of Hollywood blockbusters, evidences a contradictory adoration and castigation of the 'outsider'. Brett Easton Ellis' novel *Glamourama* (1998) (London: Picador) explicitly stages this scenario organised as it is around characters who are models *and* terrorists. We might also note here the parallel strategy of Jillian Becker's *Hitler's Children* in which the RAF are characterised as 'gangsters' (rather than guerrilla fighters). To quote Becker: 'Outside the court and the prison, the gang continued to demand attention with acts of violence and destruction. It has the romantic, aesthetic, and even erotic fascination for many people which bandit gangs have always had – especially and predictably, though not exclusively, for the young' (1978, 17).
48. As Deleuze and Guattari remark (in relation to Heidegger): 'is there anything worse, said Nietzsche, than to find oneself facing a German when one was expecting a Greek?' (*WP* 108–9). It is in this 'grey zone and indiscernability where for a moment the combatants on the ground are confused', that 'the thinker's tired eyes mistakes one for the other – not only the German for a Greek but the fascist for a creator of existence and freedom' (*WP* 109). I will return to this point, and this quotation, in my conclusion.
49. Simon Tormey's unpublished paper, 'Difference, "Creative Power" and Contemporary Political Praxis: The Case of the *Zapatistas*', presented at the *Experimenting with Intensities: Science, Philosophy, Politics, the Arts* Conference (2004), Trent University, is a good example of this kind of project. Utilising Deleuze's *Difference and Repetition* Tormey makes a convincing argument for the Zapatistas being involved in an 'immanent' politics beyond representation.
50. And this mapping would have to attend to the relations between any guerrilla, or indeed avant-garde group, and the multitude as a whole (democracy).
51. This essay is an earlier version of 'On the Production of Subjectivity', *Chaosmosis: An Ethico-aesthetic Paradigm* (1995b), pp. 1–32. For an exhaustive account of Guattari's solo project, and an impressive bibliography of his writings, see Gary Genosko, *Felix Guattari: An Aberrant Introduction* (2002) (London: Continuum). See also Stephen J. Arnott's informative essay on Guattari which involves a transversal connection to the writings on ritual by Victor Turner (Arnott, 'Liminal Subjectivity and the Ethico-Aesthetic Paradigm of Felix Guattari' at http://limen.mi2.hr/limen1-2001/stephen_arnott.html), and also Paul Bains' exploration of the importance of Raymond Ruyer's writings for Deleuze and Guattari's ethico-aesthetic conception of subjectivity

in his essay, 'Subjectless Subjectivities', *A Shock to Thought: Expression after Deleuze and Guattari* (2002) (Ed. B. Massumi) (London: Routledge), pp. 101–16.

52. Deleuze's text is one of the appendices to *The Logic of Sense* (1990) (Trans. M. Lester and C. Stivale) (Ed. C. V. Boundas) (New York: Columbia University Press).
53. This is of course to critique Marx – or rather to critique those Marxists that insist on a crude economic determinism.
54. These being two of *The Three Ecologies* (2000) (Trans. I. Pindar and P. Sutton) (London: Athlone Press) of Guattari's last work.
55. In a sense 'The History of Art' has often involved itself in foregrounding this type of Western-centred subjectivity (namely the artist genius). To follow Guattari is not to disavow the work that has been done in decentring such artist-centred models (precisely reactionary models), indeed it might be to explore the specific production of subjectivity involved in various representations of artists – and understand how these are complicit with wider socio-political factors.
56. We might add further, along with Guattari, that with the end of the cold war the issue of subjectivity – and of the production of subjectivity – is becoming increasingly important in the West itself, as is the need to think the latter through in terms of the three ecologies of the environment, society and the psyche. Again, this is the subject of Guattari's last book, *The Three Ecologies*, in which he points out that solutions to certain global problems can only come about by addressing questions of Western lifestyle, and of creating a new *style* of living (Guattari 2000). In this, the possibility of environmental disaster or the possibility of nuclear devastation (two of the possibilities produced by capitalism), as with so many other pressing problems, are intimately tied to questions to do with the production of subjectivity.
57. Hardt and Negri also devote a significant portion of *Empire* to this issue. See the section on 'The Sociology of Immaterial Labour' (*E* 289–94).
58. This Janus faced nature of technology is nothing new. Adorno and Horkheimer, in *The Dialectic of the Enlightenment* (1979) (Trans. J. Cumming) (London: Verso), make a similar, if more extreme argument, put simply, that the advances in technology have given us the tools to ease much of the world's suffering, and yet that very technology is used precisely to inflict extreme suffering.
59. And this collectivisation of subjectivity is not just to do with external relations, but also internal ones as it were. As Guattari remarks:

    the term 'collective' should be understood here in the sense of a multiplicity that develops beyond the individual, on the side of the *socius*, as well as on this side (so to speak) of the person, that is, on the side of pre-verbal intensities that arise more from a logic of the affects than from a well-circumscribed, comprehensive logic. (*S* 196)

60. Alain Badiou attends to this rupturing quality of the event, and of a continuing fidelity to this event, in his book, *Ethics: An Essay on the Understanding of Evil* (2001) (Trans. P. Hallward) (London: Verso). For Badiou, an event is always a *supplement* to a given historical situation, and is indeed an experience that lifts the human from animal to subject (Badiou 2001, 41). As Badiou remarks:

    To be faithful to an event is to move within the situation that this event has supplemented, by *thinking* … the situation 'according to' the event. And this,

> of course – since the event was excluded by all the regular laws of the situation – compels the subject to *invent* a new way of being and acting in the situation. (2001, 42)

61. See for example Guattari's analysis of three paintings by Balthus, 'Cracks in the Street' (Trans. A. Gibault and J. Johnson), *Flash Art* (1987), 135, 82–5, in which the paintings – in their organisation and style (the mobilisation of a variety of expressive components and multiple signifying/asignifying registers) – produce what Guattari calls a 'fractalization, processualization and existential recomposition' leading to 'modalities of individual and/or collective subjectivation which stand in the way of dominant subjective formations' (*CS* 85).
62. Christopher Gray makes a similar point in relation to the Situationists:

> What was basically wrong with the SI was that it focussed exclusively on the intellectual critique of society. There was no concern whatsoever with either the emotions or the body ... What needs understanding is the state of paralysis everyone is in. Certainly all conditioning comes from society but it is anchored in the body and mind of the individual, and that is where it must be dissolved. Ultimately the problem is an *emotional*, not an intellectual one. (1989, 75)

63. Although there is not space to develop this line of enquiry here we might note that this fear can also be characterised as a fear (and hence avoidance) of death. Eugene Holland in *Deleuze and Guattari's* Anti-Oedipus*: Introduction to Schizoanalysis* (1999) (London: Routledge) attends briefly to this, in relation to capitalist development (see pp. 8–9).
64. For a more sober account of the possibilities of moving beyond typical subjectivity see the title essay of Deleuze's *Desert Islands, and Other Texts 1953–1974* (2004) (Trans. M. Taormina) (Ed. D. Lapoujade) (New York: Semiotext(e)). In this essay it is unclear to Deleuze whether Guattari's ontological curtain between people and things can ever be drawn, and indeed that any possibilities will need to mobilise more than just the individual but precisely collective imagining, or simply myth. I quote Deleuze here at length:

> To that question so dear to the old explorers – 'which creatures live on deserted islands?' – one could only answer: human beings live there already, but uncommon humans, they are absolutely separate, absolute creators, in short, an Idea of humanity, a prototype, a man who would almost be a god, a woman who would be a goddess, a great Amnesiac, a pure Artist, a consciousness of Earth and Ocean, an enormous hurricane, a beautiful witch, a statue from Easter island. There you have a human being who precedes itself. Such a creature on a desert island would be a desert island itself, insofar as it imagines and reflects itself in its first moment. A consciousness of the earth and ocean, such is the desert island, ready to begin the world anew. But since human beings, even voluntarily, are not identical to the movement that puts them on the island, they are unable to join with the *élan* that produces the island; they always encounter it from an outside, and their presence in fact spoils its desertedness. The unity of the deserted island and its inhabitant is thus not actual, only imaginary, like the idea of looking behind the curtain when one is not behind it. More importantly, it is doubtful whether the individual imagination, unaided, could rise itself up to such an admirable identity; it would require the collective imagination, what is most profound in it, i.e. rites and mythology. (*DES* 11)

4 From Geophilosophy to Geoaesthetics

1. In Chapter 2 the virtual was configured as the realm of affect. Here, as a kind of corrective, I attend more to the virtual's temporal aspect, which is to say I turn from Deleuze's Spinozism to his Bergsonism.
2. See Smithson's *Robert Smithson: Collected Writings* (1996) (Ed. J. Flam) (Berkeley: University of California Press). For an overview of Smithson's work see Hobbs, *Robert Smithson: A Retrospective View* (1983) (Duisberg: Wilhelm Lehmbruck Museum).
3. For an account of sculpture's movement beyond the gallery, as well as to its relationship to landscape and architecture (and to the variety of positions taken by artists in relation to these coordination points) see Rosalind Krauss' seminal essay 'Sculpture in the Expanded Field', reprinted in *The Art of Art History: A Critical Anthology* (1998) (Ed. D. Preziosi) (Oxford: Oxford University Press), pp. 281–98. One might argue that in attending to the structural possibilities inherent in the expanded field, i.e. giving a relational account of various practices, Krauss loses sight of each work's singularity. Her discussion of Smithson's *Spiral Jetty* would be a case in point, indeed we might say that Krauss attends to the context of the jetty – but does not actually walk along the jetty itself (Krauss 1998, 295–6).
4. In his essay 'Specific Objects', in *Art in Theory 1900–1990: An Anthology of Changing Ideas* (1992) (Ed. C. Harrison and P. Wood) (Oxford: Blackwell), pp. 809–13, Judd identifies a new direction in art characterised by a turn to 'three dimensionality' and a concomitant break with anthropomorphic shapes, or indeed any form of illusionism or representation. Indeed, Judd gives us a concise description of representation, as it 'appears' within painting:

   Except for a complete and unvaried field of colour or marks, anything spaced in a rectangle and on a plane suggests something in and on something else, something in its surround, which suggests an object or figure in its space, in which there are clearer instances of a similar world – that's the main purpose of painting. (Judd 1992, 811)

   As Smithson also remarks in his essay on 'Donald Judd', in *Robert Smithson: The Collected Writings* (1996), pp. 4–6:

   With Judd there is no confusion between the anthropomorphic and the abstract. This makes for an increased consciousness of structure, which retains a remote distance from the organic. The 'unconscious' has no place in his art. His crystalline state of mind is far removed from the organic floods of 'action painting'. He translates his concepts into artifices of fact, without any illusionistic representations. (*CW* 5)

   In terms of Chapter 2 we might see Judd's practice as involving a radical break with cliché. For Judd this meant also turning to materials that did not already contain art historical references, hence his interest in steel, plexiglass and the like. See also Robert Morris, 'Notes on Sculpture: 1–3', in *Art in Theory 1900–1990: An Anthology of Changing Ideas* (1992a) (Ed. C. Harrison and P. Wood) (Oxford: Blackwell), pp. 813–22, and 'Notes on Sculpture: 4', in *Art in Theory 1900–1990: An Anthology of Changing Ideas* (1992b) (Ed. C. Harrison and P. Wood) (Oxford: Blackwell), pp. 868–73.

5. For a more exhaustive survey of Smithson's practice see Schapiro, *Earthwards: Robert Smithson and Art after Babel* (1997) (Berkeley: University of California Press), and more recently, Reynolds, *Robert Smithson: Learning from New Jersey and Elsewhere* (2004) (Cambridge, MA: MIT Press), and Roberts, *Mirror-Travel: Robert Smithson and History* (2004) (New Haven: Yale University Press).
6. This is to simplify somewhat Adorno's notion of criticism and his own use of the categories transcendent and immanent. In fact, for Adorno both of these forms of criticism have advantages – but also drawbacks: transcendent criticism allows a vantage point 'outside' of ideology and thus the possibility of a critique of the whole but in so doing locates itself at a kind of fictitious (and utopian) Archimedean Point. It also tends towards escapism, and to sweeping (barbaric) generalisations. Immanent criticism, on the other hand, seeks to grasp the contradictions within concrete phenomena (i.e. culture). It works to reveal the contradictions between the objective idea and its pretension but as such it can overlook the general ideological character of society (it neglects to link the object back to the life processes that produced it). Ultimately, of course, it is a form of *dialectical* criticism, moving between the two 'perspectives', which Adorno advocates (see Adorno's essay 'Cultural Criticism and Society', in *Prisms* (1981) (Trans. S. Weber and S. Weber) (Cambridge, MA: MIT Press), pp. 17–34, and especially pp. 23–33). It is worth pointing out here that the notion of criticism, as Adorno deploys it, is of a fundamentally different nature to the notion of philosophy, as Deleuze and Guattari understand it. The first is critique, almost by definition, the second, again by definition, is creative and affirmative. This is not to say that one must be oblivious to the history, the 'life processes', that for example produce Deleuze and Guattari's philosophy, but it is to say that Adorno's critical operation presumes the always already ideological character of philosophy and thus can operate as a kind of trap for thought.
7. In a tantalising footnote Ernst Bloch is given as an example of a thinker of immanent utopias (*WP* 224, n12).
8. It is the same operation, or inversion, that ideology performs as mapped out in the early Marx. For example, with religion: God, who is a product of man is then abstracted out and made into that which apparently produces man (transcendence is here precisely a product, albeit *masked*, of immanence). See Lucio Colletti's 'Introduction' to Marx's *Early Writings* (1975) (London: Penguin), pp. 7–56, and especially p. 48.
9. The term 'anoriginal' is taken from Andrew Benjamin's work where it is used to give: 'original complexity an ontological foundation' (Benjamin, 'Time, Question, Fold' available at www.basilisk.com/V/virtual_deleuze_fold_112.html). As Benjamin remarks:

   The point of such an undertaking is to indicate that the complexity in question does not involve an amalgam of simples that could ever be further reduced, but rather that there is complexity *ab initio*. In order to identify this other origin the term 'anoriginal' has been used. In sum, what it seeks to name is this complex possibility. (1997, 5)

10. See Deleuze's discussion of the Stoics in *The Logic of Sense* (1990) (Trans. M. Lester and C. Stivale) (Ed. C. V. Boundas) (New York: Columbia University Press), where bodies and states of affairs (i.e. substance) are portrayed as just

one element of a larger 'ground' that includes effects and incorporeal events (*LS* 6): 'The highest term therefore is not being, but *Something (aliquid)*, insofar as it subsumes being and non-being, existence and inherence' (*LS* 7).

11. This is precisely the argument set out in Henri Focillon's *The Life Forms of Art* (1992) (Trans. C. Beecher Hogan and G. Kubler) (New York: Zone Books). Here the work of art is 'an attempt to express something that is unique, it is an affirmation of something that is whole, complete, absolute. But it is likewise an integral part of a system of highly complex relationships' (Focillon 1992, 31). Art emerges from this complexity but does not necessarily resemble these conditions. Furthermore art works back on these conditions, for example, in relation to space, Focillon points out: 'A work of art is situated in space. But it will not do to say it simply exists in space: a work of art treats space according to its own needs, defines space and even creates such space as may be necessary to it' (1992, 65).
12. This is to follow Henri Bergson's account of memory and temporality (the celebrated cone). See *MM* 150–63.
13. Jacques Derrida has a more nuanced notion of the virtual – as it pertains to the object (and specifically the art object) – however, he remains within the 'closed system' of the actual inasmuch as the virtual is understood, inevitably, as virtual discourse, which reinstates an order of logocentrism (the latter 'being' the 'closed system' *par excellence*) on even the most mute of objects:

    That is to say, these silent works are in fact already talkative, full of virtual discourses, and from that point of view the silent work becomes an even more authoritarian discourse – it becomes the very place of a word that is all the more powerful because it is silent, and that carries within it, as does an aphorism, a discursive virtuality that is infinitely authoritarian, in a sense theologically authoritarian. (Derrida quoted in Brunette and Willis 1994, 13)

14. For Bergson's major statement on this see *MM* 77–131.
15. As Deleuze remarks: 'Intuition leads us to go beyond the state of experience toward the conditions of experience. But these conditions are neither general nor abstract. They are no broader than the conditioned: they are the conditions of real experience' (*B* 27).
16. It is important to point out that Massumi's understanding of the virtual, at least in his essay 'The Autonomy of Affect', in *Deleuze: A Critical Reader* (1996) (Ed. P. Patton) (Oxford: Basil Blackwell), pp. 217–39, is that it is the realm of affect. The 'seeping edge' then is the point at which that which is immanent to experience (affect) becomes conceptualised within experience (specifically with language) (Massumi 1996, 217–39). This is not however to contradict a more Bergsonian notion of the virtual as the relation between affect and its articulation is inevitably a temporal one.
17. Massumi pursued this line of argument in a recent paper, 'Living Memory', presented at the *Life's (Re)emergence: Philosophy, Culture, and Politics* Conference (2003), Goldsmiths College, London.
18. Antonio Negri also attends to this 'edge' – which he names '*kairos*' – where invention and innovation take place:

    From this perspective, what I call *kairos* is an exemplary temporal point, because Being is opening up in time; and at each instant that it opens up it must be invented – it must invent itself. *Kairos* is just this: the moment when

> the arrow of Being is shot, the moment of opening, the invention of Being on the edge of time. We live at each instant on this margin of Being that is endlessly being constructed. (Negri 2004b, 104)

See also Negri's *Time for Revolution* (2003) (Trans. M. Mandarini) (London: Continuum) where Negri remarks: '*Kairos* is the power to observe the fullness of temporality at the moment it opens itself onto the void of being, and of seizing this opening as innovation' (2003, 158).

19. For an interesting contemporary take on Smithson's notion of crystal objects see the exhibition catalogue, Bradley, Bretton-Meyer and Webster, *My Head is on Fire but my Heart is Full of Love* (2002) (Copenhagen: Charlottenborg). The exhibition itself contained some of Smithson's objects, but also utilised Smithson's writings in the organisation of the show, which itself brought together modern and contemporary art under a thematic of 'psychedelic minimalism'.
20. See Deleuze's book on *Kant's Critical Philosophy: The Doctrine of the Faculties* (1984) (Trans. H. Tomlinson and B. Habberjam) (London: Athlone Press) for a discussion of this revolution in time (and encapsulated by Hamlet's phrase 'The time is out of joint'):

> As long as time remained on its hinges, it is subordinate to movement: it is the measure of movement, interval or number. This was the view of ancient philosophy. But time out of joint signifies the reversal of the movement-time relationship. It is now movement that is subordinate to time. Everything changes, including movement ... this is the first great Kantian reversal. (*K* vii)

21. Ilya and Emilia Kabokov are particularly attuned to this 'freezing' that Judd's sculptures perform. Here they are from 'Donald Judd', *Artists' Favourites: Act 1*, Exhibition Handout (2004), London, ICA, 5 June–23 July.

> The first time we saw the work of Donald Judd was at the Philadelphia Museum of Art in 1990. Before that we did not know much about him. Once we encountered his pieces we were instantly impressed. They had a huge impact on us. The most astonishing thing about his works was that time seemed to disappear around it. All other art objects at the time were quite ordinary by comparison, while Judd's sculptures were frozen in time or were even freezing time. The boxes appeared to be some strange, unexplainable anomaly. (2004, 11)

22. Here, for example, is Smithson writing about Science Fiction films as an important source material for artists:

> The movies give a ritual pattern to the lives of many artists, and this includes a kind of 'low-budget mysticism', which keeps them in perpetual trance. The 'blood and guts' of horror movies provides for their 'organic needs', while the 'cold steel' of Sci-Fi movies provide for their 'inorganic needs'. Serious movies are too heavy on 'values', and so are dismissed by the more perceptive artists. Such artists have X-ray eyes, and can see through all of that cloddish rubbish that passes for 'the deep and the profound' these days. (*CW* 16)

23. A case in point would be Smithson's account of a crystallography of laughter:

> Let us now define the different types of Generalised Laughter, according to the six main crystal systems: the ordinary laugh is cubic or square

(Isometric), the chuckle is a triangle or pyramid (Hexagonal), the titter is prismatic (Orthorhombric), the snicker is oblique (Monoclinic), the guffaw is asymmetric (Triclinic). To be sure this definition only scratches the surface, but I think it will do for the present. If we apply this 'ha-ha-crystal' concept to the monumental models being produced by some of the artists in the Park Place group, we might begin to understand the fourth-dimensional nature of their work. From here on in, we must not think of Laughter as a laughing matter, but rather as the 'matter-of-laughs'. (*CW* 21)

In a resonance with Deleuze, Smithson mentions Lewis Carroll and the 'grin without the cat' as an anthropomorphic example of this 'laugh-matter', or what we might call, following Smithson–Deleuze, this 'matter-event'. Smithson's point is that such a description is entirely suited to the 'New Monuments' of minimalism (*CW* 22).

24. We might compare this with what Deleuze says about time in *Cinema 2: The Time Image* (1989) (Trans. H. Tomlinson and H. Galeta) (London: Athlone Press), although here it is the crystal, rather than the mirror, that allows for 'time travel':

Time has to split at the same time as it sets itself out or unrolls itself: it splits in two dissymmetrical jets, one of which makes all the present pass on, while the other preserves all the past. Time consists of this split, and it is this, it is time, that we *see in the crystal*. The crystal-image was not time, but we see time in the crystal. We see in the crystal the perpetual foundation of time, non-chronological time, Cronos and not Chronos. This is the powerful, non-organic Life which grips the world. The visionary, the seer, is the one who sees in the crystal, and what he sees is the gushing of time as dividing in two, as splitting. (*C2* 81)

See also Massumi's 'Painting: the Voice of the Grain', in *Bracha Lichtenberg Ettinger: Art Working 1985–1999* (2000) (Amsterdam: Palais des Beaux-Arts), pp. 9–32, for an interesting utilisation of the notion of the time-crystal in relation to contemporary art, and specifically the photocopied/painted surfaces of Bracha Lichtenberg Ettinger's work:

Lichtenberg Ettinger's paintings function to preserve the evanescence of things: their always coming too early to be what they should become, and to late to remain what they would have been. Freeze-framing the too-early-and-too-late captures the image in what Deleuze would call a time-crystal. The time-crystal holds together, as accompanying facets, what in the linear unfolding of things are successive beats, the risings and fallings, in the rhythm of interweaving. (Massumi 2000, 11)

25. See my Chapter 3 for a discussion of the minor in relation to art practice.
26. It is to this notion of inorganic life that Deleuze returns in his last writings. In *Pure Immanence: Essays on a Life* (2001) (Trans. J. Rajchman) (New York: Zone Books) Deleuze gives us the example of young children – who might as yet have no, or next to no, individuality as such (they all resemble one another) – but who do have singularities: 'a smile, a gesture, a funny face – not subjective qualities. Small children, through all their sufferings and

weaknesses, are infused with an immanent life that is pure power and even bliss' (*I* 30). It is this life of immanence that runs parallel to any psychosocial notions of individuality: 'the singular life immanent to a man who no longer has a name, though he can be mistaken for no other' (*I* 29). For Deleuze this life, or 'great health', is the proper subject of literature and we might say of art also (see also Deluze's *Essays Critical and Clinical* (1998) (Trans. D. W. Smith and M. A. Greco) (London: Verso), and Daniel W. Smith's informative introductory essay, 'Introduction: "A Life of Pure Immanence": Deleuze's "Critique et Clinique" Project', pp. xi–lv.

27. For a different, more expanded take on the body without organs, understood as our bodies, but also the body of the earth and the non-organic flows that move across it and indeed constitute it, see Delanda, *A Thousand Years of Nonlinear History* (1991) (New York: Zone Books). Delanda offers a history/geology of the last one thousand years of the West in terms of these flows and their stratification:

    the flows of lava, biomas, genes, memes, norms, money (and other 'stuff') are the source of just about every stable structure that we cherish and value (or, on the contrary, that oppresses or enslaves us). We could define the BwO in terms of these unformed, destratified flows, as long as we keep in mind that what counts as destratified at any given time and in any given space is relative. (Delanda 1997, 260–1)

28. Smithson, in another essay, 'A Museum of Language in the Vicinity of Art', in *Robert Smithson: The Collected Writings* (1996), pp. 138–42, also lays out a parallel project of 'abstract cartography'. Again, there are many similarities between this project and the Deleuzoguattarian project, especially the rhizomatics mapped out in Chapter 1. In the essay Smithson notes that:

    From *Theatrum Orbis Terrarum* of Orrelius (1570) to the 'paint'-clogged maps of Jasper Johns, the map has exercised a fascination over the minds of artists. A cartography of uninhabitable places seems to be developing – complete with decoy diagrams, abstract grid systems made of stone and tape (Carl Andre and Sol le Witt), and electronic 'mosaic' photomaps from NASA ... Lewis Carroll refers to this abstract kind of cartography in his *The Hunting of the Snark* (where a map contains 'nothing') and in *Sylvie and Bruno Concluded* (where a map contains 'everything') (*CW* 92)

29. Smithson's 'theoretical' resources here, as he himself remarks elsewhere, are Freud (notions of the 'oceanic') and the Freudian psychoanalyst Anton Ehrenzweig (notions of the unconscious as 'de-differentiated') (*CW* 102). See Ehrenzweig's *The Hidden Order of Art: A Study in the Psychology of Artistic Imagination* (1993) (London: Weidenfeld). See also Lyotard's preface to the French edition, 'Beyond Representation', reprinted in *The Lyotard Reader* (1989) (Trans. J. Culler) (Ed. A. Benjamin) (Oxford: Basil Blackwell), pp. 155–68.
30. For Smithson art does not involve a wild destratification, but what we might call the development and maintenance of a 'strategic zone', a space of experimentation between the strata and the outside (in fact a place in which one might encounter the outside). See Deleuze's *Foucault* (1988b) (Trans. S. Hand) (Minneapolis: University of Minnesota Press), especially pp. 120–2.

31. Craig Owens makes a similar point in his essay 'The Allegorical Impulse: Toward a Theory of Postmodernism', reprinted in *The Art of Art History: A Critical Anthology* (1998) (Ed. D. Preziosi) (Oxford: Oxford University Press), pp. 315–28. Here he is discussing the *Spiral Jetty* in relation to allegory:

    The site-specific work often aspires to a prehistoric monumentality; Stonehenge and the Nazca lines are taken as prototypes. It's 'content' is frequently mythical, as that of the *Spiral Jetty*, whose form was derived from a local myth of a whirlpool at the bottom of the Great Salt Lake; in this way Smithson exemplifies the tendency to engage in a *reading* of the site, in terms not only of its topographical specifics but also of its psychological resonances. (1998, 318)

    Although agreeing in kind with Owen's notion of allegory in relation to Smithson, one might want to question whether *reading* is the right term for Smithson's encounter with the site. Indeed, it would seem that Smithson's response and attitude is precisely one of *not* reading.
32. The contemporary artist Moriko Mori makes a similar, albeit more poetic, point about the *Spiral Jetty*:

    Staged at the best possible location within a vast nature, the *Spiral Jetty* transcends time and space. It makes me feel the earth's life force and its power of regeneration. I was awakened by something wild, something passionate that rose from deep inside. A door to the sacred world of another dimension. A dynamic installation within nature. Liberated from the natural law of life and death, which governs all living beings, as well as the continuous series of life and death, the external and the internal merged into one. (2004, 14)

33. One might note here other 'prehistoric' monuments, such as the Nazca lines, that are made not for humans (they cannot be seen from 'on the ground') but for 'impossible beings', beings from a hidden past or a yet-to-be future.
34. See J. G. Ballard's essay 'Robert Smithson as a Cargo Cultist', in *Robert Smithson: Dead Tree* (2000) (Ed. B. Conley and J. Amrhein) (Brooklyn: Pierogi), p. 31.
35. For an account of the jetty's re-emergence, and for a record of a trip there (with photographs of the now white jetty) see S. Husband's 'Ever Decreasing Circlers', *Observer Magazine*, 25 April 2004, 22–9).
36. As Smithson remarks in his essay 'A Cinema Atopia', *Robert Smithson: The Collected Writings* (1996), pp. 138–42, echoing Deleuze's own thoughts: 'One thing all film has in common is the power to take perception elsewhere' (*CW* 138). In this essay Smithson outlines a form of geo-cinema in which 'all films would be brought into equilibrium – a vast mud field of images forever motionless' (*CW* 142). Smithson also outlines the construction of a literal geo-cinema, made in a cave or cavern, and made out of crude materials. This geo-cinema shows just one film – a record of its own construction.

5 From Possible Worlds to Future Folds

1. See the exhibition catalogue *Gerhard Richter* (1991a) (London: Tate Gallery) for a selection of these Abstracts. As with the previous chapter there is a

coincidence of dates between the art and the philosophy (the original French publication of *The Fold: Leibniz and the Baroque* (1993a) (Trans. T. Conley) (Minneapolis: University of Minnesota Press) was 1988).

2. Perhaps the most 'Deleuzian' attitude to take towards Richter would be to look at his whole body of work in much the same way as Deleuze looks at Bacon's *oeuvre* and to extract concepts from this examination. This is a task that requires a book in itself, and is one that I leave for another time.
3. The work of art can, in this sense, be understood as the 'voice' of the Other. See for example Deleuze's essay, 'The Exhausted', *Essays Critical and Clinical*, (1998) (Trans. D.W. Smith and M.A. Greco) (London: Verso), pp. 152–74, for a discussion of Beckett in relation to the idea that 'Others are *possible worlds*' (*ECC* 157). See also the end of my Chapter 4 for a discussion of what happens in a world without others (which is to say, a world *without* possible worlds) albeit discussed through the possible world of Michel Tournier's novel *Friday*.
4. It is in this sense that all painting can be understood as landscape painting. In fact all art might be said to produce landscapes in that every art work expresses its own particular possible world.
5. And not just artistic subjectivities but subjectivity in general, the latter understood as the product of a distinct world-view expressed through a particular *style* of life.
6. In Bergson's terms these two floors are precisely matter and memory, or the actual and the virtual. We might compare Deleuze–Leibniz's statement: 'On its own account each monad conveys the entire world independently of others and without influx, while every body receives the impression and influx of others, and that is the totality of bodies; that is the material universe that expresses the world' (*F* 106), with Bergson's differentiation between an image and a *represented* image:

   > Now, here is the image which I call a material object; I have the representation of it. How then does it not appear to be in itself that which it is for me? It is because, being bound up with all other images, it is continued in those which follow it, just as it prolonged those which preceded it. To transform its existence into representation, it would be enough to suppress what follows it, what precedes it, and also that which fills it, and to retain only its external crust, its superficial skin. That which distinguishes it as a present image, as an objective reality, from a image is the necessity which obliges it to act through every one of its points upon all the points of all other images, to transport the whole of what it receives, to oppose every action an equal and contrary reaction, to be, in short, merely a road by which pass, in every direction, the modifications propagated throughout the immensity of the universe. I should convert it into representation if I could isolate it, especially if I could isolate its shell. (*MM* 35–36)

   For Bergson an image/object exists in virtual connection with every other image/object, however for myself, a 'centre of indetermination', parts of this virtuality are effaced so as to allow the actual image, my particular world in Leibniz's terms, to emerge.
7. As Bergson remarks: 'The objects which surround my body reflect its possible action upon them' (*MM* 21).
8. Andrew Murphie has written well on this notion of a 'clear zone' specifically in relation to new technologies. See his 'Putting the Virtual back into VR', in

A Shock to Thought: Expression after Deleuze and Guattari (2002) (Ed. B. Massumi) (London: Routledge), pp. 188–214. To lift just one moment from the essay, Murphie points out that missile guidance systems express their own particular world in their extraction of only certain data from the world. This amounts to saying that their particular 'zone of clarity' allows them, as Murphie remarks, to operate more effectively and more destructively (2002, 189–90).

9. For a discussion of the tick's world in relation to this ethology (and to Von Uexküll) see *ATP* 257.
10. Deleuze quotes Leibniz: 'our body is a type of world full of an infinity of creatures that are also worthy of life' (*F* 109). Our bodies contain other monads, the monads of our organs, that contain still other monads, *ad infinitum*. It is the *viniculum*, a kind of sticky screen, which holds, or coheres, this stuff together. Deleuze also remarks on that third type of monad not 'caught' within the relations of dominated and dominata. These are inorganic bodies that are folded within matter much like felt (*F* 115). Deleuze also characterises these as 'defective' monads that 'await on the outside', but they can also be understood as tendencies, containing as they do their own 'inner law' or 'force' (*F* 116–17).
11. As Deleuze remarks: 'If the Baroque has been associated with capitalism, it is because the Baroque is linked to a crisis in property, a crisis that appears at once with the growth of new machines in the social field and the discovery of new living beings in the organism' (*F* 110).
12. Along what Deleuze–Leibniz calls the 'fluxion', or simply the 'line of flight' (*F* 115).
13. For Deleuze's most thorough account of this folding of subjectivity see his book on *Foucault* (1988b) (Trans. S. Hand) (Minneapolis: University of Minnesota Press), and especially pp. 94–103. Deleuze reads Foucault's later works as specifically attending to the fold of modern subjectivity (which had begun with the Greeks). We are given an illustration of this with the notion of the ship understood as nothing more than a folding of/in the sea (the inside as constituted by the folding of the outside). See also my discussion of the appendix of the *Foucault* book below.
14. For Bergson's major statement on this see chapter 3 'On the Survival of Images' in *MM* 28–32.
15. There are many slippages in Deleuze's use of the terms virtual and potential. In *The Fold* the first two often appear synonymous, nevertheless I am inclined to follow Brian Massumi's definition of potential as the 'transition state between the virtual and the actual, logically distinct from both' (See Massumi's 'Introduction: Like a Thought', in his edited collection *A Shock to Thought: Expression After Deleuze and Guattari* (2002b) (London: Routledge), pp. xiii–xxxix, especially p. xxxvi).
16. Monads, on the upper floor, are entirely enclosed and non-communicating, however it might be said that on the lower floor they are always and everywhere in a kind of communication, the latter understood as the interpenetration and interconnection of all things in the world.
17. To confuse art with that which it produces can be to substitute philosophy or politics for art. In such an operation art's specific character, its specific force, is overlooked. We might say that which is ontologically prior, as cause, is taken as effect. A consequence of this is that art history can often attend to everything but the actual workings of art (that is, to the discursive and

institutional context and implications of the art object). The event is missed in an exhaustive survey of the *scene* and *effects* of the event. In connection to this is the operation of deconstruction. Here the event, or simply the production of new forms, can never be genuinely 'new' but must 'appear' in recognisable form. Hence for Derrida the impossibility of improvisation, but the importance of still attempting this impossibility. This is a track many writers on Richter have followed: the paintings as a presentation of the unpresentable, as impossible possibles and so on. See note 24 below.

18. We might note here the connections between art, as an event, and other events (for example more explicity 'political' acts) that might likewise have an aesthetic character, which is to say rupture our world.
19. To quote Deleuze, writing on Proust: 'friendship never establishes anything but false communication, based on misunderstandings, and frames only false windows. This is why love, more lucid, makes it a principle to renounce all communication' (*P* 42).
20. Lyotard opposes this view to the one he attributes – through Vincent Descombe – to Leibniz ('It should not be said that each of these experiments is merely a subjective perspective on Being that is its single totality or its single kingdom, and that Leibniz after all expressed the truth of perspectivism in metaphysical discourse' (*LYO* 190)). As we have seen Deleuze's reading of Leibniz orientates itself against such a reading and in fact brings Leibniz much closer to Lyotard.
21. Deleuze and Guattari explicitly attend to this towards the end of the chapter on art in *What is Philosophy?*:

    Are there not as many different planes as universes, authors, or even works? In fact, universes, from one art to another as much as in one and the same art, may derive from one another, or enter into relations of capture and form constellations of universes, independently of any derivation, but also scattering themselves into nebulae of different stellar systems, in accordance with qualitative distances that are no longer those of space and time. (*WP* 196)

    Deleuze and Guattari end this paragraph on multiplicity with a comment on its relationship to the One: 'Universes are linked together or separated on their lines of flight, so that the plane may be single at the same time as universes are irreducibly multiple' (*WP* 196).
22. A number of other commentators follow this particular line of Badiou's. Peter Hallward for example, whose book, *Absolutely Postcolonial: Writing Between the Singular and the Specific* (2001) (Manchester: Manchester University Press), brings Deleuze's philosophy (and that of Spinoza and Leibniz) together with Islamic, Buddhist and avant-garde literature in mapping out a philosophy of the singular over the specific. In such a 'system', as Hallward remarks, 'modes exist as so many extended or explicated degrees of a purely implicated divine intensity' (2001, 8).
23. The famous parable from Buddhism seems apposite here: man's suffering in the world is like an arrow stuck in his side. The question of where the arrow came from is less important, indeed is in some senses irrelevant, compared with the question of how to remove it. We might also take note of the last few lines of Deleuze's study of Hume: 'Philosophy must constitute itself as

the theory of what we are doing, not as a theory of what there is. What we do has its principles; and being can only be grasped as the object of a synthetic relation with the very principles of what we do' (*H* 133).

24. Stefan Germer, for example, in his 'Retrospective Ahead', *Gerhard Richter* (1991) (London: Tate Gallery), pp. 31–9, gives an account of Richter's practice as caught in a kind of deferred longing. This is also the case, for Germer, with individual pictures. For example, Germer reads Richter's Photo Paintings as an instance of Derrida's *différance*: 'The trace left by Richter's intervention in the appearance of a pictorial given can be defined using the term "*différance*" as coined by Jacques Derrida: it deviates from an already existing meaning, whilst at the same time deferring the positing of a new meaning' (Germer 1991, 26). Germer continues:

    The unfocussed and blurred zones in the Photo Paintings thus function strategically, annulling a given content without formulating one with which to replace it. We are constantly confronted with pictures that, awkwardly enough, can only be described in negative terms: they are neither photographs nor paintings, although possessing some of the characteristics of both. The blurred zones of the Photo Paintings direct a 'stop making sense' at the viewer, who – thwarted by the lack of authorial prescription of meaning – attempts to resolve the contradictions, in order to arrive at an unequivocal interpretation. This effort is doomed to failure, as Richter's pictures do not permit resolution of this dilemma in favour of either the signifier or the signified. Content is only arrived at by means of a negation of form, form only as a negation of content: which means that the whole project of representation is called into question. (1991, 26)

    A similar reading is given to Richter's Townscapes, Colour Charts and Grey Paintings, all of which in their own way are involved in this melancholy logic of *différance*. Germer eventually arrives at the Abstracts, which again are 'read' as profoundly allegorical: 'For the Abstract paintings are defined by the difference between experience and its representation; in other words they are allegorical in nature' (Germer 1991, 31). Germer goes on:

    Richter's paintings can be understood as a form of communication that is cancelled in the very act, even though the painter's desire to communicate with his viewers via the painting persists. The melancholy character of such a production stems from a simultaneous awareness of the necessity of utopia – Richter has called painting 'the highest form of hope' – and recognition of its inaccessibility. (1991, 31)

    Other commentators have also positioned Richter's sensibility in this melancholy double bind, for example as a 'product of an endlessly idealistic, endlessly disillusioned Germany' (Ascherson 1991, 38). To a certain extent my own chapter on Richter's Abstracts is written to rescue them from this melancholy and deconstructive science (and this might well involve reading them *contra* Richter himself).

25. As we shall see Deleuze does in fact attend to a notion of allegory in *The Fold* – specifically as it is mapped out in Walter Benjamin's writings. It is not within the scope of this book to compare Deleuze's 'allegorical impulse' with those above, though what can be said is that Deleuze is interested in allegory inasmuch as it foregrounds the idea of distinct points of view on the world,

rather than the more usual (and I think negative) utilisation of allegory, developed especially from Paul de Man, as that which defers presence and foregrounds a notion of *re*presentation, albeit one in crisis.

26. Thanks to Robert Garnett for first suggesting this alternative take on Richter's Abstracts.
27. For a typical deconstruction of typical theories of artistic expression see Hal Foster's essay on 'The Expressive Fallacy', in *Recordings: Art, Spectacle, Cultural Politics* (1985) (Seattle: Bay Press), pp. 59–77.
28. Deleuze himself suggests the possibility of understanding abstract painting as a monad in which there is no longer a window to an outside but rather 'an opaque grid of information on which the ciphered line is written' (*F* 27).
29. Of course, with new, and faster, technology these worlds are increasingly being realised. The fractal worlds of the Mandelbrot set would be a case in point.
30. In the terms put forward in *A Thousand Plateaus*, we move from milieus to territories:

    [A territory] is by essence marked by 'indexes', which may be components taken from any of the milieus: materials, organic products, skin or membrane states, energy sources, action-perception condensates. There is a territory precisely when milieu components cease to be directional, becoming dimensional instead, when they cease to be functional to become expressive. (*ATP* 314–15)

31. 'And this, first of all, is what makes painting abstract: summoning forces, populating the area of plain, uniform colour with the forces it bears, making the invisible forces visible in themselves' (*WP* 181).
32. It is Harold Rosenberg who most clearly identified this move from painting a picture to painting *as* event. Here he is from 'The American Action Painters':

    At a certain moment the canvas began to appear to one American painter after another as an arena in which to act rather than a space in which to reproduce, redesign, analyse or 'express' an object, actual or imagined. What was to go on the canvas was not a picture but an event. (1970, 36)

    We might say that Richter, as a contemporary painter, is an inheritor of this tradition, although his paintings are events *and* pictures at the same time.
33. And in fact all the subsequent Abstracts require a yes/no decision in terms of deciding when they are 'finished'.
34. In the sense that every form of life is made up from a different combination of the same four elements (i.e. DNA).
35. And it is also the case that any one Abstract might express more than one world. As Sean Rainbird remarks:

    [Richter's] book *128 Details from a Picture*, made in 1978, provides further evidence of [Richter's] examining the efficacy and potential of painting as a vehicle of reality. A single abstract painting was photographed by the artist 128 times from different angles, suggesting in didactic fashion the infinite perceptual possibilities – and myriad realities – arising from each abstract painting that contains not a mimetic representation of reality, but rather an equivalent and equally convincing pictorial reality. (1991, 13)

We might note also Richter's Mirror Paintings, in which a new 'world' is pictured with each encounter (those in the Guggenheim in Bilbao for example which reflect not only the spectator but, through the extensive top windows, the different atmospheric conditions). Although this is an extreme example we might say that all of Richter's paintings (and perhaps all art?) involves this interaction with 'outside' conditions and thus makes every encounter singular.

36. Again, as Sean Rainbird remarks:

    Richter also chooses a carefully circumscribed although intrinsically flexible range of paint applications. Initially this involved using dry or wet brushes of different widths and stiffness. Latterly he has also used long spatulas with straight though flexible edges to distribute paint in sweeping movements of the arm and upper body. (1991, 20)

    Rainbird continues with a musical analogy: 'If canvas, brushes and spatulas might find a parallel with the score and system of notation in music, then colour is what determines the quality of what in music would be touch, timbre, tone and register' (1991, 20).
37. Every painter has his or her particular technique of 'applying paint to canvas' in this sense. We might note here Jackson Pollock's 'drip' technique, Helen Frankenthaler's 'staining' or, more recently, the routing of a layered surface achieved by power tools in the 'paintings' of DJ Simpson (for a selection of the latter's work see Riese, *New Abstract Painting Painting Abstract Now* (2003) (Leverkusen: Museum Morsbroich).
38. Modern art is that which specifically tends towards this second type of painting (Deleuze and Guattari mention Seurat, Mondrian, and Dubuffet) (*WP* 194). It is in this sense that Richter might be understood as a specifically modern painter. As Deleuze and Guattari remark, literature and music also oscillate between their own two poles, which is to say their history is also a history of the relationship between the technical and aesthetic planes of composition (*WP* 195).
39. A published list of all Richter's works since 1962.
40. Andrew Benjamin attends to these two types of repetition in his collection of essays *Object Painting* (1994) (London: Academy Editions). To simplify somewhat, representation, for Benjamin, is the repetition of the simple and of a content that is always already predetermined. This is opposed to a repetition 'in terms of an ontology and temporality of becoming' (Benjamin 1994, 24). As Benjamin remarks: 'Becoming is the ontology proper to the art object since it is only in terms of becoming that it is possible for the work to work' (1994, 24). Benjamin's subsequent essays are concerned with precisely what this 'work' might entail as regards different objects. Importantly, Benjamin calls attention to the way in which this second type of repetition 'overcomes the work of the negative' by allowing for a present in which the repetition of the same gives way to other possibilities' (Benjamin 1994, 11).
41. We might say that the modern city is also involved in this repetition, which is to say the various modernities the world over (Asia's modernity, Africa's modernity, etc.) are not *representations* of an originary European modernity but *repetitions* of the modern.
42. In connection to this, and in the field of contemporary art, we might note Jeremy Deller's *The Battle of Orgreave*, a restaging of the British miner's

original 'battle' with the police in 1984, and which ended up as not just a representation of the original Strike battle, but in fact as a kind of repetition of that event.

43. As demonstrated by Richter's decision to destroy all works before 1962 and to number subsequent works from this 'beginning'.
44. The paintings might however be thought of as 'rhythmic characters' as Deleuze calls them in his book on Francis Bacon:

    Rhythm would cease to be attached to and dependent on a Figure: *it is rhythm itself that would become the figure, that would constitute the Figure*. This is exactly what Oliver Messiaen said about music when he distinguished between active rhythm, passive rhythm, and attendant rhythm, and demonstrated that they no longer referred to characters that have rhythm, but themselves constitute rhythmic characters. (*B* 71–2)

45. To quote Richter:

    Accept that I can plan nothing. Any consideration that I make about the 'construction' of a picture is false and if the execution is successful then it is only because I partially destroy it or because it works anyway, because it is not disturbing and looks as though it is not planned. Accepting this is often intolerable and also impossible, because as a thinking, planning human being it humiliates me to find that I am powerless to that extent, making me doubt my competence and any constructive ability. The only consolation is that I can tell myself that despite all this I *made* the pictures even when they take the law into their own hands, do what they like with me although I don't want them to, and simply come into being somehow. (*RIC* 123)

    Richter is addressing the complex relation between intention and non-intention here. We might productively compare this with Deleuze–Leibniz's difficult notion of causality. For the latter causality is a fiction inasmuch as the two floors, of matter and of the soul, are distinct. However 'ideal causes' do operate as when we attribute to something occurring within the soul (e.g. pain) a physical cause, or to something happening 'in the world' (e.g. voluntary movement) an immaterial cause. It is this 'ideal cause' that operates as the fold between the two regimes, or two floors, of the Baroque house. Thus, the 'consolation' for Richter that he *made* the paintings, even though he did not *intend* or necessarily control their particular character.
46. As Richter remarks: 'My method or my expectation which, so to speak, drives me to painting, is opposition ... Just that something will emerge that is unknown to me, which I could not plan, which is better, cleverer, than I am' (1992, 1042). The same is true for Deleuze's Bacon who explicitly paints against cliché understood as figuration and narrative (and specifically as incarnated in the photograph) (see *FB* 87–92, and my Chapter 2).
47. The found photograph works to evacuate Richter's subjectivity. At the same time Richter *requires* the photograph as a ground or starting point from which to make the painting. Hence the importance of Richter's archive of images (as seen in the exhibition/catalogue *Gerhard Richter: Atlas* (2003) (London: Whitechapel)).
48. It is in this sense that Kant's aesthetic, and especially the notion of a 'disinterested' response to art, continues to be important in thinking about the rupturing and transformative force of contemporary art.

49. For example, the 'Happening' as outlined by Allan Kaprow in his 1960 essay 'Assemblages, Environments and Happenings', reprinted in *Art in Theory 1900–1990: An Anthology of Changing Ideas* (1992) (Ed. C. Harrison and P. Wood) (Oxford: Blackwell), pp. 703–9. To quote Kaprow

> A critical turning point has been reached in a major area of avant-garde effort, which I believe is entirely to the good but which is forcing upon us the possibly disagreeable task of revising some cherished assumptions regarding the nature of the plastic arts. Certain advanced works being done at this moment are rapidly losing their traditional identities and something else, quite far-reaching in its implications is taking their place. (1991, 703)

For Kaprow this new kind of art involves breaking with those 'conditions set down by the structure of the house', and the concomitant development of an expanded notion of art (Kaprow 1991, 704). Kaprow gives a series of rubrics for this kind of art, all of which are relevant to Deleuze's definition of performance. They are:

> A *The line between art and life should be kept as fluid, and perhaps indistinct, as possible* ... B *Therefore, the source of themes, materials, actions, and the relationships between them are to be derived from any place or period* except *from the arts, their derivatives, and their milieu* ... C *The performance of a Happening should take place over several widely spaced, sometimes moving and changing locales* ... D *Time, which follows closely on space considerations, should be variable and discontinuous* ... E *Happenings should be performed once only* ... F *It follows that audiences should be eliminated entirely.* (Kaprow 1991,706–8)

See also Carolee Schneeman's 'from The Notebooks', in *More than Meat Joy: Performance Works and Selected Writings*, (1997) (Ed. B. R. McPherson) (Kingston: McPherson and Co), pp. 9–19, where performance (or a performance *work*) is defined as: 'an extension of the formal-metaphorical activity possible within a painting or construction', and thus one in which the audience is offered different 'potentialities for sensate involvement' (Schneeman 1979, 9).

50. In interview Deleuze develops this line of argument further:

> The minimalist art of Tony Smith presents us with the following situation: a car speeding along a dark motorway lit only by the car's headlamps, with the tarmac hurtling by in the windscreen. It's a modern version of the monad, with the windscreen playing the part of a small illuminated area ... The move towards replacing the system of a window and a world outside with one of a computer screen in a closed room is something that's taking place in our social life: we read the world more than we see it. (*N* 157–8)

We might add, and as I argue later in this chapter, that with the World Wide Web we are witnessing the opening up of this closed monad into an expanded Baroque, or nomadology.

51. Guy Debord gives us a similar definition of 'unitary urbanism' as that which:

> is defined first of all by the use of the ensemble of arts and technics as means contributing to an integral composition of the milieu. This ensemble must be envisaged as infinitely more far-reaching than the old domination of architecture over the traditional arts ... Unitary urbanism must, for example,

dominate the acoustic environment as well as the distribution of different varieties of food and drink. It must include the creation of new forms and the *détournement* of previous forms of architecture, urbanism, poetry and cinema ... The most elementary unit of unitary urbanism is not the house, but the architectural complex. (Debord 1989, 26)

52. It is in this sense that the Situationists are very much the inheritors of a Surrealist attitude. To quote from the English Section of the former:

    [The Surrealists] saw quite rightly, that the most vital role a revolutionary avant-garde could play was to create a *coherent group experimenting with a new life-style,* drawing on new techniques, which were simultaneously self-expressive and socially disruptive, of extending the perimeters of lived experience. Art was a series of free experiments in the construction of a new libertarian order. (Clarke *et al.* 1994, 6)

53. Guattari makes a similar call for 'a new urban planning' in his essay 'Space and Corporeality: Nomads, Cities, Drawings', in *Semiotext(e)/Architecture* (1992) (Trans. H. Zeitland and H. Zeitland) (Ed. H. Zeitland) (New York: Semiotext(e)), pp. 18G1–25G8, although for Guattari this is a project that can, and must, begin in the present: 'In fact, the means to change life and to create a new style of activity, new social values are within our reach. Only the desire and the public will to carry out such transformations is lacking' (*SC* 120G3).
54. In fact, we might say more accurately that Walter Benjamin's *flâneur* is often *moving towards* an open monad (for example, in the use of hashish). Benjamin's Charles Baudelaire too has moments of interconnectivity. Here is Benjamin quoting the latter, in relation to new technologies:

    Moving through this traffic involves the individual in a series of shocks and collisions. At dangerous crossings, nervous impulses flow through him in rapid succession, like the energy from a battery. Baudelaire speaks of a man who plunges into the crowd as into a reservoir of electric energy. Circumscribing the experience of shock, he calls this man 'a *kaleidoscope* equipped with consciousness.' (1974, 133)

    Indeed, Baudelaire/Benjamin's *flâneur* is more involved in a joyous affirmation of the city than in the distance and revulsion characterised by Friedrich Engels (and to a lesser extent Edgar Allan Poe), although in each of these writers the encounter is still privileged. We might say in fact that *Flâneurie* here is the art of encountering different worlds.
55. Although we must also note that the city can produce alienated subjectivities, or 'closed in' monads. Hence the 'blasé' attitude of the city dweller that Georg Simmel refers to, and which we can still see in today's cities:

    The blasé attitude results first from the rapidly changing and closely compressed contrasting stimulation of the nerves ... A life in boundless pursuit of pleasure makes one blasé because it agitates the nerves to their strongest reactivity for such a long time that they finally cease to react at all ... This psychological source of metropolitan blasé attitude is joined by another source which flows from the money economy. The essence of the blasé attitude consists in the blunting of discrimination. (Simmel 1992,132)

56. In *A Thousand Plateaus* the city, however striated, is likewise characterised as a site of deterritorialisation:

> Must we not say the same of the city itself? In contrast to the sea, the city is the striated space par excellence; the sea is a smooth space fundamentally open to striation, and the city is the force of striation that reinparts smooth space, puts it back into operation everywhere, on earth and in other elements, outside, but also inside itself. The smooth spaces arising from the city are not only those of world-wide organisation, but also of counterattack combining the smooth and the holey and turning back against the town: sprawling, temporary, shifting shanty towns of nomads and cave dwellers, scrap metal and fabric, patchwork, to which the striations of money, work, or housing are no longer even relevant. (*ATP* 481)

In *What is Philosophy?* a notion of the city is developed further and is characterised as the very precondition of philosophy, understood as a form of creative deterritorialisation: 'It is in this first aspect that philosophy seems to be something Greek and coincides with the contribution of cities: the formation of societies of friends or equals but also the promotion of relationships of rivalry between and within them ...' (*WP* 4). For Deleuze and Guattari the city, in both books, involves the production of a territory on the deterritorialised earth, which then operates as a site for new relative deterritorialisations (hence capitalism) and absolute deterritorialisations (hence philosophy) (see especially the section on 'Geophilosophy' in *WP* 85–113).

57. Constant's 'New Babylon' project is a realisation, of sorts, of Chtcheglov's formulations, or, returning to Deleuze–Leibniz, it is certainly an actualisation of a set of virtualities and a realisation at least on one level, although it remains unrealised on another. Here is Peter Wollen writing on this project:

> Constant called for a playful rather than a functional urbanism, a projection into the imaginary futures of the discoveries made by the Lettrist method of *dérive*, drifting journeys through actually existing cities to experience rapid, aimless changes of environment (*'ambience'*) and consequent changes of psychological state. Constant had been inspired by Pinot Gallizio, who had become the political representative of the gypsies who visited Alba, to build a model for a nomadic encampment. From this he developed to building architectural models of a visionary city ('New Babylon'), as well as making blueprints, plans and elevations, moving out of painting altogether. (1989, 15–16)

Another realisation of sorts of Chtcheglov's 'Unitary Urbanism' was the work of the *Archigram* group, especially in their 'utopian' projects such as 'Walking City', which might be seen to follow from Chtcheglov's definition of mobile architecture ('The mobile house turns with the sun. It's sliding walls enable vegetation to invade life. Mounted on tracks, it can go down to the sea in the morning and return to the forest in the evening' (Chtcheglov 1989, 24)). As Archigram remark: 'If "Walking City" is the heroic statement of mobilised architecture it represents but the most magnificent audacity of a series of Archigram projects that constantly revolve around flexing, moving, transferring' (Herron 1998, 118).

58. Deleuze makes this argument specifically in relation to music, and the 'move' to a post-war serialism (for example with Boulez). We might say that John Cage operates as the bridge here between an explicitly musical definition of Deleuze's 'new harmony' and one that names the expanded field of 'performance art', and indeed the avant-garde practices of the 1960s in general.
59. This is the coming of the 'New Barbarians' predicted by Hardt and Negri (*E* 213–18), and perhaps most explicitly mapped out in Donna Haraway's 'Cyborg Manifesto': Science, Technology, and Socialist Feminism in the Late Twentieth Century', in *Simians, Cyborgs and Women: The Reinvention of Nature* (1991) (London: Routledge), pp. 149–65. It is important to point out that technological development in itself does not provide for dissonant, radical or emancipatory subjectivities. Indeed, one need only track the military development of cyborg and AI technologies (see, for example, Delanda's *War in the Age of Intelligent Machines* (1991) (New York: Zone Books)). In the terms of this chapter we might say that attention needs to be turned to what kind of monads or subjectivities (fascist? communist? *revolutionary*?) produce, and are produced by, these technologies. This is the important business of Guattari's work on the production of subjectivity (see Chapter 3).
60. The obvious example of contemporary times being the practice of Jake and Dinos Chapman. See, for example, the work in Chapman and Chapman, *Hell* (2003) (London: Jonathan Cape, Saatchi Gallery).
61. Stelarc's performances of the 1970s might be seen as an exploration of the body's limits (i.e. pain); experiments to discover what a body is capable of. As such, they can be read through the optic of Spinoza as precisely ethological/ethical experiments. With his more recent work, with communication technologies and robotic prosthesis, we might see a more explicitly Leibnizian theorisation of the body (relationships between the dominata and dominated) and of how the body moves from being an autonomous closed monad to being something more open (a move, according to Stelarc, which amounts to switching from a psychoanalytic account of subjectivity to a cybernetic one):

    Imagine the consequences and advantages of being a split body with voltage-in, inducing the behaviour of a remote agent and voltage-out, for your body to control peripheral devices. This would be a more complex and interesting body – not simply a single entity with one agency but one that would be a host for a multiplicity of remote and alien agents of different physiologies and in varying locations. (Stelarc 1997, 66)

    It is, of course, via the World Wide Web that this expanded body is produced. Indeed we might say that the World Wide Web is a model of the 'New Baroque' involving as it does a new kind of resonance between the two levels of the monad – precisely an opening out of the closed house. It is here that we return to the subject matter of Chapter 1: the 'New Baroque' in art is art understood rhizomatically, specifically in the foregrounding of multiplicity and interconnectivity.
62. And the question of whether a subject can access this ground (that a folding can simultaneously experience the unfolded) is perhaps the religious question of our time.

Conclusion

1. See Chapter 2, pp. 46–7.
2. See for example Asger Jorn's *Open Creation and its Enemies* (1994) (Trans. F. Tompsett) (London: Unpopular Books) for an example of this 'counter-knowledge', in this case involving the construction of an alternative scientific system.
3. Antonio Negri in *Time for Revolution* (2003) (Trans. M. Mandarini) (London: Continuum), argues convincingly that the construction of a people also involves this future orientation. For Negri, this creative opening up to the potentiality of the future begins with *naming* (Negri 2003, 147–58). An interesting comparison might be made between Negri's act of naming, and the work of art. A crucial question here would be whether a people can be called into being without a linguistic utterance (i.e. through a bloc of sensations that is irreducible to signification).
4. As Williams remarks:

   By 'Residual' I mean that some experiences, meanings and values which cannot be verified or cannot be expressed in terms of the dominant culture, are nevertheless lived and practised on the basis of the residue – cultural as well as social – of some previous social formation ... A residual culture is usually at some distance from the effective dominant culture, but one has to recognize that it may get incorporated in it. This is because some part of it, some version of it – and especially if the residue is from some major area of the past – will in many cases have been incorporated if the effective dominant culture is to make sense in those areas. It is also because at certain points a dominant culture cannot allow too much of this practice and experience outside itself, at least without risk. Thus the pressures are real, but certain genuinely residual meanings and practices in some important cases survive. (1980, 40–1)

   Williams goes on to outline the sources of what he calls 'Emergent' cultures, whilst at the same time alerting us to the importance of 'very precise analysis, between residual-incorporated and residual not incorporated, and between emergent-incorporated and emergent not incorporated' (Williams, 'Base and Superstructure in Marxist Cultural Theory', in *Problems in Materialism and Culture: Selected Essays* (1980) (London: Verso), p. 41). Although this particular inside/outside paradigm of political thought is increasingly open to question, it nevertheless remains an important point that any given present is made up of a multiplicity of 'times' each with their own specificity and potentialities.
5. Paul Ricoeur puts this well in his essay 'Life in Quest of Narrative', in *On Ricoeur: Narrative and Interpretation* (1991) (Ed. D. Wood) (London: Routledge), pp. 20–33. For Ricoeur this mythopoetic function, as I have been calling it, is to be understood as a world produced by the literary text, and specifically the reader's involvement with that text:

   the sense or significance of a narrative stems from the intersection of the world of the text and the world of the reader. The act of reading thus becomes the critical moment of the entire analysis. On it rests the narrative's capacity to transfigure the experience of the reader ... To speak of a world of the text is to stress the feature belonging to every literary work of opening before it a horizon of possible experience, a world in which it would be possible to live. A text is not something closed in upon itself, it is the projection of a new universe distinct from that in which we live. To appropriate a work through reading is to unfold the world horizon implicit in it which includes actions, the characters and the events of the story told. As a result, the reader belongs at once to the work's horizon of experience in imagination and to that of his or her own real action. The horizon of expectation and the horizon of experience continually confront one another and fuse together. (Ricoeur 1991, 26)

6. We might understand Richter's Abstracts as traitors in this sense. Traitor paintings for traitor-subjectivities.
7. As Deleuze and Guattari remark in the plateau '1730: Becoming-Intense, Becoming-Animal':

   Our first principle was: pack and contagion, the contagion of the pack, such is the path becoming-animal takes. But a second principle seemed to tell us the opposite: wherever there is a multiplicity, you will also find an exceptional individual, and it is with that individual that an alliance must be made in order to become-animal. There may be no such thing as a lone wolf, but there is a leader of the pack, a master of the pack, or else the old deposed head of the pack now living alone, there is the loner, and there is the demon. Willard has his favourite, the rat Ben, and only becomes rat through his relation with him, in a kind of alliance of love, then of hate. Moby-Dick in its entirety is one of the great masterpieces of becoming; Captain Ahab has an irresistible becoming-whale, but one that bypasses the pack or the school, operating directly through a monstrous alliance with the Unique, the Leviathan, Moby-Dick. (*ATP* 243)

8. Although not within the scope of these concluding remarks an interesting project would be to locate Barney's complex *Cremaster* cycle of films within Deleuze's film 'history'. For example, the notion of opsigns and sonsigns would seem to be particularly pertinent in relation to Barney:

   Pure optical and sound images, the fixed shot and the montage-cut, do define and imply a beyond of movement. But they do not strictly stop it, neither in the characters nor even in the camera. They mean that movement should not be perceived in a sensory-motor image, but grasped and thought in another type of image ... the pure optical and sound image, its opsigns and sonsigns, are directly connected to a time-image which has subordinated movement. (*C2* 22)

   This time-image, and the break with the sensory-motor schema (i.e. *narrative*) involves:

   the rise of situations to which one can no longer react, of environments with which there are now only chance relations, of empty or disconnected any-space-whatevers replacing qualified extended space. It is here that situations no longer extend into action or reaction in accordance with the requirements of the movement-image. These are pure optical and sound situations, in which the character does not know how to respond, abandoned spaces in which he ceases to experience and to act so that he enters into flight, goes on a trip, comes and goes, vaguely indifferent to what happens to him, undecided as to what must be done. (*C2* 272)

This is not to say that the *Cremaster* films abandon the movement-image altogether. Indeed, we might say that a film such as *Cremaster 3*, although involved in opsigns and sonsigns, also stages a kind of *hyper* movement-image, or even an absurd one, in its programmatic direction (the climbing of the Chrysler building, the overcoming of the 'architect').

9. A very recent example of this kind of practice is John Bock's 'Retrospective', *Klutterhammer*, at the ICA London in 2004, which stages less a survey of previous works than an idiosyncratic and chaotic collection of the artist's influences, from art works to pop culture, presented in an equally idiosyncratic series of home made buildings and passages. As Bock remarks in relation to the show: 'This is my history' (2004).
10. See also Kodwo Eshun's account of Sun Ra's myth-science in his essay 'Synthesising the Omniverse', *More Brilliant than the Sun: Adventures in Sonic Fiction* (1988) (London: Quartet), pp. 154–63. As Eshun remarks, Sun Ra's myth is one of the *post*human:

Soul affirms the human. Ra is disgusted with the human. He desires to be alien, by emphasising Egypt over Israel, the alien over the human, the future over the past. In his Myth-Science systems, Ancient Africans are alien Gods from a despotic future. Sun Ra is the end of soul, the replacement of God by a Pharaonic Pantheon. (1998, 155)

For a further exploration of this myth-science in relation to science fiction and 'Afrofuturism' see *Last Angel of History* (1995) directed by J. Akomfrah, distributed by Black Audio Film Collective.

11. Again Kodwo Eshun is interesting on this point as it relates to the music of Sun Ra. Here he is from the aforementioned essay:

Traditionally 20th C science sterilises all myth: myth starts where science stops. But the recording medium acts as an interface between science and myth. Every medium opens up a continuum from technology to magic and back again. Magic is just another name for a future, an as-yet unknown medium, a logic identified by both Arthur C. Clarke – 'Any sufficiently advanced technology becomes indistinguishable from magic' – and Samuel Delaney: 'At the material level, our technology is becoming more and more like magic.' Ra's Myth-Science extends the technology magic continuum into sound. (1998, 160)

For Eshun new technologies, and specifically musical technologies, from synthesisers to turn tables, open up new worlds. See also Paul D. Miller's *Rhythm Science* (2004) (Massachusetts: MIT Press) for a parallel account to that of Eshun's. For an interesting example of myth production in relation to new technology see the activities of CCRU as they appear in *Mute* magazine and at www.ccru.net. See also CCRU's essay 'Who is Pulling Your Strings?', in *Frozen Tears* (Ed. J. Russell) (2001) (Birmingham: Article Press), pp. 329–45.

12. Brian Massumi has attended to this complex utilisation of affect, specifically by the mass media, in two recent papers, at the *Neuroaesthetics* Conference at Goldsmiths College, London, and at *The Ethics and Politics of Virtuality and Indexicality* Conference at the University of Leeds, both in 2005. To drastically reduce the complexity of Massumi's argument, we might say that the media increasingly operates on a self-consciously affective register – as a kind of nervous system – utilising the temporally indeterminate aspect of the event as singular point in an ever expanding exercise of power (what we might call a colonisation of the virtual).

Bibliography

Adorno, T. (1973) *The Jargon of Authenticity* (Trans. K. Tarnowski and F. Will) (London: Routledge, Keegan and Paul).

Adorno, T. (1978) *Minima Moralia: Reflections from Damaged Life* (Trans. E. F. N. Jephnott) (London: Verso).

Adorno, T. (1981) 'Cultural Criticism and Society', in *Prisms* (Trans. S. Weber and S. Weber) (Cambridge, MA: MIT Press), pp. 17–34.

Adorno, T. (1984) *Aesthetic Theory* (Trans. C. Lenhardt) (London: Routledge, Keegan and Paul).

Adorno, T. and M. Horkheimer (1979) *Dialectic of Enlightenment* (Trans. J. Cumming) (London: Verso).

Agamben, G. (1993) *The Coming Community* (Trans. M. Hardt) (Minneapolis: University of Minnesota Press).

Alÿs, F. (2005) *Walking Distance from the Studio* (Ostfildern: Hatje Cantz Publishers).

Ansell Pearson, K. (1997) *Viroid Life: Perspectives on Nietzsche and the Transhuman Condition* (London: Routledge).

Ansell Pearson, K. (1999) *Germinal Life: The Difference and Repetition of Deleuze* (London: Routledge).

Arnott, S. J. (2001) 'Liminal Subjectivity and the Ethico-Aesthetic Paradigm of Felix Guattari', available at http://limen.mi2.hr/limen1–2001/stephen_arnott.html, accessed 12 October 2005.

Ascherson, N. (1991) 'Revolution and Restoration: Conflicts in the Making of Modern Germany', in *Gerhard Richter* (London: Tate Gallery), pp. 33–9.

Association Metaworx (ed.) (2004) *Metaworx: Approaches to Interactivity* (Zurich: Birkhauser).

Atelier Van Lieshout (2005) available at http://ateliervanlieshout.com, accessed 15 October 2005.

Attali, J. (1985) *Noise: The Political Economy of Music* (Trans. B. Massumi) (Manchester: Manchester University Press).

Aust, S. (1987) *The Baader-Meinhof Group: The Inside Story of a Phenomenon* (Trans. A. Bell) (London: The Bodley Head).

Backhouse, J. (2004) 'The Invisible Insurrection of a Million Minds: Networking and Cultural Resistance from *The Sigma Project* to *Luther Blisett*', dissertation, Goldsmiths College, University of London (unpublished).

Badiou, A. (1999) *Deleuze: The Clamour of Being* (Trans. L. Burchill) (Minneapolis: University of Minnesota Press).

Badiou, A. (2001) *Ethics: An Essay On the Understanding of Evil* (Trans. P. Hallward) (London: Verso).

Badiou, A. (2002) paper presented at *Return(s) to Marx* Conference, London, Tate Modern Gallery, May 31–June 1.

Badiou, A. (2003) 'Seven Variations on the Century', *Parallax*, vol. 9, no. 27, 72–80.

Bains, P. (2002) 'Subjectless Subjectivities', in *A Shock to Thought: Expression After Deleuze and Guattari*, Ed. B. Massumi (London: Routledge), pp. 101–16.

Ballard, J. G. (2000) 'Robert Smithson as a Cargo Cultist', in *Robert Smithson: Dead Tree*, Ed. B. Conley and J. Amrhein (Brooklyn: Pierogi), p. 31.

Bank (2000) *Bank* (London: Black Dog Publications).

Bann, S. (1998) 'Three Images for Kristeva: From Bellini to Proust', *Parallax*, vol. 4, no. 8, 65–79.

Barney, M. (2002) 'Artists Project', *Tate: International Arts and Culture*, no. 2, 58–60.

Barthes, R. (1973) *Mythologies* (Trans. A. Lavers) (London: Palladin).

Barthes, R. (1977a) 'From Work to Text', in *Image/Music/Text* (Trans. and Ed. S. Heath) (London: Fontana) pp. 155–64.

Barthes, R. (1977b) 'The Death of the Author', in *Image/Music/Text* (Trans. and Ed. S. Heath) (London: Fontana), pp. 142–8.

Bataille, G. (1980) *Prehistoric Painting: Lascaux or the Birth of Art* (Trans. A. Wainhouse) (London: Macmillan).

Bataille, G. (1991) *The Accursed Share: An Essay on General Economy, Volume 1: Consumption* (Trans. R. Hurley) (New York: Zone Books).

Becker, J. (1978) *Hitler's Children: The Story of the Baader-Meinhof Gang* (London: Panther Books).

Benjamin, A. (1995) 'Introduction', in *Complexity: Architecture/Art/Philosophy*, Ed. A. Benjamin (London: Academy Editions), p. 7.

Benjamin, A. (1994) *Object Painting* (London: Academy Editions).

Benjamin, A. (1997) 'Time, Question, Fold', available at http://www.basilisk.com/V/virtual_deleuze_ fold_112. html, accessed 12 October 2005.

Benjamin, W. (1974) 'Some Motifs in Baudelaire', in *Charles Baudelaire: A Lyric Poet in the Era of High Capitalism* (Trans. H. Zorn) (London: Verso), pp. 109–54.

Benjamin, W. (1997a) 'A Berlin Chronicle', in *One Way Street* (Trans. E. Jephcott and K. Shorter) (London: Verso), pp. 293–346.

Benjamin, W. (1997b) 'Critique of Violence', in *One Way Street* (Trans. E. Jephcott and K. Shorter) (London: Verso), pp. 132–54.

Benjamin, W. (1999a) 'The Storyteller: Reflections on the Work of Nikolai Leskov', in *Illuminations* (Trans. H. Zorn) Ed. H. Arendt (London: Pimlico), pp. 83–107.

Benjamin, W. (1999b) 'The Work of Art in the Age of Mechanical Reproduction', in *Illuminations* (Trans. H. Zorn) Ed. H. Arendt (London: Pimlico), pp. 211–44.

Bergson, H. (1988) *Creative Evolution* (Trans. A. Mitchell) (London: Dover Publications).

Bergson, H. (1991) *Matter and Memory* (Trans. N. M. Paul and W. S. Palmer) (New York: Zone Books).

Bock, J. (2004) *Klutterhammer*, exhibition handout, London, ICA, 27 September–7 November.

Bogue, R. (1989) *Deleuze and Guattari* (London: Routledge).

Bogue, R. (1996) 'Gilles Deleuze: The Aesthetics of Force', in *Deleuze: A Critical Reader*, Ed. P. Patton (Oxford: Basil Blackwell), pp. 257–69.

Bogue, R. (1999) 'Art and Territory', in *A Deleuzian Century?*, Ed. I. Buchanan (Durham: Duke University Press), pp. 85–102.

Bogue, R. (2003) *Deleuze on Music, Painting and the Arts* (London: Routledge).

Bogue, R. (2004) *Deleuze's Wake: Tributes and Tributaries* (Albany: State University of New York Press).

Bonami, F. and M-L. Frisa (eds.) (2003) *Dreams and Conflicts: The Dictatorship of the Viewer (50th Venice Biennale)* (Venice: Marsillo), pp. 319–415.

Bourriaud, N. (1998) *Relational Aesthetics* (Trans. S. Pleasance, F. Woods and M. Copeland) (Paris: Les Presses du Reel).
Bourriaud, N. (2002) *Postproduction* (Trans. J. Herman) Ed. C. Schneider (New York: Lukas and Steinberg).
Bracewell, M. (2003) 'New Image Glasgow to Young British Art: Introducing the 1990s', *New Formations*, no. 50, 22–7.
Bradley, W., H. Bretton-Meyer and T. Webster (2002) *My Head is on Fire but my Heart is Full of Love* (Copenhagen: Charlottenborg Udstillingsbygning).
Brown, K. M. (2002) 'Djungel Dwelling', in *Simon Starling: Djungel* (Dundee: Dundee Contemporary Arts), pp. 23–36.
Brunette, P. and D. Willis (1994) 'The Spatial Arts: An Interview with Jacques Derrida', in *Deconstruction and the Visual Arts*, Ed. P. Brunette and D. Willis (Cambridge: Cambridge University Press), pp. 9–32.
Buchanan, I. (2000) *Deleuzism: A Metacommentary* (Edinburgh: Edinburgh University Press).
Buhlman, V. (2004) 'Volatile Milieu: The Poetics of Interactivity', in *Metaworx: Approaches to Interactivity*, Ed. Association Metaworx (Zurich: Birkhauser).
Burgin, V. (1986) 'The End of Art Theory', in *The End of Art Theory* (London: Macmillan), pp. 140–204.
C. CRED (2005) available at http://ccred.org, accessed 15 October 2005.
CCRU (2005) available at http://ccru.net, accessed 15 October 2005.
CCRU (2001) 'Who is Pulling Your Strings?', in *Frozen Tears*, Ed. John Russell (Birmingham: Article Press), pp. 329–45.
Celant, G. (1992) 'from *Art Povera*', in *Art in Theory 1900–1990: An Anthology of Changing Ideas*, Ed. C. Harrison and P. Wood (London: Blackwell), pp. 886–9.
Chapman, J. and D. Chapman (2003) *Hell* (London: Jonathan Cape/Saatchi Gallery).
Chtcheglov, I. (1989) 'Formulary for a New Urbanism (1953)', in *An Endless Adventure ... An Endless Passion ... An Endless Banquet: A Situationist Scrapbook*, Ed. I. Blazwick (London: Verso), pp. 24–5.
Cilliers, P. (1998) *Complexity and Postmodernism: Understanding Complex Systems* (London: Routledge).
Clark, T., C. Gray, C. Radcliffe and D. Nicholson-Smith (1994) *The Revolution of Modern Art and the Modern Art of Revolution* (London: Chronos Publications).
Clarke, T. J. (1992) 'On the Very Idea of a Subversive Art History', paper presented at *Association of Art Historians* Conference, University of Leeds.
Clarke, T. J. (1999) *Farewell to an Idea: Episodes from a History of Modernism* (New Haven: Yale University Press).
Colebrook, C. (2002) *Gilles Deleuze* (London: Routledge).
Colletti, L. (1975) 'Introduction' to *Early Writings*, by K. Marx (London: Penguin), pp. 7–56.
Cremaster 3 (2005) Written and directed by M. Barney, and B. Gladstone, distributed by Palm Pictures.
Debord, G. (1989) 'Toward a Situationist International', in *An Endless Adventure ... An Endless Passion ... An Endless Banquet: A Situationist Scrapbook*, Ed. I. Blazwick (London: Verso), pp. 26–8.
Delanda, M. (1991) *War in the Age of Intelligent Machines* (New York: Zone Books).
Delanda, M. (1997) *A Thousand Years of Nonlinear History* (New York: Zone Books).
Delanda, M. (2002) *Intensive Science and Virtual Philosophy* (London: Continuum).

de Man, P. (1983a) 'The Rhetoric of Temporality', in *Blindness and Insight: Essays in the Rhetoric of Contemporary Criticism* (London: Methuen), pp. 187–228.

de Man, P. (1983b) 'Literary History and Literary Modernity', in *Blindness and Insight: Essays in the Rhetoric of Contemporary Criticism* (London: Methuen), pp. 142–65.

Deleuze, G. (1977) 'Nomad Thought' (Trans. J. Wallace), in *The New Nietzsche*, Ed. D. B. Allison (New York: Dell Publishing), pp. 142–9.

Deleuze, G. (1983) *Nietzsche and Philosophy* (Trans. H. Tomlinson) (London: Athlone Press).

Deleuze, G. (1984) *Kant's Critical Philosophy: The Doctrine of the Faculties* (Trans. H. Tomlinson and B. Habberjam) (London: Athlone Press).

Deleuze, G. (1988a) *Bergsonism* (Trans. H. Tomlinson and B. Habberjam) (New York: Zone Books).

Deleuze, G. (1988b) *Foucault* (Trans. S. Hand) (Minneapolis: University of Minnesota Press).

Deleuze, G. (1988c) *Spinoza: Practical Philosophy* (Trans. R. Hurley) (San Francisco: City Light Books).

Deleuze, G. (1989) *Cinema 2: The Time-Image* (Trans. H. Tomlinson and R. Galeta) (London: Athlone Press).

Deleuze, G. (1990) *The Logic of Sense* (Trans. M. Lester and C. Stivale) Ed. C. V. Boundas (New York: Columbia University Press).

Deleuze, G. (1991a) *Empiricism and Subjectivity: An Essay on Hume's Theory of Human Nature* (Trans. C. V. Boundas) (New York: Columbia University Press).

Deleuze, G. (1991b) *Masochism: Coldness and Cruelty* (Trans. J. McNeil) (New York: Zone Books).

Deleuze, G. (1992a) *Expressionism in Philosophy: Spinoza* (Trans. M. Joughin) (New York: Zone Books).

Deleuze, G. (1992b) *Cinema 1: The Movement Image* (Trans. H. Tomlinson and B. Habberjam) (London: Athlone Press).

Deleuze, G. (1993a) *The Fold: Leibniz and the Baroque* (Trans. T. Conley) (Minneapolis: University of Minnesota Press).

Deleuze, G. (1993b) 'Language: Major and Minor', in *The Deleuze Reader* (Trans. and Ed. C. V. Boundas) (New York: Columbia University Press), pp. 145–51.

Deleuze, G. (1994) *Difference and Repetition* (Trans. P. Patton) (New York: Columbia University Press).

Deleuze, G. (1995) *Negotiations: 1972–1990* (Trans. M. Joughin) (New York: Columbia University Press).

Deleuze, G. (1998) *Essays Critical and Clinical* (Trans. D. W. Smith and M. A. Greco) (London: Verso).

Deleuze, G. (1999) 'Cold and Heat', in *Photogenic Painting* (Trans. D. Roberts) Ed. S. Wilson (London: Black Dog Publishing), pp. 61–77.

Deleuze, G. (2000) *Proust and Signs* (Trans. R. Howard) (London: Athlone Press).

Deleuze, G. (2001) *Pure Immanence: Essays on a Life* (Trans. J. Rajchman) (New York: Zone Books).

Deleuze, G. (2003) *Francis Bacon: The Logic of Sensation* (Trans. D. W. Smith) (London: Continuum).

Deleuze, G. (2004) *Desert Islands and Other Texts: 1953–1974* (Trans. M. Taormina) Ed. D. Lapoujade (New York: Semiotext(e)).

Deleuze, G. and F. Guattari (1984) *Anti-Oedipus: Capitalism and Schizophrenia* (Trans. R. Hurley, M. Seem and H. R. Lane) (London: Athlone Press).

Deleuze, G. and F. Guattari (1986) *Kafka: Towards a Minor Literature* (Trans. D. Polan) (Minneapolis: University of Minnesota Press).

Deleuze, G. and F. Guattari (1988) *A Thousand Plateaus* (Trans. B. Massumi) (London: Athlone Press).

Deleuze, G. and F. Guattari (1994) *What is Philosophy?* (Trans. H. Tomlinson and G. Burchell) (London: Verso).

Deleuze, G. and C. Parnet (1987) *Dialogues* (Trans. H. Tomlinson and B. Habberjam) (London: Athlone Press).

Derrida, J. (1976) *Of Grammatology* (Trans. G. C. Spivak) (Baltimore: John Hopkins University Press).

Derrida, J. (1987) *The Truth in Painting* (Trans. G. Bennington and I. McLeod) (Chicago: University of Chicago Press).

Derrida: The Movie (2002) Directed by A. Z. Kofman and K. Dick, distributed by Jane Doe Film.

Easton Ellis, B. (1998) *Glamourama* (London: Picador).

Ehrenzweig, A. (1993) *The Hidden Order of Art: A Study in the Psychology of Artistic Imagination* (London: Weidenfeld).

Elsaesser, T. (1999) 'Antigone Agonistes: Urban Guerrilla or Guerrilla Urbanism? The Red Army Faction, *Germany in Autumn* and *Death Games*', in *Giving Ground: The Politics of Propinquity*, Ed. J. Copjec and M. Sorkin (London: Verso), pp. 276–302.

Eshun, K. (1998) *More Brilliant Than the Sun: Adventures in Sonic Fiction* (London: Quartet Books).

Fietzek, G. (ed.) (2002) *Documenta XI: The Catalogue* (London: Art Books International).

Focillon, H. (1992) *The Life of Forms in Art* (Trans. C. Beecher Hogan and G. Kubler) (New York: Zone Books).

Ford, S. (2000) *Wreckers of Civilisation: The Story of COUM Transmissions and Throbbing Gristle* (London: Black Dog Publications).

Foster, H. (1985) 'The Expressive Fallacy', in *Recodings: Art, Spectacle, Cultural Politics* (Seattle: Bay Press), pp. 59–77.

Foster, K. (1972) 'Critical History of Art or a Transfiguration of Values', *New Literary History*, vol. 3, no. 1, 459–70.

Genosko, G. (2002) *Felix Guattari: An Aberrant Introduction* (London: Continuum).

Germer, S. (1991) 'Retrospective Ahead', in *Gerhard Richter* (London: Tate Gallery), pp. 31–9.

Goodchild, P. (1996) *Gilles Deleuze and the Question of Philosophy* (Madison: Fairleigh Dickinson University Press).

Gray, C. (1989) ' "Those Who Make Half a Revolution Only Dig Their Own Graves": The Situationists Since 1969', in *An Endless Adventure ... An Endless Passion ... An Endless Banquet: A Situationist Scrapbook*, Ed. I. Blazwick (London: Verso), pp. 73–5.

Guattari, F. (1987) 'Cracks in the Street' (Trans. A. Gibault and J. Johnson), *Flash Art*, 135, 82–5.

Guattari, F. (1992) 'Space and Corporeality: Nomads, Cities, Drawings' (Trans. H. and H. Zeitland), in *Semiotext(e)/Architecture*, Ed. H. Zeitland (New York: Semiotext(e)), pp. 118G1–125G8.

Guattari, F. (1995a) 'On Machines' (Trans. V. Constantinopoulos), in *Complexity: Architecture/Art/Philosophy*, Ed. A. Benjamin (London: Academy Editions) pp. 8–12.

Guattari, F. (1995b) *Chaosmosis: An Ethico-aesthetic Paradigm* (Trans. P. Bains and J. Pefanis) (Sydney: Power Publications).

Guattari, F. (1996a) 'Subjectivities: for Better and for Worse' (Trans. S. Thomas), in *The Guattari Reader*, Ed. G. Genosko (Oxford: Basil Blackwell), pp. 193–203.

Guattari, F. (1996b) *Soft Subversions* (Trans. D. L. Sweet and C. Wiener) (New York: Semiotext(e)).

Guattari, F. (1998) 'Pragmatic/Machine: Discussion with Félix Guattari (19 March 1985)', in *The Two-Fold Thought of Deleuze and Guattari: Intersections and Animations*, by C. J. Stivale (New York: Guilford Press), pp. 191–224.

Guattari, F. (2000) *The Three Ecologies* (Trans. I. Pindar and P. Sutton) (London: Athlone Press).

Hallward, P. (2001) *Absolutely Postcolonial: Writing Between the Singular and the Specific* (Manchester: Manchester University Press).

Hardt, M. and A. Negri (2000) *Empire* (Cambridge, MA: Harvard University Press).

Harraway, D. (1991) 'A Cyborg Manifesto: Science, Technology, and Socialist Feminism in the Late Twentieth Century', in *Simians, Cyborgs and Women: The Reinvention of Nature* (London: Routledge), pp. 149–65.

Hemment, D. (1997) 'E is for Ekstasis', *New Formations*, no. 31, 23–38.

Herron, R. (1998) 'Mobile Projects', in *Concerning Archigram*, Ed. D. Crompton (London: Archigram Archives), pp. 118–21.

Hirschorn, T. (2003) Paper presented at *Field Work: Reports from the Fields of Visual Culture* Conference, London, Victoria Milo Gallery, 16–17 May.

Hobbs, R. (1983) *Robert Smithson: A Retrospective View* (Duisberg: Wilhelm Lehmbruck Museum).

Holland, E. (1999) *Deleuze and Guattari's* Anti-Oedipus*: Introduction to Schizoanalysis* (London: Routledge).

Husband, S. (2004) 'Ever Decreasing Circlers', *Observer Magazine*, 25 April, 22–9.

In Love with Terror (2002) Directed by B. Lewis, distributed by BBC/Mentorn.

Jameson, F. (1977) 'Afterword: Reflections in Conclusion', in *Aesthetics and Politics*, Ed. R. Taylor (London: New Left Books), pp. 196–213.

Jorn, A. (1994) *Open Creation and Its Enemies* (Trans. F. Tompsett) (London: Unpopular Books).

Judd, D. (1992) 'Specific Objects', in *Art in Theory 1900–1990: An Anthology of Changing Ideas*, Ed. C. Harrison and P. Wood (Oxford: Blackwell), pp. 809–13.

Kabokov, I. and E. Kabokov (2004) 'Donald Judd', *Artists' Favourites: Act 1*, exhibition handout, London, ICA, 5 June–23 July, p. 11.

Kaprow, A. (1992) 'from *Assemblages, Environments and Happenings*', in *Art in Theory 1900–1990: An Anthology of Changing Ideas*, Ed. C. Harrison and P. Wood (Oxford: Blackwell), pp. 703–9.

Kelley, M. (1995) 'Myth Science', in *Öyvind Fahlström: The Installations* (Ostfildern: Hatje Cantz Publishers), pp. 19–27.

Krauss, R. (1998) 'Sculpture in the Expanded Field, in *The Art of Art History: A Critical Anthology*, Ed. D. Preziosi (Oxford: Oxford University Press), pp. 281–98.

Krauss, R. (1999) *A Voyage on the North Sea: Art in the Age of the Post-Medium Condition* (London: Thames and Hudson).

Kristeva, J. (1989) 'Jackson Pollock's Milky Way: 1912–1956', *Journal of Philosophy and the Visual Arts* (London: Academy Editions), pp. 35–9.

Lambert, G. (2002) *The Non-Philosophy of Gilles Deleuze* (London: Continuum).

Land, N. (1993) 'Making it With Death: Remarks on Thanatos and Desiring-Production', *Journal of the British Society for Phenomenology*, vol. 24, no. 1, 66–76.

The Last Angel of History (1995) Directed by J. Akomfrah, distributed by Black Audio Film Collective.

Lotringer, S. (2004) 'Foreword: We, the Multitude' to *A Grammar of the Multitude: For an Analysis of Contemporary Forms of Life*, by P. Virno (Trans. I. Bertoletti, J. Cascaito and A. Casson) (New York: Semiotext(e)), pp. 7–19.

Lowndes, S. (2003) *Social Sculpture: Art, Performance and Music in Glasgow; A Social History of Independent Practice, Exhibitions and Events since 1971* (Glasgow: Stopstop).

Lyotard, J-F. (1984) *The Postmodern Condition: A Report on Knowledge* (Trans. G. Bennington and B. Massumi) (Manchester: Manchester University Press).

Lyotard, J-F. (1988) *Peregrinations: Law, Form, Event* (New York: Columbia University Press).

Lyotard, J-F. (1989a) 'Philosophy and Painting in the Age of Their Experimentation: Contribution to an Idea of Postmodernity' (Trans. M. Minich Brewer and D. Brewer), in *The Lyotard Reader*, Ed. A. Benjamin (Oxford: Basil Blackwell), pp. 181–95.

Lyotard, J-F. (1989b) 'Beyond Representation' (Trans. J. Culler), in *The Lyotard Reader*, Ed. A. Benjamin (Oxford: Basil Blackwell), pp. 155–68.

Lyotard, J-F. (1991) 'Critical Reflections' (Trans. W. G. J. Niesluchawski), *Artforum*, vol. 29, no. 8, 92–3.

Lyotard, J-F. (1993) *Libidinal Economy* (Trans. I. H. Grant) (London: Athlone Press).

Marx, K. and F. Engels (1970) *The German Ideology: Part One*, Ed. C. J. Arthur (London: Lawrence and Wishart).

Massumi, B. (1993) *A User's Guide to Capitalism and Schizophrenia: Deviations from Deleuze and Guattari* (Cambridge, MA: MIT Press).

Massumi, B. (1996) 'The Autonomy of Affect', in *Deleuze: A Critical Reader*, Ed. P. Patton (Oxford: Basil Blackwell), pp. 217–39.

Massumi, B. (2000) 'Painting: The Voice of the Grain', in *Bracha Lichtenberg Ettinger: Artworking 1985–1999* (Amsterdam: Palais des Beaux-Arts), pp. 9–32.

Massumi, B. (2002a) *Parables for the Virtual: Movement, Affect, Sensation* (Durham: Duke University Press).

Massumi, B. (2002b) 'Introduction: Like a Thought', in *A Shock to Thought: Expression After Deleuze and Guattari*, Ed. B. Massumi (London: Routledge), pp. xiii–xxxix.

Massumi, B. (2003) 'Living Memory', *Life's (Re)emergence: Philosophy, Culture, and Politics* Conference, paper presented at Goldsmiths College, University of London, 23 May.

Massumi, B. (2005a) 'First Dialectic: Edges of the Envelope', *Neuroaesthetics* Conference, paper presented at Goldsmiths College, University of London, 12 May.

Massumi, B. (2005b) 'The Future Birth of the Affective Event', *The Ethics and Politics of Virtuality and Indexicality* Conference, paper presented at University of Leeds, 30 June– 3 July.

Meinhof, U. (2001a) 'Armed Anti-Imperialist Struggle', in *Hatred of Capitalism: A Semiotext(e) Reader*, Ed. C. Kraus and S. Lotringer (New York: Semiotext(e)), p. 63.

Meinhof, U. (2001b) 'Armed Anti-Imperialist Struggle (and the Defensive Position of the Counterrevolution in its Psychologic Warfare Against the People)' (Trans. S. Huth), in *Hatred of Capitalism: A Semiotext(e) Reader*, Ed. C. Kraus and S. Lotringer (New York: Semiotext(e)), pp. 273–80.

Melville, S. (1981) 'Notes on the Re-emergence of Allegory, the Forgetting of Modernism, the Necessity of Rhetoric, and the Conditions of Publicity in Art and Art Criticism', *October*, no. 19, 33–48.

Michaux, H. (1999) *Henri Michaux* (London: Whitechapel Art Gallery).

Miller, P. D. (2004) *Rhythm Science* (Cambridge, MA: MIT Press).

Mori, M. (2004) 'Robert Smithson: *Spiral Jetty*', *Artists' Favourites: Act 1*, exhibition handout, London, ICA, 5 June–23 July, p. 14.

Morris, R. (1992a) 'Notes on Sculpture 1–3', in *Art in Theory 1900–1990: An Anthology of Changing Ideas*, Ed. C. Harrison and P. Wood (Oxford: Blackwell), pp. 813–22.

Morris, R. (1992b) 'Notes on Sculpture 4', in *Art in Theory 1900–1990: An Anthology of Changing Ideas*, Ed. C. Harrison and P. Wood (Oxford: Blackwell), pp. 868–73.

Mulholland, N. (2002) 'Learning from Glasvegas: Scottish Art after the "90" ', *Journal of the Scottish Society for Aesthetics*, vol. 7, 61–9.

Murphie, A. (2002) 'Putting the Virtual Back into VR', in *A Shock to Thought: Expression After Deleuze and Guattari*, Ed. B. Massumi (London: Routledge), pp. 188–214.

n55 (2005) available at http://www.n55.dk, accessed 15 October 2005.

Nacking, Å. (1999) 'Interview with Superflex', *Afterall*, 0, 52–61.

Negri, A. (1991) *The Savage Anomaly: The Power of Spinoza's Metaphysics and Politics* (Trans. M. Hardt) (Minneapolis: University of Minnesota Press).

Negri, A. (2003) *Time for Revolution* (Trans. M. Mandarini) (London: Continuum).

Negri, A. (2004a) *Subversive Spinoza: (Un)contemporary Variations*, Ed. T. S. Murphy (Manchester: Manchester University Press).

Negri, A. (2004b) *Negri on Negri: Antonio Negri in Conversation with Anne Dufourmantelle* (Trans. M. B. DeBevoise) (London: Routledge).

Nelson, M. (2000) *Extinction Beckons* (London: Matt's Gallery).

Nelson, M. (2001) *A Forgotten Kingdom*, Ed. W. Bradley (London: ICA).

Nietzsche, F. (1997) *A Nietzsche Reader* (Trans. and Ed. R. J. Hollingdale) (London: Penguin).

Olkowski, D. (1999) *Gilles Deleuze and the Ruin of Representation* (Berkeley: University of California Press).

O'Sullivan, S. (2000) 'In Violence: Three Case Studies Against the Stratum', *Parallax*, vol. 6, no. 2, 104–9.

O'Sullivan, S. (2001) 'Writing on Art (Case Study: The Buddhist Puja)', *Parallax*, vol. 7, no. 4, 115–21.

O'Sullivan, S. (2003) 'Review of *Political Physics*', by John Protevi, *Parallax*, vol. 9, no. 1, 126–7.

O'Sullivan, S. (2005a) 'Four Moments/Movements for an Expanded Art Practice (Following Deleuze, Following Spinoza)', *The Issues (in Contemporary Culture and Aesthetics)*, vol. 1, 67–8.

O'Sullivan, S. (2005b) 'The New Moderns', *The Showroom Annual* (London: The Showroom Gallery), pp. 46–51.

O'Sullivan, S. (2005c) 'Ten Concepts Following Cathy Wilkes' Practice', *Afterall*, vol. 12, 65–70.

Owens, C. (1998) 'The Allegorical Impulse: Toward a Theory of Postmodernism', in *The Art of Art History: A Critical Anthology*, Ed. D. Preziosi (Oxford: Oxford University Press), pp. 315–28.

Patton, P. (2000) *Deleuze and the Political* (London: Routledge).

Patton, P. and J. Protevi (eds.) (2003) *Between Deleuze and Derrida* (London: Continuum).

Paz, O. (1990) 'Nature, Abstraction, Time', in *Alternating Currents* (Trans. H. Lane) (New York: Arcade Publishing), pp. 28–31.

Pollock, G. (1993) 'The "View from Elsewhere": Extracts from a Semi-public Correspondence about the Visibility of Desire', in *Twelve Views of Manet's Bar*, Ed. B. R. Collins (New Jersey: Princeton University Press), pp. 278–315.

Preziosi, D. (1991) *Rethinking Art History: Meditations on a Coy Science* (New Haven: Yale University Press).

Protevi, J. (2001) *Political Physics* (London: Athlone Press).

Rainbird, S. (1991) 'Variations on a Theme: The Paintings of Gerhard Richter', in *Gerhard Richter* (London: Tate Gallery), pp. 11–21.

Rajchman, J. (1998) *Constructions* (Cambridge, MA: MIT Press).

Rajchman, J. (2000) *The Deleuze Connections* (Cambridge, MA: MIT Press).

Read, H. (1974) *A Concise History of Modern Painting* (London: Thames and Hudson).

Rees, A. L. and F. Borzello (eds.) (1986) *The New Art History* (London: Camden Press).

Reynolds, A. (2004) *Robert Smithson: Learning from New Jersey and Elsewhere* (Cambridge, MA: MIT Press).

Richter, G. (1991a) *Gerhard Richter* (London: Tate Gallery).

Richter, G. (1991b) 'Notes 1996–1990', in *Gerhard Richter* (London: Tate Gallery), pp. 108–24.

Richter, G. (1992) 'from "Interview with Benjamin Buchloh" ', in *Art in Theory 1900–1990: An Anthology of Changing Ideas*, Ed. C. Harrison and P. Wood (Oxford: Blackwell), pp. 1036–47.

Richter, G. (2003) *Gerhard Richter: Atlas* (London: Whitechapel).

Ricoeur, P. (1991) 'Life in Quest of Narrative', in *On Paul Ricoeur: Narrative and Interpretation*, Ed. D. Wood (London: Routledge), pp. 20–33.

Riese, V. (ed.) (2003) *New Abstract Painting Painting Abstract Now* (Leverkusen: Museum Morsbroich).

Roberts, J. L. (2004) *Mirror-Travel: Robert Smithson and History* (New Haven: Yale University Press).

Rogoff, I. (2000) *Terra Infirma: Geography's Visual Cultures* (London: Routledge).

Rogoff, I. (2003) 'Engendering Terror', in *Geography and the Politics of Mobility*, Ed. U. Bieman (Wien: Generali Foundation), pp. 48–63.

Rosenberg, H. (1970) *The Tradition of the New* (London: Paladin).

Schapiro, G. (1997) *Earthwards: Robert Smithson and Art after Babel* (Berkeley: University of California Press).

Schmitz, E. (forthcoming) *Ambient Mode: Poetics and Politics of Dispersed Engagements* (New York: Lukas and Steinberg).

Schneeman, C. (1997) 'From The Notebooks', in *More than Meat Joy: Performance Works and Selected Writings*, Ed. B. R. McPherson (Kingston: McPherson and Co.), pp. 9–19.

Serres, M. (1995) *Genesis* (Trans. G. James and J. Nielson) (Ann Arbor: University of Michigan Press).
Simmell, G, (1992) 'The Metropolis and Mental Life', in *Art in Theory 1900–1990: An Anthology of Changing Ideas*, Ed. C. Harrison and P. Wood (Oxford: Blackwell), pp. 130–5.
Smith, D. W. (1998) 'Introduction: "A life of Pure Immanence": Deleuze's "Critique et Clinique" Project', in *Essays Critical and Clinical*, by Gilles Deleuze (Trans. D. W. Smith and M. A. Greco) (London: Verso), pp. xi–lv.
Smithson, R. (1996) *Robert Smithson: The Collected Writiings*, Ed. Flam (Berkeley: University of California Press).
Spector, N. (2003) *Matthew Barney: The Cremaster Cycle*, exhibition handout, New York, Guggenheim, February 21–June 11.
Spinoza, B. (1951) 'A Political Treatise', in *Works of Spinoza: Volume One* (Trans. R. H. M. Elwes) (New York: Dover Publications), pp. 287–387.
Stahl, O. (2001) '*Die Meinhof hat Alles Verraten*: Ulrike Meinhof: Memories, Forgettings, Remembrances', dissertation, University of Leeds (unpublished).
Stelarc, (1997) 'Parasite Visions', *Art and Design*, no. 56, 66–9.
Stammheim: The Trial of the RAF (1985) Directed by R. Hauff, distributed by Bioskop.
Stivale, C. (1998) *The Two-Fold Thought of Deleuze and Guattari: Intersections and Animations* (New York: Guilford Press).
Superflex (2005) available at http://www.superflex.net, accessed 15 October 2005.
Tormey, S. (2004) 'Difference, "Creative Power" and Contemporary Political Practice: The Case of the Zapatistas', paper presented at *Experimenting with Intensities: Science, Philosophy, Politics, the Arts* Conference, Trent University, 12–14 May.
Toscano, A. (2004) 'Preface: The Coloured Thickness of a Problem', to *The Signature of the World: What is Deleuze and Guattari's Philosophy?*, by E. Alliez (Trans. E. R. Albert and A. Toscano) (London: Continuum), pp. ix–xxv.
Tournier, M. (1985) *Friday*, (Trans. N. Denny) (New York: Pantheon Books).
Transnational Republic (2005) available at http://www. transnationalrepublic.org, accessed 15 October 2005.
Vague, T. (1994) *Televisionaries: The Red Army Faction Story 1963–1993* (Edinburgh: AK Press).
Warburg, A. (1998) 'Images From the Region of the Pueblo Indians of North America', in *The Art of Art History: A Critical Anthology*, Ed. D. Preziosi (Oxford: Oxford University Press), pp. 177–206.
Wilkes, C. (2001) *Cathy Wilkes* (Glasgow: The Modern Institute).
Williams, R. (1980) 'Base and Superstructure in Marxist Cultural Theory', in *Problems in Materialism and Culture: Selected Essays* (London: Verso), pp. 31–49.
Wollen, P. (1989) 'Bitter Victory – The Situationist International', in *An Endless Adventure … An Endless Passion … An Endless Banquet: A Situationist Scrapbook*, Ed. I. Blazwick (London: Verso), pp. 9–16.
Wood, P. (1994) 'Truth and Beauty: The Ruined Abstraction of Gerhard Richter', in *Art has No History: The Making and Unmaking of Modern Art*, Ed. J. Roberts (London: Verso), pp. 180–99.
Zizek, S. (2004) *Organs Without Bodies: Deleuze and Consequences* (London: Routledge).

Index